'To Hell with Culture'

'To Hell with Culture'

Anarchism and Twentieth-Century British Literature

Edited by

H. GUSTAV KLAUS AND STEPHEN KNIGHT

UNIVERSITY OF WALES PRESS
CARDIFF
2005

British Library Cataloguing-in-Publication Data
A catalogue record for this book is available from the British Library.

ISBN 0-7083-1898-3

The publishers wish to acknowledge the financial support of the Higher Education Funding Council for Wales in the publication of this book.

Printed in Wales by Dinefwr Press, Llandybïe

Contents

Notes on Contributors

Kathleen Bell is a Senior Lecturer at De Montfort University, where she teaches twentieth-century literature. Her publications are chiefly on twentieth-century poetry and popular fiction.

Valentine Cunningham is Professor of English Language and Literature at the University of Oxford and Fellow and Tutor in English at Corpus Christi College, Oxford. He has written extensively about Victorian literature, the Thirties, Spanish Civil War writing and literary theory. His most recent book is *The Victorians: An Anthology of Poetry and Poetics.*

Paul Gibbard is Research Editor for the Complete Works of Voltaire at the Voltaire Foundation, Oxford. He wrote his doctoral thesis on anarchism in English and French writing of the *fin de siècle.*

Victor Golightly lectures in English at Trinity College, Carmarthen, and is a past editor of *New Welsh Review.* He has recently completed a Ph.D. thesis at the University of Wales Swansea, on the modernism of W. B. Yeats, Dylan Thomas and Vernon Watkins. His paper 'Writing with Dreams and Blood: Dylan Thomas, Marxism and 1930s Swansea' was published in *Welsh Writing in English* in 2003.

David Goodway is Senior Lecturer in History, School of Continuing Education, University of Leeds. He is the author of *London Chartism, 1838–1848* and (with Colin Ward) *Talking Anarchy,* and has edited *For Anarchism* (in the History Workshop Series) and *Herbert Read Reassessed,* as well as collections of the political writings of Read, Comfort and Maurice

Brinton. He is currently completing a book on anarchism and British writers since *c.*1880, in which there will be chapters on both Huxley and Comfort.

Katie Gramich is Senior Lecturer in English at Bath Spa University College. A graduate of the universities of Wales, London and Alberta, she has research interests in Welsh cultural studies, women's writing, post-colonial and twentieth-century literature. Recent publications include editions of *The Rebecca Rioter* by Amy Dillwyn and *Queen of the Rushes* by 'Allen Raine' and a bilingual anthology of *Welsh Women's Poetry, 1460–2001.*

H. Gustav Klaus is Professor of the Literature of the British Isles at the University of Rostock. He has published widely on nineteenth- and twentieth-century working-class writing. His most recent monographs are *Factory Girl* (1998) and *James Kelman* (2005). With Stephen Knight he has co-edited *The Art of Murder* (1998) and *British Industrial Fictions* (2000).

Stephen Knight is a Professor of English Literature at Cardiff University. He has written widely on medieval and modern literature, recently publishing books on Robin Hood and crime fiction. He has a special interest in Welsh literature in English and his most recent book is *One Hundred Years of Fiction* (2004) in the 'Writing Wales in English' series.

William K. Malcolm has spent a quarter of a century engaged in research on James Leslie Mitchell. His doctoral thesis from the University of Aberdeen was published in 1984 as *A Blasphemer & Reformer: A Study of James Leslie Mitchell/Lewis Grassic Gibbon.* A director of the Grassic Gibbon Centre at Arbuthnott, he edits the Centre's newsletter, *The Speak of the Place.* He has recently finished editing a miscellany of Mitchell's uncollected writings, including correspondence, notebooks, essays and manuscripts.

John Rignall is Reader in the Department of English at the University of Warwick. He has published widely on nineteenth- and early twentieth-century fiction, his titles including *Realist Fiction and the Strolling Spectator* (1992), an edited collection of essays, *George Eliot and Europe* (1997), and the *Oxford Reader's Companion to George Eliot* (2000), of which he was the general editor.

Raimund Schäffner teaches English Literature at the University of Heidelberg. He has published two books, *Politik und Drama bei David*

Edgar and *Anarchismus und Literatur in England*, as well as many articles on contemporary British political drama, English poetry and prose writing since the seventeenth century and post-colonial literature.

Christian Schmitt-Kilb is lecturer in English Literature at the University of Rostock. His research interests include English literature and culture in the sixteenth century as well as twentieth-century British fiction and drama. His study *'Never was the Albion Nation without Poetrie': Poetik, Rhetorik und Nation im England der frühen Neuzeit* was published in 2004.

Heather Worthington is a lecturer in English at Cardiff University. Her research has focused on crime fiction in the nineteenth century and her book on *The Rise of the Detective: Crime Fiction in Early Nineteenth Century Popular Fiction,* will be published in 2005.

Acknowledgements

The editors and publishers would like to thank the following for their permission to quote passages held in copyright: Extracts from *A Poet in the Family* (1947; republished as Part 1 of *Goodbye, Twentieth Century* [London, Pimlico, 2001]) are reprinted by permission of The Peters Fraser and Dunlop Group Limited on behalf of Dannie Abse © Dannie Abse, 1974; Eve and Jonathan Bates for extracts from Ralph Bates, *Lean Men* and *The Olive Field*; Rachel Trezise and Parthian Books for extracts from *In and Out of the Goldfish Bowl*; Jean Faulks for extracts from Ethel Mannin, *Women and the Revolution*; David Higham Associates for extracts from Herbert Read, *Poetry and Anarchism*; James Kelman and Secker & Warburg for extracts from *The Good Times*, *A Disaffection*, *How Late it Was, How Late* and *Translated Accounts*; Mark Ravenhill and Methuen Publishing for extracts from *Shopping and Fucking* and *Some Explicit Polaroids*; Iain Sinclair and Granta Books for extracts from *Lights Out for the Territory*; Christopher Sinclair-Stevenson and the estate of John Cowper Powys for extracts from John Cowper Powys, *Letters* and *Wolf Solent*; Enda Walsh and Nick Hern Books (*www.nickhernbooks.co.uk*) for extracts from *Disco Pigs*; John Williams and Bloomsbury Publishing for extracts from *Cardiff Dead*. Extracts from *White Powder, Green Light* by James Hawes, published by Jonathan Cape, are used by permission of The Random House Group Limited. Extract from *Sheepshagger* by Niall Griffiths, published by Jonathan Cape, is used by permission of The Random House Group Limited.

The editors and publishers apologize to any copyright holders whom they have been unable to contact, though they have made strenuous efforts in all cases. They will rectify in any further edition any omissions notified.

1

Introduction

H. GUSTAV KLAUS AND STEPHEN KNIGHT

1.

> But there is *one* field about which you don't have to know *anything*, where you
> can be certain that you will never make a fool of yourself even though you may
> pronounce the most outrageous nonsense. This is anarchism and its doctrine.[1]

John Henry Mackay, an expatriate Scot, author of a *roman-à-clef* about
anarchism, was only slightly exaggerating when, in 1932, he was looking
back at an embattled life as a propagandist for the cause in Germany; and
his observation has lost nothing of its pertinence. The confusions about
anarchism, ranging from its equation with terrorism to its identification with
disruption and chaos, are legion. The flak it has taken from the two dominant forces of the labour movement, state communism and Social
Democracy, has not helped either. For the one, anarchism came to embody
the 'infantile disorder' (Lenin) of left-wing communism; for the other,
it was a mix-up of lofty ideas by dreamers: unpractical, unrealistic,
irresponsible.

The only allowance one can make for the continued existence of such
lazy notions about the movement is that the 'river of anarchy' (Marshall) is
fed by many different sources and tributaries. No one thinker can command
undisputed allegiance among its followers. To the old catch-phrase 'Ni Dieu
ni maître' one could add 'ni maître-penseur'. The various, but also comple-
mentary, schools and positions to be found under the anarchist umbrella
ought to be read in conjunction, so as to distil the essence of the creed.[2]

To proceed to the core elements of anarchism it may help, first of all, to mark it off, on the left, from the hierarchical and authoritarian set-up of Marxist-Leninist Communism and, on the right, from the advocates of an anarcho-capitalism, that is, economic libertarians who repudiate the state only to favour the market as a self-regulating instance. Nor should anarchism as a social movement be confounded with the privatized hedonistic 'lifestyle anarchism' (Bookchin) lately rampant in the west.

The whole history of anarchist thought in the nineteenth century can be seen as an attempt to reconcile the two seemingly incompatible beliefs in true individual freedom and necessary cooperative effort, and thus to combine the two sources of human energy, individual and social. In some early thinkers such as Godwin, but especially Stirner, both faced with *anciens régimes*, the freedom of the individual is privileged; in others, such as Proudhon and Kropotkin, building in part on a now-available reservoir of working-class experience, a better balance between the two tenets is achieved, based on notions of cooperation and mutuality.

Importantly, then, anarchism stands not only for liberty, the absence of rulers and the emancipation of individuals, but also for equality and human solidarity. From very early on, it has written on its banner the ending not only of the domination of man by man, or man by the state, but also of that of woman by man. For anarchism is deeply distrustful of authority in any form, the authority of state, government and bureaucracy no less than that of the paterfamilias – though there have at times been, for example from Proudhon's pen, some ugly misogynist outpourings. Anarchism also views the 'experts of knowledge' with a critical eye, and while there have been differing views about the 'authority of competence', many writers in the anarchist tradition, starting with William Godwin and including prominently in our time Noam Chomsky and James Kelman, have not tired of challenging precisely the controlling interest of elites and self-appointed experts.

Nor has the currently fashionable concept of 'empowerment' of hitherto oppressed or disadvantaged groups a place in the edifice of anarchism, for empowerment as commonly understood can easily become a self-serving act, devoid of solidarity. It can turn into careerism, it can individualize or sectionalize victories and successes, whereas anarchism (excepting the extreme individualism of Max Stirner and his adherents) couples self-initiative and a do-it-yourself approach with mutual aid between individuals and groups.

Out of the collapse of communism and the crisis of Social Democracy, following the latter's reluctant adoption of neo-liberal policies, many of anarchism's contentions have emerged relatively unscathed. Easy, given its refusal to dirty its hands in the corridors of power, might be one response. It is true that the short life and small scale of anarchist experiments in history can be held against it. But the point is whether its central tenets have stood the test of time.

Take the stand on decentralization. More than fifty years ago, the British anarchist weekly *Freedom* proclaimed: 'Anarchism and Syndicalism are not ashamed to pronounce their Regionalism.' And it went on to cite the case of six railway workers from south Wales who had collected 3,200 signatures for a letter of protest against 'the reckless and inefficient Railway Executive' and demanded 'complete control over the Western Region by our regional officers'.[3] At the time this fell on deaf ears. Today the idea of the regions as relatively autonomous and more manageable communities, and with it the devolution of power, has caught on all over Europe, even though anarchists may not be comforted by the prospect of Brussels bureaucrats watching over these affairs.

Beyond regionalism, decentralization implies organization from the bottom up. In the political sphere anarchists have therefore championed participatory democracy, which includes the election of non-permanent delegates, respecting the decisions of their constituents, instead of representatives bound only by their conscience. The decisions were ideally to be reached by consensus, following extensive discussions – no doubt often an inhibiting process. Over the last decades, the 'new social movements' (of women, ecologists and pacifists) through their successors, the non-governmental organizations and what today is loosely called the anti-globalization move-ment, have displayed features much more akin to anarchist principles than to the structure and outlook of the centralized labour organizations of the past. A vast array of local and regional initiatives and projects, action and monitoring groups, makes for heterogeneous composition: out goes the class basis of the subject of history. Exchanges and cooperation take place across ideological divides between environmentalists, trade unionists, peasant activists, church people and anarchists. Networking is the watchword, and it applies from the local to the global level. Spokespeople have replaced leaders.

Yet the trajectory of the German Greens, once a radical movement unit-ing pacifists and environmentalists, is a sad reminder of the truth of the old anarchist adage that power invariably corrupts. Since entering parliaments and governments at communal, regional and national level, they have dis-carded most of their fundamental principles (rotation in office went first). The final sell-out came in 1999, when a majority of the party supported the bombing of Yugoslavia without even a UN mandate, and their economic recipes today are indistinguishable from liberal ones.

The economy is the crux of anarchism. In the past it had set its hopes on the collectivization of the land and the factories, the mines and docks. These were to be run and controlled by the producers themselves, always taking account of local needs, rather than by planners in a remote centre. A confederation between the parcelled-out units of production and distribution would ensure supply and exchange on a larger scale. The thrust was, and is, clearly as much against bigness as against the capitalist mode itself. 'Downsize' could be the watchword, if it had not been irremediably tainted by the ruthless capitalist practice of making people redundant. 'Small is beautiful' (Schumacher) remains the preferred slogan. But anarchists in today's world are not at all united about whether to rely on these older recipes or accept a mixed economy with a 'tamed' capitalism, or even accord the arch-enemy 'state' some protective function against the 'global players'. However, any anarchist economic thinking worth its salt will surely have to retain the important distinction, currently more than ever erased, between private property for immediate consumption (such as a car or house, which may be the fruit of the labour of an individual) and, say, the natural resources of the earth, to which no individual can lay a claim; similarly with the private appropriation by capital of the results of labour socialized on a vast scale, or the results of scientific research carried out by groups of scientists and often enough supported by public funding. Meanwhile small-scale solutions are being practised day by day. The springing up of countless cooperatives, especially in the food sector, a direct response to the ecological crisis, is proof that self-initiative and self-reliance are alive.

Some of these cooperative models hark back, often unknowingly on the part of the agents, to the pioneering socialist experiments of the first half of the nineteenth century.[4] These practically lived utopias had fallen into disrepute when Marxism triumphed, in the guise of 'scientific' socialism, over its 'utopian' cousin. Engels's influential distinction first appeared in French in 1880, four years after the First International, which had been riven by dissensions between the followers of Marx and those of Proudhon and Bakunin, had been formally disbanded. For that matter, the later Kropotkin also came to reject utopianism.

Anarchism, finally, has an honourable record of anti-militarism. On the few occasions its supporters took up arms en masse – we are not talking here of those adherents of the 'propaganda by deed' who *in extremis* resorted to the assassination of rulers – this was regarded as an act of self-defence. In the case of the Spanish Civil War and Revolution armed resistance was mounted against Franco's coup and his Fascist allies from Germany and Italy. But during the two great conflagrations of the twentieth century and in many lesser, if not less atrocious, military conflicts anarchists have been war-resisters, prepared to risk imprisonment or internment for their acts of civil disobedience.

In Alex Comfort's war novel *The Power House* (1944), set on the other side of the Channel, a disaffected French officer reflects that in having joined the army he 'was humouring a lunatic; the State is a lunatic in these days':

> 'You have to humour a lunatic. Otherwise he kills you. I have a girl I'm going to marry; that's sane – I have a job and a life, and I don't want to lose them – that's sane. The government declares war, puts up a row of little men for me to shoot at, then boom! They shoot back, and I'm dead.'
> . . .
> The choices were to co-operate and be killed, refuse and be killed, or protest and be killed at leisure. The beauty of it is that you can't possibly win.

Towards the end of the book, a character called Claus, who has seen the worst – exile from Germany in 1933, Spain 1936–8, internment camps on both sides of the Pyrenees and now one in occupied France – and who to all intents and purposes appears to his guards like a madman, has this engaging dream:

> There is only one responsibility – to the individual who lies under your own feet. To the weak, your fellows.
> The weak do a great deal – every woman who hides a deserter, every clerk who doesn't scrutinize a pass, every worker who bungles a fuse, saves some-body's life for a while. Somebody will start, though it needs no starting, an International League of the Weak, president, Til Eulenspiegel, Simplicissimus, Schweik, or anyone else you like, a league against all citizens, armies (whether of occupation or liberation), against understrappers, jailers, orators and fools.[5]

2.

This brings us to the literature of anarchism, for the present work is neither primarily about its teachings nor an attempt to put the anarchist case. Our aim is to trace how perceptions and misperceptions of anarchist ideas and practices have infiltrated British writing over the last one hundred years. We start where Raimund Schäffner's groundbreaking study of anarchism and literature in the nineteenth century left off, in the 1900s, and review several key figures and texts in a series of case studies.

The opening essay deals with Joseph Conrad's fictional engagements with anarchism. To most students of English literature *The Secret Agent* (1907) remains the best-known novel about the movement. Unfortunately, to many it is also the only one with which they are familiar. Conrad's critique of the anarchists is merciless. Except for the figure of the Professor, they are a pathetic, false and self-deluded lot; but, intriguingly, the representatives of law and order and the institutions of bourgeois society fare little better in this novel.

Closely on its heels came G. K. Chesterton's *The Man Who Was Thursday* (1908), whose collection of anarchists is even more scurrilous, but, unlike Conrad, the author shows concern for the common man. And his portrait of the one true anarchist in the novel remains ambivalent. Lucian Gregory, 'the anarchic poet', at one point cries: 'An artist is identical with an anarchist . . . An artist disregards all governments, abolishes all conventions. The poet delights in disorder only.' The notion that the artist, every major artist, disrupts and destroys as he creates, that he is a breaker of rules, untied by obligations of gratitude or obedience, and that therefore all art is per se anarchist, never wears out. It is an *épater les bourgeois* view of the artist, with just enough of a trace of truth in it to be not totally wrong. But Chesterton knew better. His narrator distances himself from 'the old cant of the lawlessness of art and the art of lawlessness', though he grants 'the red-haired revolutionary' an 'arresting oddity' and towards the end of the novel lets him rehearse the anarchist case.[6]

In the work of two Scottish writers of the 1920s, James C. Welsh and James Leslie Mitchell (better known under his later pseudonym 'Lewis Grassic Gibbon'), there are echoes of the syndicalist movement active around the First World War. Glasgow had its own lively anarchist-syndicalist scene around the indefatigable, if idiosyncratic figure of Guy Aldred. Again, the attitudes of the writers are ambivalent. In part they appear fascinated by the rousing potential of anarcho-syndicalism, in part they remain sceptical or, in the case of Welsh's *The Morlocks* (1924), horrified by what they fear as its excesses. Syndicalism's subterranean influence can also be felt in Welsh fiction in this and following decades. It exists both as a critique of centralist leftism and also, into Raymond Williams's work and beyond, as the concept behind continuing Welsh affiliation to a dynamic, self-managing community, whether industrial or rural.

It is not until the late 1930s that we find a substantial number of writers openly embracing anarchism and congregating, during the war years, around the journal *Now*. They were clearly inspired by the events in Spain, as Herbert Read's pastoral 'Song for the Spanish Anarchists' (1939) demonstrates:

> The golden lemon is not made
>   but grows on a green tree:
> A strong man and his crystal eyes
>   is a man born free.
>
> The oxen pass under the yoke
>   and the blind are led at will:
> But a man born free has a path of his own
>   and a house on the hill.
>
> And men are men who till the land
>   and women are women who weave:
> Fifty men own the lemon grove
>   and no man is a slave.[7]

The Spanish tragedy moved all the writers on the left, and drew some of them, like Ralph Bates, into combat. It also divided them, as it did the left in general. (An earlier litmus test, followed by mutual recriminations, had been the suppression of the Kronstadt rising of Soviet sailors.) For someone who shared the socialist-communist analysis of the Spanish situation, Bates's representation of the anarchists is remarkably fair-minded. For members of the Independent Labour Party (ILP), and especially those with friends among the anarchists, like Ethel Mannin (or George Orwell, or the protagonist of Ken Loach's film *Land and Freedom* [1995], who shifts from a communist to an ILP/POUM position),[8] the Popular Front government installed in Madrid and Barcelona was betraying the Revolution. Mannin was impressed by the powerful personality and fiery rhetoric of Emma Goldman, with whom she shared a platform on Spain in 1938, but displayed unease about the American anarchist's domineering behaviour, which did not leave much chance for a discussion between equals. The split in the Anarchist Federation of Britain in 1945, of which Mannin gave a fictionalized account in *Comrade, O Comrade; Or Low-Down on the Left* (1947), hardly came as a surprise to her.

There were writers who flirted only very briefly with anarchism, such as Ethel Carnie, who in 1925 contributed some poems to *Freedom*; others who were attracted by its anti-militarism; and there were those in whom anarchist ideas fermented a long time before surfacing quietly. Among the latter one may count John Cowper Powys, whose late (post-1945) novels assert anarchism without qualification. AE's last work *The Avatars* (1933) also belongs here. A part-futurist, part-regressive fantasy, its rage against the state and an alienated life can be read as a rediscovery of the freedom-of-nature brand of anarchism represented in the early twentieth century by Emma Goldman's journal, *Mother Earth*. Aldous Huxley's pacifist turn, and his sympathies for the anarchists, as expressed in his answer to the questionnaire about his stand on the Spanish Civil War, came after he emerged from a deep personal crisis. It took some time for the full vision to mature in his fiction. But late in life he surprised readers, used to regarding the author of *Brave New World* as an anti-utopian, with *Island* (1962), an affirmative utopia conceived along libertarian lines, if doomed through foreign intervention.

But the most substantial gathering of anarchist-inspired writers at any time in Britain was the *Now* circle, composed of many conscientious objectors, among them Alex Comfort, D. S. Savage, Julian Symons and George Woodcock. Symons it was who took issue with the all-inclusive editorial policy of the journal, which for his taste gave room to irreconcilable views. His criticisms were later acknowledged by Woodcock when he launched the new series in 1943 with the statement: 'So far as their social content is concerned, the volumes of NOW will be edited from an anarchist point of view.'[9]

Anarchism's fortunes ran low in the 1950s and 1960s, despite the efforts of dedicated individuals such as Comfort, who addressed the founding meeting of the Campaign for Nuclear Disarmament in 1955, and Colin Ward, who in a hostile climate doggedly edited the pocket review *Anarchy* from 1961 to 1970. In its pages many forward-looking ideas on education, housing and ecology were first aired and pragmatic solutions for the here and now envisaged.

Anarchism revived in the wake of 1968, but how the new impulses sedimented into literature, to the present, still awaits close examination. Theatre is an area that deserves examination, especially the work of Mark Ravenhill and Enda Walsh, but the most significant literary voice to have emerged in Britain in the last decades of the twentieth century, whose project can be linked to some aspects of anarchism, is James Kelman. The author's uncompromising stance on vernacular language and narrative voice is as exemplary as his practical support for countless campaigns. Kelman enjoys great prestige among younger writers in Britain, even though their works are largely devoid of the high moral ground occupied by their peer. The 'gritty realist' school in contemporary Scottish or Welsh fiction, or in the current drama of the British Isles, proto-anarchist though many of its characters and sentiments appear, is imbued with a purely negative conception of freedom. It has appropriated the destructive urge of anarchism, but without anarchism's concomitant 'creative passion' (Bakunin) and cooperative vision.

Not every thinker, writer or practitioner whose work has an anarchist dimension has been happy to be conscripted into its camp. A. S. Neill was wary of the label, although his educational principles, as practised in Summerhill, appear thoroughly compatible with anarchist ones. Kelman prefers to call himself a 'libertarian Socialist', which has the advantage of pairing the two principal pillars on which the house of anarchism with its many rooms rests. No matter the name, it is in the end the extent of writers' affinities with anarchist attitudes and projects that is relevant.

3.

'To hell with culture!' Our title has been borrowed from a wartime booklet by Herbert Read, who in turn had taken it from Eric Gill. How could a fine artist make such a shocking statement, and how could an erstwhile Professor of Fine Arts, ceramics specialist at the Victoria and Albert Museum, and poet approve of it? Gill was fed up with seeing 'culture as a thing added like sauce to otherwise unpalatable stale fish!'[10] And Read was concerned, like William Morris and Eric Gill, to end the segregation between culture and life, and the elevation of the former to a higher realm with purely decorative functions:

> My belief is that culture is a natural growth – that if a society has a plenitude of freedom and all the economic essentials of a democratic order, then culture will be added without any excessive striving after it. It will come naturally as the fruit to the well-planted tree.[11]

Read here goes back to the original meaning of 'culture', the tending of plants, and from then on to cultivation, the tending of minds, that is education, always of prime importance in anarchist thought. So far from reaching for the gun, like a famous Nazi (whom Read quotes), when he hears the word 'culture', Read would like to award it a proper status in the communal life that he envisions. Literature, then, has a place in the anarchist universe, and there should be room, too, in the reading lists and discussions of the academy for the literature of anarchism.

NOTES

[1]   John Henry Mackay, *Abrechnung: Randbemerkungen zu Leben und Arbeit* (Freiburg, 1976 [1932]), p. 107 (my translation – HGK). Quoted from Raimund Schäffner, *Anarchismus und Literatur in England: Von der Französischen*

Revolution bis zum Ersten Weltkreig (Heidelberg, 1997), p. 6. Mackay's novel *Die Anarchisten* had been published in 1891 and an English translation appeared in the same year.

2   Good recent digests of anarchism as a doctrine and social movement can be found in David Goodway's introduction to his edited collection, *For Anarchism: History, Theory and Practice* (London, 1989), and, at greater length, in Peter Marshall, *Demanding the Impossible: A History of Anarchism* (London, 1992) and Jean Préposiet, *Histoire de l'anarchisme* (Paris, 1993). Among older works, George Woodcock's *Anarchism: A History of Libertarian Ideas and Movements* (New York, 1962) and Daniel Guérin's *L'anarchisme: De la doctrine à l'action* (Paris, 1965) are still essential reading.

3   *Freedom*, 21 July and 8 September 1951, repr. in *Mankind is One: Selected Articles from the Anarchist Weekly Freedom* (London, 1952), p. 142.

4   Cf. H. Gustav Klaus, 'Early Socialist Utopias in England 1792–1848', in *The Literature of Labour: Two Hundred Years of Working-Class Writing* (Brighton, 1985), pp. 22–45.

5   Alex Comfort, *The Power House* (London, 1944), pp. 118, 319.

6   G. K. Chesterton, *The Man Who Was Thursday* (Harmondsworth, 1937 [1908]), pp. 10–12, 183.

7   Herbert Read, 'A Song for the Spanish Anarchists', in John Lehmann and Stephen Spender (eds), *Poems for Spain* (London, 1939), p. 93.

8   POUM (Partido Obrero de Unificación Marxista) was a radical left-wing organization, principally based in Catalonia, with which the ILP had links. 'Land and Freedom' (*Tierra y Libertad*) is an old anarchist slogan.

9   George Woodcock, 'Note to Readers', *Now*, n.s., I (1943), 2.

10 Eric Gill, *Sacred & Secular &c* (London, 1940), p. 173. Read uses this as an epigraph to his pamphlet, *To Hell with Culture: Democratic Values are New Values* (London, 1941), p. 7.

11 Read, *To Hell with Culture*, p. 52.

2

Conrad and Anarchism: Irony, Solidarity and Betrayal

JOHN RIGNALL

Conrad the ironist might have appreciated the irony of contributing to a serious consideration of the relations between anarchism and literature with a literary response to anarchism as relentlessly negative and roundly contemptuous as his own. *The Secret Agent* and the two short stories which immediately preceded it, 'The Informer' and 'An Anarchist', present the representatives of anarchism as a gallery of grotesque, pathetic or absurd creatures who are the objects of a derision that never lets up. Conrad clearly had no sympathy for anarchists or their cause, but at the same time he was, just as clearly, deeply exercised by them and angrily aroused by what they represented, for at least a year and a half; that is, in the period between December 1905, when he wrote 'An Anarchist' and the summer of 1907 when he finished the book version of *The Secret Agent*. He was, indeed, more exercised and more engaged than he ever cared to acknowledge.

In September 1906 he urged Galsworthy, to whom he had sent part of the manuscript of *The Secret Agent*, not to take it too seriously: 'The whole thing is superficial and is but a *tale*'; and he claimed 'I had no idea to consider anarchism politically – or to treat it seriously in its philosophical aspect'.[1] Looking back at the genesis of the novel in the Author's Note of 1920, he made light of his knowledge of the subject: 'the subject of *The Secret Agent* – I mean the tale – came to me in the shape of a few words uttered by a friend in a casual conversation about anarchists or rather anarchist activities'.[2] Those few words uttered by the friend, Ford Madox Ford, about the Greenwich bomb that blew up Martial Bourdin back in February 1894 were '"Oh that fellow was half an idiot. His sister committed suicide

afterwards." These were absolutely the only words that passed between us'
(p. 9). Ford recalls the incident and the words rather differently, and even
though Ford is a notoriously unreliable witness, with a cavalier attitude
towards fact and truth, the novel and the two preceding stories present clear
evidence that he did indeed offer more assistance than a passing remark, and
that he provided Conrad with anarchist literature, memoirs and contacts, just
as he claims in *A Personal Remembrance*.[3] Through him Conrad met Helen
Rossetti, Ford's cousin, who with her sister Olive and brother Arthur had, as
teenagers in the mid-1890s, produced an anarchist journal, *The Torch*, in
their family home in north London (they were the children of William
Michael Rossetti, brother of Dante Gabriel and Christina, who was an official in the Inland Revenue). Conrad read numbers of *The Torch* and other
anarchist journals: the figure of the Professor is probably inspired by a
Professor Merizoff who features in an American journal of the 1880s;[4] and
he generally embarked on a programme of reading and research about anarchism which he never admitted he had undertaken. The Author's Note to *A
Set of Six* (1908), the collection in which 'The Informer' and 'An Anarchist'
appeared in book form after their original publication in *Harper's Monthly
Magazine* in 1906, is even more evasive about the origins of those stories:

> Of 'The Informer' and 'The Anarchist' I will say next to nothing. The pedigree
> of these tales is hopelessly complicated and not worth disentangling at this dis-
> tance of time. I found them and here they are. The discriminating reader will
> guess that I have found them within my mind; but how they or their elements
> came in there I have forgotten for the most part; and for the rest I really don't
> see why I should give myself away more than I have done already.[5]

Conrad's claim that he has found them in his own mind is consistent with
his aesthetic, as set out in the manifesto preface to *The Nigger of the
Narcissus*, where he maintains that the artist descends within himself and
finds there the terms of his appeal. But there is a marked defensiveness here:
'give myself away'. What does he fear to give away? The secret of his own
creativity? In fact, what he is refusing to give away is his sources, or rather,
the fact that he took anarchism seriously enough to explore it, to read up about
it and do some groundwork of a Zolaesque kind. For what the two stories
reveal quite clearly is the extent of his research. Although 'An Anarchist' was
actually written just before 'The Informer' in December 1905, and published
in *Harper's* in August 1906, 'The Informer' being published in December
of that year, in *A Set of Six* that order is reversed, and it is in that order that
they will be dealt with here.

The narrator of 'The Informer', a collector of Chinese bronzes and porce-
lain, is visited by a Mr X from Paris, who is keen to see his collection and
comes with the recommendation of a good friend – a friend in whose essential
frivolousness and undiscriminating enthusiasm for interesting human types
one can discern an unflattering image of the 'friend' of the Author's Note to
The Secret Agent, namely Ford Madox Ford. Mr X is a cultivated upper-
class anarchist, announced by the friend as 'a revolutionary writer whose
savage irony has laid bare the rottenness of the most respectable institutions'
(p. 74) but also as 'the active inspirer of secret societies, the mysterious
Number One of desperate conspiracies' (p. 74). Wont to dine while in
London in a very good restaurant, which is frequented also by the narrator,
we are shown him eating out: 'His meagre brown hands emerging from
large white cuffs came and went breaking bread, pouring wine, and so on,
with quiet mechanical precision' (p. 75). Not so much dining out, then, as
taking the sacrament of sophisticated bourgeois life. At one of these dinners
he talks to the narrator about his involvement with anarchists and tells the
story of how a London cell, based in a house in Hermione Street owned by
the grown-up children of a government official, came to be suspected of
having a police informer in its ranks. The middle-class owners of the house are
a sister and brother: the sister, dubbed 'our young Lady Amateur of anarchism'
(p. 84), is a striking young woman and her brother a 'serious youth' (p. 85)
who prints anarchist publications in the basement. Up in the attic 'a comrade, nick-named the Professor' (p. 88), is working on perfecting detonators,
while the man in charge of the whole set-up is 'a very able young fellow called
Sevrin' (p. 83), to whom the young Lady Amateur is clearly emotionally
attached. In order to flush out the spy Mr X comes to London and arranges
for a bogus police raid on the premises. The raid has the planned effect and
the man who betrays himself as the police informer is Sevrin, who takes
poison. The young Lady Amateur is devastated and, after the thoughtful Mr
X sends her Sevrin's diary setting out his treachery to the cause in daily detail,
she goes to Florence and then into retreat in a convent – actions which Mr X
describes as 'Gestures! Gestures! Mere gestures of her class' (p. 101).

The sources that Conrad refuses to identify in his Author's Note are easy
to discern in this story; the house in Hermione Street and its owners are
clearly modelled on the Rossettis: Conrad had had a meeting with Helen
through Ford's introduction. In the story the three Rossetti children, Olive,
Helen and Arthur, are conflated into two and made young adults rather than
the teenagers they really were during their anarchist phase. The young Lady
Amateur is the age of Helen as she was when Conrad met her in 1906 and,
to judge from a photo of Helen, shares the same facial features: 'big-eyed,

broad-browed face and [. . .] shapely head' (p. 84). The printing press in the basement producing anarchist pamphlets was a feature of the Rossetti household, while Arthur was a serious youth much given to chemistry and chemical experiments with explosive substances.

Moreover, the Rossettis' anarchist journal, *The Torch*, played a crucial role in the other story, 'An Anarchist', since the historical event on which it is based – an attempted break-out by prisoners from the French penal colony on St Joseph's island off the coast of French Guiana – was reported in the journal. Conrad must have read that report since he used the name of one of the anarchist prisoners, Simon Biscuit, for a figure in the story.

The anarchist of the title, a French mechanic, is found working for an international food company on an island in a great South American river by the narrator, a lepidopterist. He is an escaped convict, and known to be such by Harry Gee, the local representative of the company, the manager of the cattle station. The mechanic is trapped on his South American island and unable to return to his native Paris. His story is one of a life ruined by a single evening of indiscretion and indulgence. Celebrating his twenty-fifth birthday, he gets drunk, suddenly begins to see life as miserable and exploited and causes a riot in a café by jumping on a table and yelling 'long live anarchism and death to capitalists'. He is arrested, tried and, after a disastrously ill-judged speech by the young socialist defence lawyer, he is sent to prison. On finishing his sentence he is unable to find work because of his prison record and is befriended by anarchists, who involve him in a bomb plot that fails. Arrested again, he is sent to a penal colony on St Joseph's island off the coast of South America. When the inmates mutiny, he stands aloof but stumbles on a revolver and a rowing boat. Two of the other anarchist conspirators, whom he holds responsible for his imprisonment, come upon him and he rows with them in the boat out to sea. He then produces his revolver and forces them to do the rowing. When a ship appears on the horizon, he shoots them, heaves the bodies overboard and is eventually rescued, only to be dropped off on the island where the unscrupulous manager of the cattle station exploits his skills as a mechanic.

So what was it about anarchists and anarchism that so exercised Conrad that he kept working away at the subject in these three very different but related texts for a year and a half? What fired his imagination and inflamed his contempt? Jacques Berthoud, in a recent article on *The Secret Agent*, argues that the novel is concerned not so much with challenging anarchism as with criticizing the liberal-progressive response to it: his real target is not the anarchists but the liberal left (like his friends Cunninghame Graham and Edward Garnett) and its belief that the human world can be improved by abstract principle and generalized feeling.[6] This is a powerful reading and does justice to the central role of irony in the novel. But in my view anarchism does exercise Conrad in its own right and the unrelenting irony in the work is not just a technique, but stands in a close relationship to anarchism itself.

From the first, Conrad stressed that his treatment of his subject in *The Secret Agent* was ironic. Writing to his publisher in 1906 while he was working on the novel he described it as 'a fairly successful and sincere piece of ironic treatment applied to a special subject – a sensational subject',[7] and he repeated that claim to Cunninghame Graham in October 1907: 'It had some importance for me as a new departure in *genre* and as a sustained effort in ironical treatment of a melodramatic subject – which was my technical intention.'[8] The implication is that irony is principally a technical matter, an artistic strategy – a point he returns to in 1920 in the Author's Note:

> even the purely artistic purpose, that of applying an ironic method of that kind, was formulated with deliberation and in the earnest belief that ironic treatment alone would enable me to say all I felt I would have to say in scorn as well as in pity. (p. 11)

However, in my view the ironic method is determined by the subject of anarchism to a greater extent than Conrad's pronouncements, with their stress on the technical, might suggest.

When he adds the subtitle 'An Ironic Tale' to 'The Informer' when it appears in *A Set of Six*, he provides a clue to the connection between subject and method. What *The Secret Agent* and the two stories have in common is a running association of anarchism with 'informing', in the sense of betrayal. Verloc, as a double agent and embassy spy, is permanently involved in betraying the cause he professes to uphold; and, more importantly, with the bomb plot he betrays Winnie's trust in him by fatally implicating the hapless Stevie. Winnie is then further betrayed by another member of the anarchist group, comrade Ossipon. Sevrin 'The Informer' betrays his comrades, while Paul in 'An Anarchist' is betrayed by the anarchists who befriend him and by the socialist lawyer, who is more concerned with making a reputation for himself than with obtaining the lightest sentence for his client. Then Paul in his turn betrays his fellow escapers. And, in betraying each other, these anarchists are at the same time betraying a fundamental principle of their political faith, a principle which is summed up in an article entitled 'Why We are Anarchists' in *The Torch*, number 5, which Conrad is likely to have read (since he seems to have read number 6, which contains the report of the revolt on St Joseph's island). The article stresses the importance, and the naturalness, of solidarity:

> We are Anarchists because we have studied the tendencies of evolution and see that all things advance from the simple to the complex, from slavery to freedom. Because we see that everything in the universe is built on the Anarchist principle of free individuals freely co-operating to produce one great whole. Because we see that the principle of solidarity of each for all and all for each, of what is good for all being good for the individual and vice versa, is the great law of nature.[9]

The principle of solidarity is the great law of nature; and this could be said to be part of the philosophical aspect of anarchism, which Conrad claims in the letter to Galsworthy of September 1906 not to have treated seriously; or rather, one might reasonably infer, not to have been able to take seriously at all. The association of anarchism with betrayal makes a fundamental mockery of that article of anarchist faith, and it is not difficult to see why it should have provoked Conrad's sardonic contempt. What he must have taken exception to is not the principle of solidarity itself, which in his maritime fiction he can honour, but the insistence that it is a law of nature. He was thoroughly opposed to such a Rousseauesque belief in a benign and meaningful nature, in the natural nobility of mankind.[10] In a well-known letter to Cunninghame Graham in 1899 he sets out his anti-Rousseau position in Rousseau's language (and Conrad's second), French:

> L'homme est un animal méchant. Sa méchanceté doit être organisée. Le crime est une condition nécéssaire de l'existence organisée. La société est essentiellement criminelle – ou elle n'existerait pas. C'est l'égoisme qui sauve tout – absolument tout – tout ce que nous abhorrons tout ce que nous aimons.

> [Man is a vicious animal. His viciousness must be organized. Crime is a necessary condition of organized existence. Society is fundamentally criminal – or it would not exist. Selfishness preserves everything – absolutely everything – everything we hate and everything we love.][11]

Clearly displayed here is not only his anti-Rousseauism but also the characteristic double vision of the ironist. The law of nature is not solidarity but selfishness, but selfishness is double-edged, preserving what is lovable as well as what is hateful. This is a highly deliberate and self-conscious double vision, which can be clearly distinguished from the self-deluding, self-deceived doubleness that characterizes Conrad's fictional anarchists. What the association of anarchism with betrayal points to is a disabling and demeaning duality: these people appear and purport to be one thing and are another. There is a striking discrepancy between appearance and being, between their words and their deeds, their rhetoric and their reality. In *The Secret Agent* Karl Yundt is a typical example: he preaches revolution, but 'the famous terrorist had never in his life raised as much as his little finger against the social edifice' (p. 47). From letters Conrad wrote between the periodical publication and the book publication of 'The Informer' it appears that he considered changing its title to 'Gestures', a change that would have highlighted the emptiness and role-playing of the anarchist figures. That hollow gesturing is summed up in the scene where Sevrin has been unmasked as an informer. As he stoops before the young Lady Amateur, as if to touch the hem of her garment, she produces the appropriate gesture: 'She snatched her skirt away from his polluting contact and averted her head with an upward tilt. It was magnificently done, this gesture of conventionally unstained honour, of an unblemished high-minded amateur' (p. 98).

These are the words of Mr X, but he, too, is as deeply implicated in ges-tural behaviour as is the young woman he mocks, leading as he does the privileged life of a cultivated bourgeois connoisseur while preaching revo-lution to the downtrodden masses. Conrad mocks his revolutionary posturing with a strategically placed descriptive detail, showing him interrupt his account 'to attack impassively, with measured movements, a *bombe glacée* which the waiter had just set down on the table' (p. 82).

The false, self-deluding, self-deceived doubleness of these anarchists is one that the ironic vision, which consciously exploits the discrepancy between surface meaning and underlying intention, is peculiarly well adapted to expose. The anarchist faith professed by would-be revolutionaries is an unwittingly ironic phenomenon in Conrad's view, and the ironic mode is the appropriate tool for its unmasking, sharing its duality but raising it to a higher level of deliberation and self-awareness. At the same time, anarchism as an ideology shares with irony a power to disturb and unsettle the very kind of complacency that most of its adherents in Conrad's world display. Harry Gee, the blusteringly affable, unscrupulous and overbearing manager of the South American cattle station in 'An Anarchist', registers its threat to a conventional bourgeois view of the world:

'But that subversive sanguinary rot of doing away with all law and order in the world makes my blood boil. It's simply cutting the ground from under the feet of every decent, respectable, hard-working person. I tell you that the con-sciences of people who have them, like you or I, must be protected in some way; or else the first low scoundrel that came along would in every respect be just as good as myself. Wouldn't he, now? And that's absurd!' (p. 144)

Cutting the ground from under the feet of those who are as respectably self-satisfied as Harry Gee is what Conrad's irony and anarchism could be said to have in common, and this may help account for the ambivalence of some of his pronouncements. While unsparing in his criticism of the hypocrisy and self-delusion of his bourgeois anarchists, in particular, Conrad repeatedly professes a certain respect for the most extreme expressions of anarchism. In the letter in French to Cunninghame Graham in 1899 he claims that he respects 'the extreme anarchists' because their hope for 'general extermination' is 'justifiable and, moreover, it is plain'.[12] It has the virtue of cutting through the obfuscations of language: 'One compromises with words. There's no end to it. It's like a forest where no one knows the way.' In another letter to the same correspondent in 1907, after completing *The Secret Agent*, he repeats the claim in relation to the figure of the Professor:

> And as regards the Professor I did not intend to make him despicable. He is incorruptible at any rate. In making him say 'madness and despair – give me that for a lever and I will move the world' I wanted to give him a note of perfect sincerity. At the worst he is a megalomaniac of an extreme type. And every extremist is respectable.[13]

Again, the Professor's stance has the qualities of simplicity and clarity that contrast with the self-deceived and deceitful rhetoric of his accomplices, and, with a characteristically ironic twist, Conrad honours the extremist with the epithet 'respectable' which would conventionally be applied to the society that he threatens. The ironist can detonate his own explosive charges.

Conrad's subversive irony has, then, some affinity with extreme forms of anarchism in its power to unsettle, although the parallel between the writer and the shabby, insignificant and demented figure of the Professor should not be pressed too far. What both call into question is the security taken for granted both by those anarchists who believe human solidarity to be guaranteed by a law of nature and by those who, like Harry Gee, accept the inequalities of existing hierarchical society as similarly ordained. That no meaningful order can safely be assumed in life is the lesson painfully learned by Paul the engineer in 'An Anarchist'. A man of the working class, he is more vulnerable and exposed to the power of others than are the bourgeois anarchists in 'The Informer', and his experience reveals the radical insecurity of existence that the unthinking are blind to: 'The principal truth discoverable in the views of Paul the engineer was that a little thing may bring about the undoing of a man' (p. 144). In his case that little thing is, ironically, a drunken feeling of solidarity with the 'multitude of poor wretches [who] had to work and slave to the sole end that a few individuals should ride in carriages and live riotously in palaces' (p. 146). Rather like the idiot Stevie in *The Secret Agent*, 'the pity of mankind's cruel lot wrung his heart' and he yells out the words that condemn him: '*Vive l'anarchie! Death to the capitalists!*' (p. 147). The momentary, emotional, unthinking commitment to solidarity with the suffering of others makes him a perpetual victim of other men. He becomes an object of surveillance – 'Watched by the police, watched by the comrades, I did not belong to myself any more' (p. 149) – and a prisoner, officially or unofficially, to the end of his days. The bitterly ironic structure of this 'Desperate Tale' is Conrad's most explicit rebuttal of the belief that the principle of solidarity, of each for all and all for each, is the great law of nature.

Betrayal reveals a world that cannot be trusted, where a little thing can bring about a man's undoing and individual life is precariously poised above an abyss. That precariousness is neatly figured in *The Secret Agent* by a glimpse of Mr Verloc leaning 'his forehead against the cold window-pane', protected by only 'a fragile film of glass' from 'the enormity of cold, black, wet, muddy, inhospitable accumulation of bricks, slates, and stones, things in themselves unlovely and unfriendly to man' (p. 54). Conrad's fictional world in these three texts is one of radical insecurity and atomized individualism. If betrayal is one experience that cuts the ground from under the characters' feet, irony is the device that does the same for the reader. In political terms that irony is even-handed, striking out not only at anarchism and its adherents, but also at the social and economic system that they seek to overthrow. In 'An Anarchist' the meat-extract manufacturing company's advertising is mocked for implying a benevolent interest in the betterment of mankind that can match the rhetoric of anarchism in its appeal to the gullible, to those like Paul the engineer with 'warm heart and weak head' (p. 161):

Of course everybody knows the B. O. S. Ltd., with its unrivalled products: Vinobos, Jellybos, and the latest unequalled perfection, Tribos, whose nourishment is offered to you not only highly concentrated, but already half digested. Such apparently is the love that the Limited Company bears to its fellowmen – even as the love of the father and mother penguin for their hungry fledglings. (p. 135)

Capitalism, too, lays bogus claim to solidarity with the human race, and its betrayals are similarly pernicious, as Paul discovers at the hands of Harry

Gee. For Conrad the ironist the two extremes meet, and he concludes his
remarks to Cunninghame Graham on *The Secret Agent* with a telling confla-
tion of capitalism and anarchism as destructive forces: 'If I had the necessary
talent I would like to go for the true anarchist – which is the millionaire. Then
you would see the venom flow. But it's too big a job.'[14]

NOTES

[1]   Frederick R. Karl and Laurence Davies (eds), *The Collected Letters of Joseph
      Conrad*, vol. 3, *1903–1907* (Cambridge, 1988), p. 354.
[2]   Joseph Conrad, *The Secret Agent* (Harmondsworth, 1963), p. 8. Further refer-
      ences to this edition will be given in the text.
[3]   Ford Madox Ford, *Joseph Conrad: A Personal Remembrance* (London, 1924),
      pp. 230–1.
[4]   Paul Avrich, 'Conrad's Anarchist Professor: An Undiscovered Source', *Labour
      History*, 18, 3 (1977), 397–402.
[5]   *A Set of Six*, The Medallion Edition of the Works of Joseph Conrad, vol. 11
      (London, 1925), p. x. Further references to this edition of the two stories will
      be given in the text.
[6]   Jacques Berthoud, '*The Secret Agent*', in J. H. Stape (ed.), *The Cambridge
      Companion to Joseph Conrad* (Cambridge, 1996), pp. 100–21.
[7]   *Letters*, 3, p. 371.
[8]   Ibid., p. 491.
[9]   *The Torch: A Revolutionary Journal of Anarchist-Communism*, n.s., 5 (31
      October 1894), 1.
[10] In *A Personal Record* he dismisses Rousseau as an 'artless moralist' with no
      imagination and a defective grasp of reality; see Joseph Conrad, *The Mirror of
      the Sea & A Personal Record*, ed. by Z. Nader (Oxford, 1988), p. 95. In *Under
      Western Eyes* (1911), too, he implicitly disparages Rousseau when he has the
      narrator observe that, 'there was something of naïve, odious and inane simplicity'
      about the unfrequented corner of Geneva where Rousseau's statue stands. And
      Conrad once again suggests an oblique relationship between Rousseau, anar-
      chism and betrayal when it is by this statue that Razumov, who has been urged
      to write something by the anarchist Julius Laspara, begins to write his confession
      to Natalia Haldin of how he betrayed her brother to the Tsarist authorities in
      St Petersburg. Cf. Joseph Conrad, *Under Western Eyes* (London, 1947 [1911]),
      pp. 290–1.
[11] Frederick R. Karl and Laurence Davies (eds), *The Collected Letters of Joseph
      Conrad*, vol. 2, *1898–1902* (Cambridge, 1986), pp. 159–60.
[12] *Letters*, 2, p. 160.
[13] *Letters*, 3, p. 491.
[14] Ibid.

3

Identifying Anarchy in
G. K. Chesterton's
The Man Who Was Thursday

HEATHER WORTHINGTON

One of G. K. Chesterton's many short essays is on the subject of telegraph poles. Chesterton relates how, with an unnamed friend, he takes a walk through 'one of those wastes of pine-wood which make inland seas of solitude in every part of Western Europe'.[1] He comments on how the apparent uniformity of the trees conveys a sort of terror: the very sameness of the trees makes them strange. At one point the pair come across a telegraph pole, and the straightness of the pole immediately reveals the illusory nature of the regularity of form of the pine-trees: '[c]ompared with the telegraph post the pines were crooked – and alive' (p. 23). In the ensuing conversation, the straightness of the poles and the imposition of order they suggest are initially denigrated.

How much better, Chesterton's companion argues, in 'all his anarchic philosophy' (p. 24), is the natural forest than the man-made object. The argument continues, with Chesterton admitting the ugliness of the telegraph pole, yet suggesting that its baseness lies not so much in its appearance or essential function, but in the uses to which it is put: for example, concealing the machinations of millionaires from the rest of society. The allegorical discussion of anarchy and order is terminated by nightfall, and the two men find themselves lost in the chaos of the forest. In an ironic turn, the very telegraph poles which they have been denigrating are the instruments of their salvation: groping their way through 'the fringe of trees which seemed to dance round us in derision [. . .] it was just possible to trace the outline of something just too erect and rigid to be a pine tree. By these, we finally felt our way home' (p. 27). Disorder, or anarchy, this essay seems to suggest, has its attractions, but order is necessary to survival.

This tension between anarchy and order is implicit in the etymology of the word 'anarchy'. In the original Greek the literal definition of 'anarchy' is 'without a leader' or 'without a ruler', a definition which has been refined over time into 'a society without government'.[2] But this relatively simple denotation also connotes 'both the negative sense of unruliness which leads to disorder and chaos, and the positive sense of a free society in which rule is no longer necessary'.[3] As the essay on telegraph poles suggests, this tension between positive and negative is evident in those writings of G. K. Chesterton that invoke the spectre of anarchy.[4] His uses of the terms 'anarchy' and 'anarchist' draw on stereotypical associations of anarchy with disorder and destruction, figured in equally stereotypical contemporary imaginings of the anarchist as the bearded, bomb-carrying nihilist, often of foreign origin, who seeks the destruction of social order to shock the certainty of authority. Yet Chesterton's own concept of the perfect society was, in the positive sense, anarchical: one in which government is unnecessary, where individuals would deal fairly and rationally with each other without recourse to a system of imposed laws. In this, his position was close to that of William Godwin, long considered as having given the first clear statement of anarchist principles in his *Enquiry Concerning Political Justice* (1793).

A society such as that advocated by Chesterton as a Distributist, arguing for a world without external government in which each man would have his 'three acres and a cow', relies on the freedom of the individual to govern his own personal and economic destiny.[5] This reliance on the individual in turn requires that the individual should have a strong sense of identity, not necessarily on a national scale, but at a personal level. Chesterton's concept of 'small is beautiful', illustrated in the many short, excellently written essays he produced, is evidence of his desire for order and containment. As he declared, '[a]ll my life I have loved frames and limits', and in the construction of identity a recognition of the limits of self is essential.[6] Before a self-regulating society can even be imagined, the individual must regulate him- or herself. Chesterton's concern with self-regulation and identity can perhaps be related both to his own early struggles to find his place in the world and to the broader question of pre-war, post-Victorian cultural and artistic identity.

The debate did not remain at the allegorical level of the telegraph-pole essay: for Chesterton the tension between positive and negative, between order and disorder, and the anxieties which that tension arouses are most clearly articulated in questions of identity. His central discussion of this matter and the text most focused on issues arising from anarchism is

The Man Who Was Thursday. This novel explores the instability of and search for personal, social and cultural identity in its depiction of Gabriel Syme and his fellow detectives/anarchists. That the novel is concerned with Chesterton's own youthful anxieties is retrospectively made apparent by his observation in his autobiography that the scepticism induced in him by, among other things, the new Impressionism in art was directly related to his own 'mood of unreality and sterile isolation', a mood in which 'I felt as if everything might be a dream [. . .] as if I had myself projected the universe from within'.[7] He goes on to describe how his revolt against this solipsism and scepticism was 'afterwards thrown up in a very formless piece of fiction called *The Man Who Was Thursday*', and directs the reader's attention to the subtitle of the work, 'A Nightmare'.[8] This subtitle refers not only to the pessimistic social and cultural nightmare induced by the 'nihilism of the Nineties', but to the dreamlike qualities of the narrative itself.[9]

In *The Man Who Was Thursday* the tension between positive and negative, between order and chaos, between, for Chesterton, optimism and pessimism, is figured not in telegraph poles and trees, but in men, specifically in the two poets Gabriel Syme and Lucian Gregory, who are the initiatory protagonist and antagonist, representing the antithesis between the new, Impressionism-linked poetic forms, which for Chesterton appeared to celebrate disorder and chaos, and the older, traditionally ordered forms. Opposition is inherent in the very names of the poets: 'Gabriel' suggests angelic status while 'Lucian' is doubly oppositional, combining suggestions of light and, with its resemblance to 'Lucifer', demonic status. This tension is then mapped on to a wider social antithesis between ordered society, figured in the detectives, and disordered society, figured in the anarchists. But as the new experimental poetry used the same basic materials as the old, and as the telegraph poles are related to and exist within the woods, so the detectives and anarchists are inextricably linked: indeed, they are one and the same. As with the telegraph poles, whose baseness lies not in their ugly utility but in the uses to which they are put, the anarchists, for whom order is shown to be essential, are the unwitting tools of capitalist interests. Sunday, the leader of the Anarchist Council, is reputed to have for his right-hand men 'South African and South American millionaires'.[10] As the Marquis de St Eustache, or Wednesday, declares, 'the rich have always objected to being governed at all. Aristocrats were always anarchists' (p. 227).

But not only culture, politics and personal identity are questioned in the novel. As in 'The Telegraph Poles', nature features as a threatening and anarchical force, here embodied in the unknowable and terrifying figure of Sunday. *The Man Who Was Thursday*, then, uses anarchy and anarchists as signifiers for the tensions and conflicts which are worked through in the narrative. This concept of the text as a locus of tension suggests that it is a serious and dry narrative, when in fact it is in many ways a comedy. One of Chesterton's great gifts as a writer was to make the serious entertaining and amusing, and *The Man Who Was Thursday* is no exception to this rule. Constructed, as the subtitle indicates, as a nightmare, the narrative opens with a scene set in the evening, where a mysterious and threatening sunset hints at the troubles that will arrive with nightfall. The novel concludes with a morning scene, when the night, and nightmare, is over, and a new day can begin. Within this structure the events recounted take place over seven days: the chaos of nightmare is contained within the order of time, paralleled by the seven anarchists, named after the days of the week, and reflecting the seven days of creation, which are the focus of the final chapter. The representation of the creation myth has religious overtones, but also speaks of the creation of order from disorder and, in the context of the novel, assigns identity, as the anarchists/detectives are reduced to their essential selves. What has been shifting and plural becomes part of a secure natural order: each individual now has a sound basis on which to build the future. The serious message of the narrative, the necessity of a sense of order to survive the chaos of existence at both a personal and a communal level, is imparted to the reader in a text that is not detective novel or adventure story, romance or moral tale, comedy or tragedy, fantastic or realist, but contains elements of all these. The text is itself anarchic.

Plurality and duality, at the level of character, identity, plot and language, are central to *The Man Who Was Thursday*, and this is apparent from the opening of the narrative. The very architecture of the suburb in which the action begins is uncertain of its identity, 'sometimes Elizabethan and sometimes Queen Anne', and its status as 'an artistic colony' is subverted by its failure to produce any art (p. 9). Each positive statement is balanced by its negative or opposite, and this is true of the poet Lucian Gregory, whose 'dark red hair parted in the middle [. . .] literally like a woman's' frames a face 'broad and brutal', seeming to blend 'the angel and the ape' (pp. 12–13). His opposite is Gabriel Syme, 'a mild-looking mortal, with a fair, pointed beard and faint, yellow hair', who is 'less meek than he looked' (p. 14). Their opposition is more than physical. Syme is 'a poet of law, a poet of order [. . .] a poet of respectability' (p. 14), while Gregory is an 'anarchic poet', arguing that '[a]n artist is identical with an anarchist', who 'disregards all governments, abolishes all conventions' (p. 15). The opposition between the two men is furthered by their secret identities: Gregory is not only anarchic in his verse, but an anarchist in fact, while Syme upholds laws not only in poetry but in his covert role as a detective. There is no indication of the genesis of Gregory's anarchism, but Syme's adherence to the law is the result of childhood experience. Born into 'a family of cranks' (p. 68), Syme, having been 'surrounded with every conceivable kind of revolt from infancy' (p. 69), chooses to revolt himself into 'the only thing left – sanity' (p. 69). But the fanaticism inherited from his parents is apparent in the fierceness with which he defends 'common sense' (p. 69), and a close encounter with the after-effects on innocent bystanders of an anarchist bomb leaves 'a spot on his mind that was not quite sane' (p. 69) with regard to anarchists and anarchy. As a result, when he is first approached by the 'philosophical policeman' (p. 75) who recruits him, Syme is closer in appearance to the anarchists he opposes than to a supporter of law and order: wrapped in an old black cloak, with long hair and beard, 'he looked a very satisfactory specimen of the anarchists upon whom he had vowed a holy war' (p. 71).

It is in the course of Syme's conversation with the policeman that Chesterton's reading of the role of the anarchists is most explicitly defined. There is 'a purely intellectual conspiracy' in which 'the scientific and artistic worlds are silently bound in a crusade against the Family and the State' (p. 74). Anarchists are divided into two groups, an outer circle of men known to the world 'who believe that rules and formulas have destroyed human happiness' (p. 79), a group with whom Chesterton himself would to some extent have sympathized, and a second, secret, inner circle. This latter is the true danger: the freedom from rule that these intellectual anarchists preach is actually the freedom of death.[11] They seek to destroy humanity. In anarchism, as in all else in *The Man Who Was Thursday*, what is visible is often a mask that conceals a different reality or identity. This is apparent in the encounter between Syme and the policeman. It is Syme's outwardly anarchist appearance that attracts the attention of the officer, who in turn is superficially an 'automatic official, a mere bulk of blue in the twilight' (p. 71). This surface appearance is rapidly subverted by the tenor of the constable's speech, which is educated and philosophical. The ensuing intellectual dialogue with Syme results in Syme's recruitment into 'the New Detective Corps for the frustration of the great conspiracy' (p. 84).

At Scotland Yard he is shown into a room 'the abrupt blackness of which startled him like a blaze of light' (p. 82). Here he meets the unseen chief of the New Detectives, 'a man of massive stature' (p. 82). The identity of this man is not overtly revealed until the closing pages of the narrative, but the astute reader will have realized before then that the chief of detectives and Sunday, the head of the Anarchist Council, are one and the same: law and anarchy are contained within a single suprahuman figure. Syme's short initial encounter with this figure ends with him passing from the darkness of the room into the light of evening with a new identity, that of a detective, an identity ratified by the small blue card 'on which was written "The Last Crusade" ' (p. 84). This change of identity is further marked by a change of dress, an alteration from the disorderly clothing which reflected his disordered campaign against anarchy to a neat and contained appearance suited to his new, ordered role. But this is not the only assumption of new identity that Syme undergoes. The sense of a passage through time and space that facilitates his rebirth as a new persona in a different world is most marked in Syme's serendipitous encounter with Gregory's branch of the anarchists and the subsequent election of Syme to the Central Council of Anarchists as Thursday.

This encounter commences in yet another location where appearances are deceptive. The 'dreary and greasy beershop' (p. 29) to which Gregory escorts Syme produces champagne and lobster mayonnaise in response to Syme's humorous request, a response which prompts him to declare that 'I don't often have the luck to have a dream like this. It is new to me for a nightmare to lead to a lobster. It is commonly the other way' (p. 30). The dreamlike quality inherent in the dislocation of appearance and reality responds to the subtitle of the novel, and Syme's reference to a nightmare is more prophetic than he realizes. In a sequence of events that combines fantasy and horror, humour and thrill, and politics and parody, Syme is drawn into the underworld of the anarchists. The table at which Syme and Gregory are seated begins to turn, gradually increasing in speed and carrying them down through the floor of the inn. The tunnel in which they are deposited is lit with red light, and leads to a round chamber. Humour and irony lighten a potentially dark and dangerous scene in the password that gains them entry, 'Mr Joseph Chamberlain' (p. 33). The ensuing description of the anarchists' secret meeting place and of their behaviour is pure parody. The passages leading to the council chamber are 'made up of ranks and ranks of rifles and revolvers, closely packed' (p. 33), and the chamber itself is made of steel, 'almost spherical in shape', lined with 'things that looked like the bulbs of iron plants, or the eggs of iron birds. They were bombs, and the very room itself seemed like the inside of a bomb' (p. 34). The portrayal of the anarchist meeting is itself heavily ironic. It is organized and run in the manner of a trade union meeting or communist gathering, with much emphasis on order and rules, each member being described as a delegate and called comrade: anarchists require order in the promulgation of disorder that is their aim. Gregory's speech in support of his own election is muted and ill-received, but Syme, in a moment of inspiration, offers a triumphant speech advocating anarchy and is elected instead of Gregory, to take on yet another identity as

Thursday, member of the Central Anarchist Council. Syme feels himself to have taken on the role of a crusading knight: the swordstick with which he has been issued 'became almost the sword of chivalry' (p. 86); his apparently coherent identity as a poet has become diffused into a multiple identity, combining the poet with the detective, the anarchist and the crusader, and the alteration in persona is reflected in his relationship with the world.

As he steps on to the boat that will take him to his first meeting with the Council, Syme has 'a singular sensation of stepping out into something entirely new; not merely the landscape of a new land, but even into the landscape of a new planet' (p. 84). The sense of otherness is compounded by the appearance of the stones of the Embankment, where he lands, which look like 'the colossal steps of some Egyptian palace' (p. 87) and the foreign aspect of Leicester Square, described as looking like 'the replica of some French or even Spanish public place' (p. 92). Anarchism is articulated as, and located in, foreign space. This was perhaps a response to the Aliens Act of 1905, itself an attempt to address the perceived problems arising from the influx of immigrants into England from Europe.[12] Distanced from Englishness and 'normality', and in contrast to Chesterton's apotheosis of the common man as one who is rooted in place and secure in identity, the anarchist is a stranger in a land made strange.

This strangeness is made clear in the descriptions of the members of the Anarchist Council, descriptions which are both stereotypical and often comedic, even scurrilous. Monday, the Secretary of the Council, has a relatively normal face, 'long, pale and intellectual' with 'a tuft of dark beard' (p. 88) but his smile has 'something unnerving in it [. . .] the last nightmare touch' (p. 90) and, on closer examination, the Secretary appears 'wasted with some disease [. . .] his eyes were alive with intellectual torture' (p. 101). As the narrative notes, '[h]e was typical of each of the tribe; each man was subtly and differently wrong' (p. 101). Tuesday, or Gogol, is described as 'a common or garden Dynamiter', with a 'bewildering bush of beard and hair' and 'the sad eyes of some Russian serf' (p. 97). Wednesday, or the Marquis de St Eustache, has a superficial French normality, but the atmosphere surrounding him is reminiscent of 'drowsy odours and of dying lamps in the darker poems of Byron and Poe' (p. 101), while his facial features declare him 'not a Frenchman; he might be a Jew; he might be something deeper yet in the dark heart of the East' (p. 102).[13] Professor de Worms, or Friday, is, '[s]ave for his intellect [. . .] in the last stages of senile decay' (p. 102). Bearded and with wrinkled grey skin, he looks 'as if some drunken dandies had put their clothes upon a corpse' (p. 103), with an aura of not merely decrepitude, 'but corruption' (p. 103). In contrast, Saturday, or Dr Bull, has the appearance of normality, combining '*savoir-faire* with a sort of well-groomed coarseness which is not uncommon in young doctors' (p. 103). His strangeness is located in the black glasses which totally obscure his eyes, reminding Syme of the 'story about pennies being put on the eyes of the dead' (p. 103).

Exceeding all these, in stature, authority and strangeness, is Sunday, the leader of the Council. A preternaturally large man, 'planned enormously in his original proportions [. . .] enlarged terribly to scale' (p. 94), Sunday evokes in Syme a sense of spiritual evil. Sunday's face seems 'too big to be possible' (p. 96), and it is only by a supreme effort of will that Syme can take his place at the table with the other Council members. Having established this strange and alien group of men, the narrative almost immediately begins to deconstruct these seemingly certain signifiers of identity. Gogol, who is most obviously and stereotypically representative of contemporary images of anarchists, is exposed by Sunday as a member of the same police agency as Syme. Stripping off his hairy disguise, Gogol is revealed as having 'thin red hair and a pale, pert face' (p. 123), while his voice, losing the heavy Polish accent, reverts to a tone that is 'clear, commercial and somewhat cockney' (p. 122). This reversion to type is repeated as the novel progresses, and each member of the Council is revealed as a detective and an ordinary man. On removing his dark glasses, Saturday, or Dr Bull, becomes 'a boyish-looking young man, with very frank and happy hazel eyes, an open expression, [and] cockney clothes like those of a city clerk' (p. 179). In the course of the duel between Syme and the Marquis de St Eustache, or Wednesday, his mask is pulled off, revealing 'the blonde, well-brushed, smooth-haired head which is common in the English constabulary' (p. 214) and which belongs to one Inspector Ratcliffe. The Secretary, or Monday, he of the sinister twisted smile, unmasks himself after the pursuit in France as yet another detective. Professor de Worms admits his own membership of the detective force, in his attempt to elicit the same information from Syme, and eventually confesses to being a thirty-eight-year-old actor by the name of Wilks, who had appropriated the identity of the real Professor de Worms so successfully that the original was now considered a bad copy.

The Anarchist Council is in fact comprised of detectives, with the exception of Sunday, who remains an unknown quantity. Far from being strange or foreign, the men are ordinary, commonplace characters, drawn into the conspiracy through their recruitment into the detective force. Once the process of revelation has commenced, the pace of the narrative quickens, literally and figuratively. The action becomes a series of pursuits in search both of other anarchists and of the truth or reality. This tilting of perception and its significance in terms of identity are articulated in the often-analysed scene in the woodlands at the commencement of the pursuit: 'The inside of the wood was full of shattered sunlight and shaken shadows. [. . .] Even the solid figures walking with him Syme could hardly see' (p. 223). The effect of the light and shadow makes those fleeing appear to be wearing black half-masks, similar to those worn by their pursuers:

> The fancy tinted Syme's overwhelming sense of wonder. Was he wearing a mask? Was anyone wearing a mask? Was anyone anything? This wood of witchery, in which men's faces turned black and white by turns, in which their figures first swelled into sunlight and then faded into formless night, this mere chaos of chiaroscuro [. . .] seemed to Syme a perfect symbol of the world in which he had been moving for three days, this world where men took off their beards and spectacles and their noses, and turned into other people. (p. 224)

The sense of confusion Syme experiences leads him to question whether there '[w]as anything that was apart from what it seemed' (p. 225). This is further mapped by Chesterton on to 'what modern people call Impressionism, which is another name for that final scepticism which can find no floor to the universe' (p. 225). Without a secure delineation of identity, meaning becomes meaningless, subject to change and interpretation. The sense of personal dislocation depicted here is brought into sharper relief by the depiction of a French peasant, who seems to represent 'common sense' (p. 228), epitomizing the 'ordinary healthy person' (p. 228) who would be immune to the lure of anarchy. The peasant's 'swarthy figure stood dark against a square of sunlight, almost like some allegorical figure of labour frescoed on a ground of gold' (pp. 228–9), secure in his identity and his locality. This is Chesterton's apotheosis of the common man, happy and content with his lot, an aspirational figure for the other characters and for the reader.

The confused and confusing pursuit in France comes to an end with the revelation of the Secretary as a detective, a revelation which redirects the pursuit and its object. The return passage to England and the chance meeting with the ex-Gogol bind the six detectives together as a coherent force, whose aim is the apprehension, in both senses of the word, of Sunday. This larger-than-life figure seems to hold the answers to the mystery that the novel has become, but there is an element of anxiety among the detectives as they consider their quest. As the Professor observes, 'I should feel a bit afraid of asking Sunday who he really is' (p. 270), not because of a fear of violence, but 'for fear he might tell me' (p. 271). Syme concludes that it is not, as Dr Bull has it, 'six men going to ask one man what he means' (p. 273), but 'six men going to ask one man what they mean' (p. 273). Meaning in the narrative is constantly changing as identities alter: as Robert L. Caserio suggests, for Chesterton 'the means to certainty is equivocal, but only equivocation can clear a path for certainty'.[14]

Chesterton's playfulness with language and the delight he takes in its potentially anarchic qualities are evident throughout the novel, recognizing both the desire to fix meaning and the impossibility of achieving such fixity. It is in the representation of Sunday, whose monstrous appearance is contradicted by the frequent playfulness and levity of his speech, that this opposition, and the anxiety it can induce, is made clear. Sunday represents both certainty – the detectives are certain that he holds the answers to their questions – and uncertainty – it is impossible to know or understand him. This opposition can be seen when the detectives finally confront Sunday, demanding answers to their questions. Sunday treats their demands for information with a levity that, on a different level, contains serious comment.

Sunday implicitly recognizes the detectives' request for certainty: 'you want me to tell you who I am, and what you are, and what this table is, and what this Council is, and what this world is' (p. 275). Although his summation seems a reiteration of their questions, by the apparently frivolous inclusion of the table Sunday moves their questions from the physical to the metaphysical, from the empirical to the philosophical.[15] And his response to Syme's reiterated plea of 'what are you?' (p. 276) is similarly couched in metaphysical terms: 'you will have found out the truth of the last tree and the topmost cloud before the truth about me. You will understand the sea, and I shall still be a riddle; you shall know what the stars are, and not know what I am' (p. 276). The only fact that Sunday offers Syme and his companions is that he 'is the man in the dark room, who made you all policemen' (p. 277). This confirmation of his dual role as detective chief and anarchist leader serves only to destabilize certainty, leaving the detectives further confused by his admission of identity. The desperate attempt to make sense of the apparently senseless is evident in the ensuing crazy and comic pursuit of Sunday. The illogicality and impossibility of dreams permeate Sunday's flight, as he moves through London first in a hansom cab, then in a commandeered fire engine, before liberating an elephant from the zoo and finally transferring to a balloon.

In the course of his flight, Sunday throws scraps of paper bearing messages back to the pursuing detectives, each addressed to a specific individual. But the messages, although perfectly coherent, are senseless: 'What about Martin Tupper *now*?' runs the message to Dr Bull (p. 279). 'Fly at once. The truth about your trouser-stretchers is known. – A Friend' is the content of the note addressed to Inspector Ratcliffe (p. 281). The recipients attempt to make sense of the contents, assuming that there is a hidden, personal meaning concealed in the words. Even in its failure, such an attempt acknowledges the desire of the individual to construct meaning in relation to the self. Another illustration of this is the misreading of the sounds heard by the pursuers as they reach the barrier of a high, impenetrable fence. Wondering if the fence marks the boundaries of Sunday's domain, the detectives interpret the noises coming from within in different ways. Syme hears 'the most horrible noises, like devils laughing and sneezing and blowing their devilish noses' (p. 282). The Secretary suggests that it is Sunday's dogs barking, dogs that Gogol shudderingly observes 'would be no ordinary dogs' (p. 283). Sunday's overwhelming influence, even in his absence, inflects the detectives' reading. It is only when they surmount the fence that the reality becomes apparent. The unearthly noises emanate from the inhabitants of the zoo in which the detectives find themselves. In spite of this commonplace explanation, the shadow cast by Sunday causes Syme to see the inhabitants of the zoo differently, as 'a glaring panorama of [. . .] strange animals [. . .]. The whole gave him a sensation, the vividness of which he could not explain, that Nature was always making quite mysterious jokes' (p. 286).

Sunday, with his joking, senseless messages and his oracular and obscure answers, is here clearly identified with the nature to which Syme refers. And it is into nature that Sunday leads the detectives as they continue their pursuit. The action moves from the town into the country, and the pursuers abandon their cabs and continue on foot 'through black thickets and [. . .] ploughed fields till each was turned into a figure too outrageous to be mistaken as a tramp' (p. 292). The external indicators of each individual's identity are gradually stripped away, preparing them for the new identity to be assumed. The journey required takes them physically through rich countryside, into parkland, which evokes in all six a remembrance of and a nostalgia for their boyhood: before they can assume their adult identities, they must metaphorically return to childhood. This final passage complete, on their arrival at Sunday's house they are issued with new clothes, exotic and theatrical costumes. But in contrast to the costumes which the detectives used in the construction of their anarchist identities, 'these disguises did not disguise, but reveal' (p. 314).

Each man is dressed according to the appropriate day of the week from which he took his anarchist identity, but here the days of the week are also the days of creation. And the aspect of creation that occurred on each day proves to embody simultaneously the essential identity of the man. Religion

and nature, order and anarchy are fused together in the creation of the world
and of the individual in the world. The week of creation is completed by
Sunday, who represents 'the Sabbath [and] the peace of God' (p. 322). He
makes a speech, in which he admits his role in manipulating and directing
the others, in forcing them into the uncertainties which have brought them
to certainty. But he gives them no clear answer. As Syme states, 'my soul
and heart are [. . .] happy and quiet [. . .] but my reason is still crying out. I
should like to know' (p. 323). It is not Sunday who enables Syme to reach
some understanding, however, but Gregory.

Gregory has been absent from much of the narrative, but the dream-state
which permits dislocation and disjunction also permits his entry into this
final scene. He is clothed totally in black, and his anarchist identity is, in
keeping with the religious metaphor, conflated with that of Satan. He is 'a
destroyer. I would destroy the world if I could' (p. 325). His impassioned
speech in support of anarchy arouses in Syme a response that articulates the
sense of opposition against which identity is constructed: the fight against
chaos which constitutes a sense of self. Syme recognizes that he and
Gregory are two sides of the same coin. Only their perspective is different:
every individual requires something against which he or she can define themselves. Then 'each thing that obeys law may have the glory and the isolation
of the anarchist [. . .] each man fighting for order may be as good and brave
a man as the dynamiter' (p. 327). And Sunday, representing the anarchy of
nature and the unknowable universe, combining in a single figure anarchy
and order, signifies the ultimate in opposition and in definition. But he is
suprahuman. What Syme has come to realize is that the common factor in
humanity is suffering uncertainty, and his final question to Sunday is 'have you
ever suffered?' (p. 328). Sunday's response is couched in biblical terminology,
' "Can ye drink of the cup that I drink of?" ' (p. 329). This biblical reference, while in keeping with the religious element implicit in Chesterton's
use of the Creation myth, does not equate Sunday with God.[16] Rather, it suggests the suffering inherent in Sunday's dual identity, a duality which can
never be resolved.

This is the culmination of the novel. Sunday's final words are dimly
heard as Syme falls into the blackness of unconsciousness. Here is the final
rite of passage, and a final rebirth. As the narrative observes, '[w]hen men
in books wake from a vision, they commonly find themselves in some place
in which they might have fallen asleep' (p. 329). Syme's awakening is totally
different: 'gradually [. . .] he knew that he was and had been walking along
a country lane' (p. 329). He is accompanied by Gregory, and they are in easy
conversation 'about some triviality' (p. 329). But Syme feels 'a crystal

simplicity in his mind [. . .] he was in possession of some impossibly good news' (p. 330). And the world in which he moves is also new-born: 'Dawn was breaking over everything in colours at once clear and timid; as if Nature made a first attempt at yellow and a first attempt at rose' (p. 330). Syme has passed through the nightmare of uncertainty and has achieved the security of identity that enables mankind to exist in anarchical nature. In a return to beginnings, Syme returns to the place where the nightmare commenced, and to the red-headed sister of Gregory, a return which implicitly promises a new beginning.

The Man Who Was Thursday is ultimately less about anarchy, anarchism or anarchists than about a search for identity. Stereotypical contemporary images of anarchism and its practitioners function as signifiers for the mental and social chaos inherent in uncertainty of identity. As 'The Telegraph Poles' suggests, in a chaotic world some order and structure is essential to survival, and to relate to the world the individual must have a strong sense of self. To hell with culture? For Chesterton, to hell with high modernist culture, certainly. Such culture questions identity and reality and destabilizes conceptions of self. But in its other sense, that of growth and development in all its guises, that which shapes and informs the self, culture creates a rational individual with an innate sense of order and right and would make external government redundant. Such culture would make possible the anarchic society visualized by Chesterton in his Distributist polemic, and should, accordingly, be preserved.

NOTES

[1]   G. K. Chesterton, 'The Telegraph Poles', *Alarms and Discursions* (London, 1926 [1910]), p. 21; further references will be inserted in the text.

[2]   Peter Marshall, *Demanding the Impossible: A History of Anarchism* (London, 1993 [1992]), p. 3.

[3]   Ibid.

[4]   As well as *The Man Who Was Thursday*, Chesterton wrote two essays directly concerned with anarchism. These are 'The Anarchist', first published in the *Daily News*, 4 December 1909, later incorporated into *Alarms and Discursions* (1910), and 'The Conversion of an Anarchist', published in *The Touchstone and the American Student Magazine*, 5 (1919), reprinted in *The Chesterton Review*, 8 (1982). In both essays, anarchists are depicted as slavish followers of the ideas of others, followers who do not really comprehend those ideas. Against this unstructured chaos Chesterton advocates common sense and order.

5   Distributism was discussed in *GK's Weekly*, a periodical edited and financed by
     Chesterton from 1925 until his death in 1936. The Distributist element of
     Chesterton's thought and its influence on his novels is discussed in Ian Boyd,
     The Novels of G. K. Chesterton: A Study in Art and Propaganda (London, 1975).

6   Cited in Margaret Canovan, *G. K. Chesterton, Radical Populist* (New York,
     1977), p. 81.

7   'Foreword: A Composite Essay from G. K. Chesterton's *Autobiography*', in
     D. J. Conlon (ed.), *G. K. Chesterton: A Half-Century of Views* (Oxford, 1987),
     p. v.

8   Ibid., p. vii.

9   Ibid., p. ix.

10   G. K. Chesterton, *The Man Who Was Thursday: A Nightmare* (Bristol, 1937
     [1908]), p. 227; further references are inserted in the text.

11   Karl Kegler suggests that in *The Man Who Was Thursday* '[t]his second variety
     of anarchism is nihilism [. . .] Chesterton regards this nihilistic anarchism as a
     purely intellectual concept that has its roots in German idealistic philosophy,
     thinking perhaps of Schopenhauer and Nietzsche.' See Kegler, 'Anarchic
     Optimism: *The Napoleon of Notting Hill* and Chesterton's Concept of Violence',
     Inklings: Jahrbuch für Literatur und Ästhetik, 14 (1996), 193–207 (199).

12   The Aliens Act was a response to perceived widespread anxiety and debate
     about the relationship between alien immigration, crime and the problems pres-
     ented by Britain's poor. Unrest in Europe during this period had increased rates
     of immigration into the country, and the eruption of terrorist acts abroad, in
     conjunction with rising crime-rates in Britain, fostered a fear of anarchism. This
     fear was further fed by contemporary scientific discourses, such as those on
     social Darwinism and eugenics.

13   Chesterton's association of anarchism and evil with Jewishness is evidence of
     what has been read as his anti-Semitism, here and elsewhere. In the context of
     this text I would suggest that he is drawing on contemporary stereotypical asso-
     ciations of Jewishness with capitalism, equally unacceptable to the modern
     reader, but part of the times in which Chesterton wrote.

14   Robert L. Caserio, 'G. K. Chesterton and the Terrorist God Outside
     Modernism', in Lynne Hapgood and Nancy L. Paxton (eds), *Outside
     Modernism: In Pursuit of the English Novel, 1900–30* (Basingstoke, 2000), p.
     66.

15   The inclusion of a table in this apparently sensible list is surely a reference to
     the issue familiar to all new students of philosophy, the Platonic and
     Aristotelian definitions of the essence of tableness.

16   According to Christopher Hollis, in an interview Chesterton specifically denied
     that Sunday represented God. Rather, he represents nature. See Hollis, *The
     Mind of Chesterton* (London, 1970), p. 58.

4

Art for Politics' Sake: The Sardonic Principle of James Leslie Mitchell (Lewis Grassic Gibbon)

WILLIAM K. MALCOLM

I am a Scotsman, an artist, and – an integral part of my being – an anarchist. My art is implicit anarchy.[1]

Thus James Leslie Mitchell, more famous as the pseudonymous Lewis Grassic Gibbon, defined his personal credo less than a year before his early death in 1935. Yet only the tag of Scotsman here – factually representing his country of birth – appears free of ambiguity. Mitchell's take on anarchism, evidently deeply felt, was typically eclectic and idiosyncratic, while his views on the personal artistic ramifications of this political standpoint deserve to be teased out in full. His art collectively can indeed be considered 'implicit anarchy' dedicated to one overriding libertarian end.[2] However, the precise political character of Mitchell's writing demands to be defined clearly to sustain comfortable judgements concerning his precise literary aims, and to enable us in turn to evaluate his final achievement as a writer.

Politically motivated art comes in all shapes and sizes, from thinly masked propaganda to the most profound paeans to fundamental human values and beliefs. Great art truly can be inspired by the political conviction lying at its very heart; Picasso's 'Guernica', for example, possesses a trenchant political power that freely transcends its artistic medium. Equally, political art – of all persuasions – can be crudely doctrinaire and ultimately forgettable. It is comparatively rare to find an individual work which marries political fervour with aesthetic poise. The 1930s, chronicled memorably by Piers

Brendon as 'the dark valley',[3] that uniquely grim era involving massive social, economic, political and even spiritual upheaval, inevitably threw up a wealth of artistic responses, mixing politics and art in endless permutations. In this article I wish to explore the peculiar relationship that evolved between the radical art and politics of Leslie Mitchell who, as Lewis Grassic Gibbon, is now securely placed amongst the foremost writers of this most sharply political period. Indeed, Gustav Klaus's percipient description in 1978 of Gibbon's epic trilogy *A Scots Quair* as constituting 'the outstanding Socialist prose work of the inter-war period'[4] has now become the accepted critical standpoint upon Mitchell's literary legacy.

I have written elsewhere about Leslie Mitchell's preferred creative method, in 'shouting too loudly', to construct a socially motivated art-form fuelled by moral indignation and directed towards formal political ends.[5] Here, I wish to examine more closely Mitchell's basic artistic motivation and his distinctive view of the function of art, as well as to trace the development of his preoccupation with the role of the artist – including his own. In particular, I intend to show the latent ambivalence of the relationship between his art and his politics in his writing and to demonstrate how his declared political motivation as a self-styled 'good anarcho-communist'[6] simultaneously stimulated his creativity and clipped his sense of artistic achievement. In the final analysis, Mitchell's willingness to sacrifice his art to his politics paradoxically yielded its own lasting aesthetic salvation.

Leslie Mitchell's literary ambitions pre-dated even his radical political disposition. At thirteen years of age, brim-full of the brashness of youth, he declared in a school essay: 'I think I will be a journalist, or perhaps an Editor, but you'll have to wait a long time before you read one of my books or newspapers!'[7] Despite these early apprehensions, and in defiance of the inauspicious cultural background that he inherited as son to a poor crofting farmer in the Mearns, three years later Leslie Mitchell's literary ambitions found a practical outlet, with his employment as cub reporter with the *Aberdeen Journal* in his local city. Within two more years, Mitchell's writing talents were further rewarded when he found increased pay and responsibility south, with the *Scottish Farmer* in Glasgow. However, following this professional high-point in 1919, Leslie Mitchell had to endure considerable tribulations before finally he could realize his adolescent aim to become a self-proclaimed 'professional writer-cratur':[8] the abrupt termination of his journalistic career, with his dismissal from the *Scottish Farmer*; severe mental anguish, culminating in nervous collapse on at least two occasions; and two unwelcome terms 'conscripted' into the Forces – as he put it in his first novel – by hunger and unemployment.[9]

Having taken the plunge professionally in September 1929, Mitchell the tyro author was exposed to additional pressures, as breadwinner for a young wife – Rebecca Middleton, wholly supportive former classmate and neighbour from Arbuthnott – and infant daughter and son, born in 1930 and 1934 respectively. The pressure of earning a living exclusively by the efforts of his pen committed Leslie Mitchell to a darg which consumed the bulk of his waking hours. 'If I took to writing (as I possibly did) owing to constitutional laziness and under the impression that authorship was an easy job, I'm being disillusioned', he lamented to his mentor, Alexander Gray, in July 1930, the depression palpable.[10] This unrelenting vocation of writing led Mitchell to stretch his talents across unfamiliar genres and encouraged him to produce pulp work, written as a self-confessed 'holiday from more serious things'.[11] His publisher file among his papers, now located at the National Library of Scotland, clinically calibrates the efforts he had to make in order to earn a passable living from his work, constantly pushing for minuscule improvements in advances and in royalty terms with publishers at home and abroad.[12]

Thus, Leslie Mitchell's career as a writer was hard earned, indeed. In addition, it was carved out against a wholly unpropitious cultural background. Both Mitchell parents were baffled by the literary prodigy born in their midst; their attitude can best be recorded as an expression of the Protestant work ethic, projected as a Calvinist denunciation of activities which seemed to be distinguished by the avoidance of hard physical graft. Half-brothers, John and George, and peers at school were also notoriously uncomprehending. Gallingly, Alexander Gray, Mitchell's enlightened teacher at Arbuthnott Public School, fought a lone battle during Mitchell's schooldays – and afterwards – to convince his protégé's family and the community at large of Mitchell's prowess and of his academic potential. As someone brought up amidst the harsh pragmatism of Scottish crofting society, therefore, Leslie Mitchell was made fully conscious of the superficial image ascribed to art of being a cosmetic enterprise, removed from real life. His parents famously subscribed to the negativity typically generated by books and writing in north-east farming circles, pouring scorn upon his literary efforts and urging him to seek semi-steady (if poorly remunerated) employment in the shape of a 'real job' contracted by a 'fee' at a neighbouring farm. First and foremost, then, writing acquired a sardonic inflection in Mitchell's life experience by offering him the simple promise of escape from the dour social reality of the present.

Given a background where cultural pride was largely defined inversely, by hostile challenging of traditional figures of authority (teachers, ministers, lawyers, politicians, journalists and landowners all being gleefully walloped at regular intervals in Mitchell's fiction and non-fiction), Mitchell himself tended to be similarly ironic in his fictional portrayal of writers and artists. The failed writer turned bitter ironist is a figure which haunts Mitchell's fiction, with Andreas van Koupa, the predatory and self-seeking gigolo from his first novel, *Stained Radiance*, personifying most completely this risible trait. Koupa is Mitchell's most critical portrait of the artist-as-idler/cynic; this lapsed revolutionary rationalizes coldly about his solipsistic decision to abandon all pretence of artistic integrity:

> I will keep me secure in the places to which I climb, fenced round with the politics and prejudices of the little bourgeois swine. I shall burn the torch of art behind their shelter, not see it blown to dust and ashes on proletcult barricades. God mine, art cries for security, for shelter. Have I not earned the so-little share of those now?[13]

A scurrilous (and probably libellous) cameo of 'Wallace Mongour', surviving among Mitchell's manuscripts, sums up admirably his opposition towards the stereotypical Scottish literary dilettante:

> Since then [adopting the name of Wallace Mongour] he has not looked back, publishing every two years or so a novel dealing with Scots life and based on intimate study of the works of the minor German dramatists, with which he is well acquainted. Every three years produces a new book of verse. As literary editor of the 'London Looker-on' he has done more than any other to keep alive interest in the Scots Renaissance, and in his charming home in Hampstead has become the centre of the movement.[14]

Leslie Mitchell was invariably sceptical when referring to serious artistic endeavour, even his own. He was patently unsuited by both his peasant rearing and his peasant temperament to assume the po-faced stance of the aesthete. In his correspondence, he indulged habitually in self-reflexive humour that poked fun at his own literary pretentions; his wry self-description as 'professional writer-cratur' is subtly self-mocking, and even his most famous production, *Sunset Song*, the first volume of the *Scots Quair* trilogy, was flippantly corrupted in his own correspondence to 'Sunstroke Song'.[15] In addition, Mitchell compulsively planted playful squibs in various publications, aimed at pinching himself out of authorial complacency and pricking any sense of elitist pomposity. Having gained professional recognition in the form of an entry in *Who's Who* in 1934 – the contemporary index to the great and the good – Mitchell couldn't resist subverting its status, and simultaneously undermining his own self-image, by listing as his recreation the glorious implausibility of 'deep-sea diving'.[16]

This impish penchant for self-parody is also evident in his fiction work, for example in the incongruous casting of the clownish Reverend Gibbon in *Sunset Song*, accorded the author's own Scots surname yet caricatured as an inveterate womanizer, hypocrite and hedonistic self-seeker. In the same book, the portrait of Tony 'the daftie' embodies a blanket warning about the dangers of books and learning, Chris's mother remonstrating with her husband, 'learning in books it was sent the wee red daftie at Cuddieston clean skite, they say'.[17] However, this witty self-recrimination is also part of a more fundamental concern in Mitchell's writing, to be discussed later, constituting a profound and serious exploration of the whole function of art, of the role of the artist and of his fundamental artistic responsibility.

In tandem with his deep-seated interest in writing, from early adulthood Leslie Mitchell demonstrated a sustained interest in left-wing politics, espousing some form of anarchism or communism for two decades from his schooldays till his death. His Scottishness may be recognized as an important cultural influence, but Mitchell minimized its political significance, categorically defining his stance in March 1934 as, 'non-Nationalist, and yet interested in this new revival of cultural and political Nationalism'. Mitchell's personal political philosophy, then, was emphatically universal in scope, sustaining an imaginative vision which rejected nationalism and internationalism within 'the vision of Cosmopolis'.[18] This political ideal was underpinned by Mitchell's emotional humanism, honed by his direct personal experience of social injustice and deprivation – in the primitive drudgery of his own family background in small-scale farming or in the detached observation of urban squalor and political repression in Glasgow in 1919, which gave birth to the radicalism of 'Red Clydeside'.

While Mitchell's political credo had a fierce moral charge at its core, then, its formal expression inevitably varied over the years. In a letter to Naomi Mitchison in 1933, Mitchell provided a useful thumbnail-sketch of his adult political development, rehearsing what he termed the 'brief history of a revoluter':

> I suppose I'm still some kind of revolutionary. I was thrown out of the Communist Party as a Trotskyist – while I was in the ranks of the Army, doing Communist propaganda. So I went Anarchist for a bit, but they're such damn fools, with their blah about Kropotkin (whose anthropology is worse than Frazer's) and Bakunin. When the last Labour Gov went west, I re-applied to join the Communists, but they refused to have anything to do with me. Brief

history of a revoluter. I once tried (and wrote a propaganda novel for it) to form a Society of Militant Pacifists – chaps who were to engage in sabotage, train-wrecking, and so on if another war came. But the Promethean Society pinched my members.[19]

Throughout his non-fiction, Mitchell assumed an interconnectedness between anarchism and communism; his personal political creeds of anarchism and communism can be conflated within the compound of anarcho-communism with little real ideological difficulty. His utopian political ideal portraying a free and just society is anarchist in conception, predicated, very like Kropotkin's, on a belief in natural human values and instincts. However, Mitchell's sympathies with Diffusionism (see note 25 for a discussion of this movement) coloured this vision, divorcing it from formal political reality and cementing it into a heavily romanticized picture of antediluvian purity preserved in a pre-civilized world. Communism then became increasingly prominent within Mitchell's political hybrid as the practical means of achieving this Diffusionist-anarchist goal, as he observed to Tom Wintringham, comrade in the anti-fascist group Writers' International, which spawned the highly influential Thirties journal *Left Review*. Mitchell explained to Wintringham in March 1934: 'You and I use Anarchism in different senses. I'm a conscious anarchist, not a laissez-faire one! . . . This is an old Communist dodge. Not that I mind – bless 'em! Communism we must have before we can have the No-state. So we're agreed, aren't we?'[20]

Mitchell's political attitude hardened perceptibly towards the end of his life, embracing, albeit reluctantly, hard-line revolutionary Marxism – just like young Ewan Tavendale in *Grey Granite* – as a vehicle offering radical political solutions to the rapidly deteriorating social conditions of the mid-Thirties. Nevertheless, Mitchell remained clear-eyed in his perception of the subordinate function of communism and of its accommodation by his anarchist ideal, defining for Eric Linklater his abolitionist view of the political necessity of CP activism as a means towards the ultimate attainment of political freedom:

I loathe organization, control, the state, and the voice of the sergeant-major. As the sole surviving specimen of Natural Man to be found in these islands, I'm naturally an anarchist. But how you or I or – more to the point – our unfortunate progeny can attain real freedom and fun without the preliminary conditioning of communism is beyond me. Communism's merely a means to an end – a nannie enforcing on the dirty little boy who calls himself Man the necessity for scrub-bing the back of his neck and keeping his regrettable bowels in order. When he grows adolescent and can do these things automatically and has ceased to smell quite so badly, he'll be a much better equipped specimen for his chosen mission of playing football with the cosmos.[21]

While Mitchell may have felt uncomfortable in his role as writer, he remained just as sharply focused in his view of the ends of art as in his left-wing politics. As with most things, his pronouncements on art are sure-footed. His artistic principles, however, require to be carefully unravelled and dissected to be fully understood.

Mitchell's artistic ideal is most effectively articulated in an aside within his mature historical essay on 'The Antique Scene', in *Scottish Scene*. Here, his belief in the ultimate force of art crystallizes into a suitably exalted proclamation: 'all art is no more than the fine savour and essence of the free life.'[22] This rather amorphous definition suggests a belief in the existence of a totally pure and universally accessible Keatsian form of objective truth, a mytho-poetic absolute, enshrining unspecified images of social and spiritual liberation. Implicit within this construct is a mild anarchist sentiment, in the allusion to the ultimate goal of 'the free life'.

It was inevitable, in fact, that Mitchell's faith in art and politics – the twin anchors of his adult philosophy – would coalesce. The relationship between the two motivating forces was problematic, however. Throughout his life the dual forces of art and politics repeatedly pulled against each other, promoting internal tensions in his aesthetic that were never fully reconciled. In his professional life, clandestine political activity in Glasgow even resulted in the forced abandonment of his dream to earn a practical living as a writer, in journalism, with his sacking from the *Scottish Farmer*. However, Mitchell's inner conflict also created a paradoxical dynamic, which animates his most mature writings.

Mitchell refined his artistic precepts in one of his last published essays, focusing specifically on the then relatively innovative art-form of film. Here, he fashions a suitably elevated view of the inordinate representational capacity of this exciting new medium to 'present the free and undefiled illusion', before taking this artistic precept a step further in his definition of the duality of its practical fulfilment. Thus, his positive image of the *verité* of film homes in on its ability to capture the desirable anarchist lifestyle enjoyed by the Punak of Borneo, viewed as 'naked, cultureless, happy, the last folk of the Golden Age'. This utopian image is then immediately counterbalanced and tempered by a realist vision of the opposite extreme, featuring 'the dead cities of Northern England, cities of more dreadful night than that dreamt by Thomson'.[23] However, Mitchell's ideal itself remains essentially unreal, as an 'illusion' – granted, one that is 'free and undefiled'; the artificiality of art, then, is final and inescapable. In his own case, Mitchell came closest to representing 'the free and undefiled illusion' in his representation of human existence at its purest and most natural. Put simply, his weakest writing – the rather glib fantasy and magic realism of his story cycles and of the pulp novels *Three Go Back, The Lost Trumpet* and *Gay Hunter* – involved the direct depiction of a Diffusionism-inspired ideal, an anarchist utopia happily stripped of the maladies of modern civilization – but thereby also divorced from the frantic social concerns of life in the twentieth century.

A confirmed realist who believed that, for the best writers, 'life, not editors or anthologists, calls forth their poetry',[24] Mitchell nevertheless remained conscious that the raw material was irremediably 'defiled' by the process of transmutation into the illusion of art. This nagging consciousness of the inherent artificiality of all art, what may be termed an all-embracing sardonicism, informed Mitchell's beliefs as a writer and manifested itself in a variety of ways in his writings. Ultimately, the recognition of all art's essential unreality allowed Mitchell to articulate clear aims and liberated him to produce literary constructs with clearly defined ulterior – and essentially utilitarian – purpose.

Mitchell's sardonic view of art was bolstered by his Diffusionist-anarchist ideal. One of the sacrosanct motifs of Mitchell's social utopia, his ideal 'No-state', is the absence from it of all of the aberrant trappings of civilization (principally religion, social stratification and war), including culture itself – as projected in his reference to the tribal Punak. In Mitchell's most concise account of his relationship with Diffusionism, a typically passionate proselytizing essay entitled 'The Diffusionist Heresy', published in the inaugural edition of the anarchist journal of the Promethean Society in 1931, he traces his gravitation towards the radical historical doctrine propounded by William J. Perry and Grafton Elliot Smith in the early decades of the twentieth century. The cardinal thesis of the Diffusionists, based upon historical research focused on early societies from diverse times and places and charting the global spread of common lines of civilized development, was that precivilized society epitomizes the natural human values of social cooperation and individual freedom uncontaminated by 'civilized' rites and customs. This pristine vision was vital in helping Leslie Mitchell to reclaim his moral belief in human goodness. In 'The Diffusionist Heresy', Mitchell hails early man, as follows: 'He was gregarious and communistic. He was Natural Man, completely lacking in culture.'[25]

Three years later, in his seminal study of 'The Land' in *Scottish Scene*, Mitchell expanded this vision of ethnic harmony to picture the arrival in

Scotland of the original Maglemosian hunters, 'dark men, and tall, without gods or kings, classes or culture, *writers or artists*, free and happy, and all the world theirs' (my emphasis).[26] Within this conception, a fundamental condition of natural happiness is that people are totally immersed in the spontaneous business of living rather than celebrating life vicariously through art.

This particular aspect of Mitchell's sardonic principle is evident throughout the first volume of *A Scots Quair*. The peasant farmers who represent the collective hero of *Sunset Song* are introduced in the Prelude in complimentary terms, as folk who respond directly to everyday life in the natural world without the mediation of art or culture. They are presented with stark simplicity, as 'the crofters, dour folk of the old Pict stock, they had no history, common folk'.[27] Following hard upon Mitchell's mock-heroic history of the Kinraddies, graphically chronicling their aristocratic lies, hypocrisies and duplicities, the crofters are mercifully well off without any formal history. Twenty pages later, a more aggressive intertextual denunciation of manufactured cultural heritage – this time targeting previous fictional accounts of Scottish country life – rounds off the Prelude. The Reverend Gibbon's abstruse literary riddle defines his new parish of Kinraddie by matching it against notorious fictional incarnations of both a romanticized and a caustically realistic nature: '. . . he was to say it was the Scots countryside itself, fathered between a kailyard and a bonny brier bush in the lee of a house with green shutters'. The folk narrator's impatient response to this pretentious analogy is soberingly down to earth, a potent combination of cynicism and naivety: 'And what he meant by that you could guess at yourself if you'd a mind for puzzles and dirt, there wasn't a house with green shutters in the whole of Kinraddie' (p. 24). The bluntly anti-intellectual stance of the narrator here is a further projection of the author's sardonic principle, calculated again to serve notice of the inherent non-reality of art, including the very novel in which it appears.

Subsequently, throughout the book Chris Guthrie's central conflict between her English and Scottish personas dramatizes at length a choice between, in essence, abstract ideas (largely superimposed by an alien imperialist culture) and life itself. The conundrum can have only one possible resolution; as her nature-loving mother had cautioned her in the innocence of her childhood: '*Oh Chris, my lass, there are better things than your books or studies or loving or bedding, there's the countryside your own, you its, in the days when you're neither bairn nor woman*' (p. 27; italics in original). And the paradox of using art to promote the happy primordial state of artlessness is most keenly expressed at the close of the novel, where Robert

Colquohoun's moving threnody for the dead crofters at the new Kinraddie war memorial is delivered in poignant acknowledgement of the legislative purpose that he inherited from their innate inarticulacy: '*They went quiet and brave from the lands they loved, though seldom of that love might they speak, it was not in them to tell in words of the earth that moved and lived and abided, their life and enduring love*' (pp. 255–6; italics in original).

While Leslie Mitchell's writing was informed by the sardonic principle derived from a combination of his cultural background and his personal political ideology, his mature view of art was totally circumscribed by its moral, social and political intention. Far from undervaluing the power of art, Mitchell's artistic standards were unremittingly severe; art of a purely escapist or esoteric form invited criticism and dismissal. In an essay in *Left Review* which constitutes his mature manifesto as a writer, Mitchell expressly proclaimed, 'I am a revolutionary writer', and his retrospective subdivision of his own canon into 'explicit or implicit propaganda' helps to untangle the dichotomy inherent within his mature aesthetic.[28] Within this collocation, Mitchell's work as a whole is categorized as 'propaganda' which possesses an overt didactic purpose. Subsequently, his history and fantasy writing can be viewed as 'implicit' propaganda, in that the mytho-poetic vision of a naturally free and spiritually uncomplicated primitive existence that is central to it only indirectly criticizes the social maladies that were rife in Thirties Britain by offering such pointed contrast.

Paradoxically, it is precisely when Mitchell constructs his 'explicit' propaganda that his art knowingly departs from the supposedly purer realm of the romantic 'free and undefiled' ideal, of mythic fantasy. This is when the author self-consciously obtrudes, wilfully shaping his narrative to fulfil an 'explicit' political purpose. Thus, while Mitchell's narrative powers serve him superbly in his social realism, the author remains terminally aware that the 'explicit' propaganda, dedicated to the exposure and denunciation of social ills and moral injustices and to the exploration of harsh political necessities, is ultimately less aesthetically pure than the expression of the human ideal. In essence, in dealing with unhappy social realities and political practicalities rather than with sanguine matters of human potentiality, his work is reduced in his own eyes to an inferior form. Conversely, in proclaiming the essential artificiality of his own creation, Mitchell is ring-fencing its political purpose.

Leslie Mitchell is most accurately classified as an exponent of what the French writer Louis Aragon defined as 'littérature engagée', that is, as a writer of maverick radicalism who freely dedicates his writing to clear social and political ends.[29] His work acquires truly serious purpose only in direct dedication to a greater cause – when it becomes explicit 'propaganda'. At its very best, art is sublimated in direct social, moral and political purpose. In fact, Mitchell was adamant that, in the final analysis, he would sacrifice art for even the merest possibility of social relief, writing unequivocally and with tremendous trenchancy in his portrait of 'Glasgow': 'There is nothing in culture or art that is worth the life and elementary happiness of one of those thousands who rot in the Glasgow slums.'[30] And Mitchell's last published novel, the romantic fantasy *Gay Hunter*, contains an icy blast of realism in an oblique metafictional reference signifying by inference the author's own disapproval of the frivolity of his lightweight genre. Completely out of context, Gay, his eponymous heroine, suddenly condemns her natural idyll in the coldest terms: 'Life an eternal picnic – it was the kind of thing that sick little imaginative novelists had dreamt of in the smoke and squalor and the unemployment queues of the fourth decade of the twentieth century.'[31] In this passage, the tension between Mitchell the writer and Mitchell the radical – his sardonic principle – is expressed as guilty self-recrimination.

Mitchell's sardonic principle is also manifested in subtler ways, however. In particular, metafictional intrusions serve as insistent reminders to the reader that the fictional world that has been crafted by the author is after all just that – an illusion. To undermine the suspension of disbelief in his writing highlights its subservient function and underlines its primacy as a political instrument. David Lodge's definition of metafiction is especially pertinent in this context. In *The Art of Fiction*, Lodge writes of this intriguing literary device, exemplified in work by early novelists like Sterne through to more modern fiction writers, such as Borges, Calvino and Barth, as 'fiction about fiction: novels and stories that call attention to their fictional status and their own compositional procedures'. The author thereby 'foregrounds the gap between art and life that conventional realism seeks to conceal'. Lodge goes on significantly to expand upon how metafiction commonly appears as 'asides' in the English novel:

> These passages acknowledge the artificiality of the conventions of realism even as they employ them; they disarm criticism by anticipating it; they flatter the reader by treating him or her as an intellectual equal, sophisticated enough not to be thrown by the admission that a work of fiction is a verbal construction rather than a slice of life.[32]

Mitchell's best work is littered with understated metafictional intrusions defining the unbridgeable interface standing between art and reality. I referred earlier to the gentle self-mockery of the satire of Reverend Gibbon in *Sunset Song*, and the most striking of Mitchell's metafictional intrusions occurs in the sequel, *Cloud Howe*, in the form of a directly autobiographical reference that must have seemed painfully near the bone to his immediate family. Chris and Cis Brown flee from Segget to Mitchell's home-patch of Arbuthnott (not, note, the fictional Kinraddie). There they find sanctuary in a croft unmistakable as Mitchell's home of Bloomfield: 'a little farm, high in the Reisk, overtopped by the wave of its three beech trees, standing up squat in the blow of the wind that came in a shoom from the Bervie braes'.[33] The autobiographical vein is capped when they meet a farmer's wife who refuses payment for milk and freshly baked cakes on account of Chris's college acquaintanceship with her son, who 'lived in London and wrote horrible books' (p. 173). Here, art and reality collide in personally framed retribution, but the passage again serves to underscore the gulf eternally separating the two fields. In the final novel of the trilogy, young Ewan Tavendale, practising Marxist anti-hero of *Grey Granite*, personifies most fully Mitchell's sardonic principle; in Ewan's materialist world-picture, absolutely everything, including his own personal happiness, has to be sacrificed to the one over-weening revolutionary cause. Mitchell also underlines – and undermines – the artifice of his urban novel less earnestly with the metafictional jibe directed at his crony, fellow writer Hugh MacDiarmid, who by this time in 1934 had emerged as the celebrated figurehead of the Scottish Literary Renaissance. Mitchell makes a crude pun on C. M. Grieve's pugnacious *nom de guerre* by representing him as 'Hugo MacDownall, the chap who wrote in Synthetic Scots'. The ingenuousness of Ewan's logical rejoinder concerning MacDiarmid's linguistic experimentation, '*Why synthetic? Can't he write the real stuff?*', constitutes a sly dig at a fellow writer increasingly committed to poetry as a self-justifying pursuit.[34] To Mitchell, as to Ewan Tavendale, the sardonic principle governing all art was absolute.

In summary, Leslie Mitchell's politics were an original amalgam of radical beliefs: of libertarian anarchism, of Diffusionist anthropology, of revolutionary Marxist-Leninism. His art was driven by political inspiration, again in a curious set of ways. A sardonic principle evolved as a key component in his mature aesthetic in response to the pragmatic attitude fomented by his peasant background. This was compounded by the abolitionist viewpoint of the Diffusionist-anarchist apologist, for whom art was segregated and held at arm's length from natural existence. While Mitchell's historical studies became a means of pursuing empirical evidence for his utopian 'No-state', his potboiling novels represented an imaginative extension of his natural mytho-poetic ideal. Just as Mitchell's sociopolitical ideal remained apolitical in nature – politics would disappear, millennium-style, from the ideal society – so his artistic ideal of the perfect 'free and undefiled illusion' was itself transitory, representing, along with all culture, social division and religion, a dispensable feature of modern life attendant upon the freak accident of civilization.

Mitchell's belief in art per se seemed to diminish in inverse proportion to the increasing militancy of his political disposition. The tension manifested between his art and his politics developed into a paradox whereby ultimately his creative art was both inspired and terminally compromised by its very political status. Finally, Leslie Mitchell found himself committed to an aesthetic that subliminally proclaimed its inherent redundancy and denied its rightful existence. Yet in the recognition of the sardonic principle underlying his efforts, Leslie Mitchell found his true literary voice.

NOTES

[1] Lewis Grassic Gibbon, 'News of Battle: Queries for Mr Whyte', *The Free Man*, 3 (17 March 1934), p. 9.

[2] Leslie Mitchell's relationship with libertarian politics is fully documented in Uwe Zagratzki, *Libertäre und utopische Tendenzen im Erzählwerk James Leslie Mitchells (Lewis Grassic Gibbons)* (Frankfurt, 1991). For the philosophical background to anarchist thought, I have relied largely upon George Woodcock's classic study, *Anarchism* (Harmondsworth, 1963).

[3] Piers Brendon, *The Dark Valley: A Panorama of the 1930s* (London, 2000).

[4] H. Gustav Klaus, 'Socialist Fiction in the 1930s: Some Preliminary Observations', in John Lucas (ed.), *The 1930s: A Challenge to Orthodoxy* (Hassocks, 1978), pp. 13–41, (p. 32). Mitchell's prominence as a radical novelist has been confirmed by a number of critical studies of left-wing literature stretching over the last twenty-five years, especially David Smith, *Socialist Propaganda in the Twentieth-Century British Novel* (London, 1978); Valentine Cunningham, *British Writers of the Thirties* (Oxford, 1988); Andy Croft, *Red Letter Days: British Fiction in the 1930s* (London, 1990). A full conspectus of Mitchell's critical treatment over the years is given in William K. Malcolm, 'A Retrospective View of James Leslie Mitchell', *Edinburgh Review*, 110 (2003), 55–73. The website of the Grassic Gibbon Centre at Arbuthnott at *www.grassicgibbon.com* has a regularly updated inventory of critical writings about Leslie Mitchell/ Lewis Grassic Gibbon.

[5] William K. Malcolm, '"Shouting Too Loudly": Leslie Mitchell, Humanism and the Art of Excess', in Margery Palmer McCulloch and Sarah M. Dunnigan (eds), *A Flame in the Mearns: Lewis Grassic Gibbon – A Centenary Celebration* (Glasgow, 2003), pp. 76–88.

[6] J. Leslie Mitchell, letter to Jean Baxter dated 17 September 1932, Aberdeen University Library (AUL), MS 2377.

7   J. Leslie Mitchell, 'Dear Robert', letter dated 5 June 1914, in 'Essay Book Kept by James Mitchell, Arbuthnott P. School, Book I', National Library of Scotland (NLS), Acc. 5325b. While Leslie Mitchell awaits a sympathetic modern biography fusing factual accuracy and critical insight, the central details of his life can be gleaned from Ian S. Munro, *Leslie Mitchell: Lewis Grassic Gibbon* (Edinburgh, 1966).

8   J. Leslie Mitchell, letter to Mr and Mrs Alexander Gray, 29 September 1929, NLS, Acc. 5325a.

9   J. Leslie Mitchell, *Stained Radiance: A Fictionist's Prelude* (London, 1930), pp. 30–1.

10 J. Leslie Mitchell, letter to Alexander Gray dated 16 July 1930, NLS, Acc. 5325a.

11 J. Leslie Mitchell, dedication to *Three Go Back* (London, 1932).

12 J. Leslie Mitchell, Publication Files, NLS, Acc. 10966.

13 Mitchell, *Stained Radiance*, p. 192.

14 J. Leslie Mitchell, 'Lowland Scots as a Literary Medium', NLS, MS 26059.

15 J. Leslie Mitchell, letter to Jean Baxter dated 17 September 1932, AUL, MS 2377.

16 *Who Was Who: A Companion to Who's Who Containing the Biographies of Those Who Died*, 3 (London, 1941), p. 947.

17 Lewis Grassic Gibbon, *Sunset Song* (Edinburgh, 1988 [1932]), p. 47. References to the Gibbon trilogy *A Scots Quair* are to the Canongate volumes scrupulously edited by Tom Crawford, published in 1988, 1989 and 1990 respectively; after a first footnote further references will be inserted in the text.

18 Lewis Grassic Gibbon, 'News of Battle: Queries for Mr Whyte'.

19 J. Leslie Mitchell, letter to Naomi Mitchison dated 10 August 1933, NLS, Acc. 5885.

20 J. Leslie Mitchell, letter to Tom Wintringham dated 8 March 1934, property of the Estate of Tom Wintringham.

21 J. Leslie Mitchell, letter to Eric Linklater dated 10 November 1934, NLS, Acc. 10282.

22 Lewis Grassic Gibbon, 'The Antique Scene', reprinted in Ian Campbell (ed.), *The Speak of the Mearns* (Edinburgh, 1994 [1934]), p. 102. All references to essays originally published in the miscellany *Scottish Scene* (London, 1934), jointly authored by Lewis Grassic Gibbon and Hugh MacDiarmid, are cited as they appear in this recent collection.

23 Lewis Grassic Gibbon, 'A Novelist Looks at the Cinema', *Cinema Quarterly*, 3 (1935), 81–5. This essay is reproduced in full, together with selected shorter fiction, non-fiction, poetry and summaries, in Valentina Bold (ed.), *Smeddum: A Lewis Grassic Gibbon Anthology* (Edinburgh, 2001), pp. 739–43.

24 Lewis Grassic Gibbon, 'Literary Lights', in Campbell (ed.), *The Speak of the Mearns*, p. 136.

25 J. Leslie Mitchell, 'The Diffusionist Heresy', *The Twentieth Century*, 1 (1931), 14–18. Mitchell published two essays in the Promethean Society's journal, *The Twentieth Century*: 'The Diffusionist Heresy', in March 1931, and 'The

Prince's Placenta and Prometheus as God', in February 1932. Both articles are permeated by a mild anarchism very much in keeping with the journal's pacifist temper, summed up by the editor, Jon Randell Evans, in the first editorial promulgating 'peace propaganda', in the form of 'active and intense propaganda until total disarmament is achieved' (*The Twentieth Century*, 1 [1931], 23–4). Accompanying contributions from R. L. Megroz, Sir Norman Angell, W. H. Auden and Aldous Huxley make firm pledges towards this pressure group's laudable, if somewhat woolly, cause.

As noted laconically by Mitchell in his 'brief history of a revoluter', incorporated in his letter to Naomi Mitchison of 10 August 1933, the Promethean Society effectively put paid to his own ambition to establish an anarchist group of a similar nature. The aims and history of this body, 'The Secular Control Group', are charted in Mitchell's fascinatingly autobiographical second novel, *The Thirteenth Disciple: Being Portrait and Saga of Malcom Maudslay in his Adventure through the Dark Corridor* (London, 1931), pp. 240–65.

Diffusionism constituted a strangely short-lived sideline in evolutionary theory during the first half of the twentieth century. While the historical researches of H. J. Massingham, William J. Perry and Grafton Elliot Smith are looked upon with a degree of scientific caution nowadays, their best works are invigorated by an enduring passion and intensity: the interested reader may be directed towards Massingham's *The Golden Age* (London, 1927), Perry's *The Growth of Civilization* (London, 1924) and Elliot Smith's *Human History* (London, 1930). Mitchell published hagiographical portraits of both Elliot Smith and Perry in *The Millgate*, 26 (1931), 579–82, and 27 (1932), 323–6, respectively, although his major historical volumes, *The Conquest of the Maya* and *Nine Against the Unknown* (both London, 1934), are more freshly energized by his Diffusionist-anarchist leanings.

[26]   Lewis Grassic Gibbon, 'The Land', in Campbell (ed.), *The Speak of the Mearns*, p. 156.

[27]   Lewis Grassic Gibbon, *Sunset Song*, p. 4.

[28]   Lewis Grassic Gibbon, 'Controversy: Writers' International (British Section)', *Left Review*, 1 (1935), 179–80. This seminal essay on Mitchell's revolutionary art is reprinted in full in David Margolies (ed.), *Writing the Revolution: Cultural Criticism from* Left Review (London, 1998), pp. 38–9.

[29]   A useful summary of Aragon's artistic theory is provided in Max Adereth, 'What is "*Littérature Engagée*"?', in his *Commitment in Modern French Literature* (1967), republished in David Craig (ed.), *Marxists on Literature* (Harmondsworth, 1975), pp. 445–85.

[30]   Lewis Grassic Gibbon, 'Glasgow', in Campbell (ed.), *The Speak of the Mearns*, p. 122.

[31]   J. Leslie Mitchell, *Gay Hunter* (London, 1934), p. 93.

[32]   David Lodge, *The Art of Fiction* (London, 1992), pp. 206–7.

[33]   Lewis Grassic Gibbon, *Cloud Howe* (Edinburgh, 1989 [1933]), p. 169.

[34]   Lewis Grassic Gibbon, *Grey Granite* (Edinburgh, 1990 [1934]), p. 31. 'Hugh

MacDiarmid' (Christopher Murray Grieve) (1892–1978), dedicatee of *Grey Granite*, expounded the linguistic theory of Synthetic Scots, which underpinned his superb poetic achievement in the early collections *Sangshaw* (Edinburgh, 1925), *Penny Wheep* (Edinburgh, 1926) and *A Drunk Man Looks at the Thistle* (Edinburgh, 1926). This theory proposed the integration of arcane and obscure Scottish words and idioms into a coherent poetic language. For full details, see Hugh MacDiarmid, 'The Case for Synthetic Scots', in *At the Sign of the Thistle: A Collection of Essays* (London, 1934), p. 185.

Acknowledgement is made to the Trustees of The National Library of Scotland in Edinburgh, to Aberdeen University Library and to the Estate of Tom Wintringham for permission to quote from letters by James Leslie Mitchell in their possession.

5

Anarcho-syndicalism in Welsh Fiction in English

STEPHEN KNIGHT

1. ANARCHO-SYNDICALIST POLITICS IN WALES

The narrators of Gwyn Thomas's bitterly sparkling comedy *The World Cannot Hear You* (1951) visit an adult education facility cum holiday home. They express concern that the charitable English owner might expect them to be brimming over 'with syndicalism and class spite'.[1] The hostility of workers to the propertied can be taken as a constant in Welsh industrial fiction, but in his identification of syndicalism as a major constituent of the workers' – or non-workers', in this case – aggression, Thomas is as astute as usual in listening to what he called 'the voices of Glamorgan'. In syndicalism he identified a strain in south Welsh political and, indeed, emotional thought that has been largely overlooked by commentators but that, in fact, not only played a major role in the political consciousness of industrial south Wales but also is represented recurrently, and even recently, as a set of ideas and values of considerable power in Welsh fiction in English.

The term syndicalism is an English-language euphemism for anarcho-syndicalism, to avoid the bomb-throwing, mad-individual connotations of anarchism. Its bitterest enemies, such as the conservative-owned newspapers of Wales like the *Western Mail* and the even more servile *Rhondda Leader*, used the full compound as a way of traducing their enemies, but no proper understanding of Welsh anarcho-syndicalism should forget the link with anarchism. Bakunin and Marx divide on the role of the state. Marx felt it would wither away under proper communism after its instruments were seized and wielded by the workers; Bakunin thought it should never, even in revolutionary hands, be given the opportunity to play a part in constructing the future. While some anarchists, oppressed to the stage of negative desperation, saw only suicidal violence as a path ahead, where they were strong and multiple those who rejected the state saw a common future in local, direct and determined resistance through their informal or formal unions, or, in French, *syndicats*. That collective anti-statism is precisely anarcho-syndicalism, though to distinguish the position from that of a reformist and gradualist unionism the French coined the phrase 'revolutionary syndicalism'.

The position of the anarcho-syndicalists was that workers could, by a range of means, mostly by strikes of varied gravity but also by violence if necessary, seize power from the present exploitative owners and continue to run the institutions seized – industry, farm, fishing fleet, for example – for the enhanced livelihood of all who worked there and their connections. There would, of course, be friendly and efficient relations with other syndicates, but no state. The syndicates are the state and anarchy is their mode of connection, or unconnection. Social relations within the syndicates will be unhierarchical, with leaders no more than recurrently elected representatives, and equally avoided will be the central bureaucracy of big unions, the entrenched power of permanent officials, the corruption of office and, most important of all in the early twentieth century, the ideas of gradual reformist change and an inherently shared interest between boss and worker. The furthest the anarcho-syndicalists would go in the direction of state-like organization is to seek an industrial union, with all the miners and related trades together, so they can exert maximal power against the mine-owners.

This heady politics is clearly a combination of the anti-state basis of anarchism and the revolutionary insurgency of Marxism. It appealed especially where regional forces were strong and federal ones weak, as in Spain and America, but for a crucial period in the history of labour relations anarcho-syndicalism played a role in Britain. The standard explanation is that elements of the position arrived from France and America by about 1905, that Tom Mann, a major evangelist for these politics, returned from Australia in 1910 (and founded the Industrial Syndicalist Educational League) and that some of the hotter heads in 'the great unrest' of 1910–14 used anarcho-syndicalism to some degree to validate their fury. In fact, the first American wave, De Leonism, was more concerned with developing industrial unions; it was the Wobblies, International Workers of the World, from 1905 on, who stressed direct action and rank-and-file control; the French influence in Britain was never strong. Other, local, factors were at work. Many of the major anarcho-syndicalists, like James Connolly from Ireland, the Glasgow leaders, Noah Ablett from the Rhondda and even the Larkin brothers in the Liverpool transport strike of 1913–14, had an anti-London, colonially conscious objection to the central state as well as a theoretical one – and the major figure, Tom Mann himself, was converted to anarcho-syndicalism in Australia. There are also native traditions of anti-statism: the Socialist League, a cradle of anarcho-syndicalism, shared William Morris's English communalist, anti-parliamentarian principles, which reached back to the seventeenth century.[2] In Wales the principle of communality was even older, as ideas of local, self-sufficient order and prosperity were enshrined in the concept and institution of the *gwerin*, the democratic mutually responsible 'folk'.[3] There is a strong resemblance in the links between native traditions and anarcho-syndicalism in Wales with those discussed by Schäffner in the case of Spain (see pp. 67–9).

This volatile mixture of ideas played a part in the intensifying conflict of the first decade of the twentieth century as profits fell, workers were pressured to bear the burden and younger unionists were less willing to be patronized, less constrained by the forces of religion and respectability, and were also in touch with worldwide radicalism. Bob Holton has claimed that: 'The idea that Syndicalism made only limited progress in Britain compared with continental Europe or the USA is another popular myth which fails to stand up to close scrutiny.'[4] In support of that view, Keith Davies has provided a detailed account of the vigour of syndicalism in Wales.[5]

A key moment was in late 1908 when the Plebs League was founded – a De Leon idea – to educate the workers to resist complicit union leaders, seen, in a classical image, as oppressive tribunes of the people. At Ruskin College, Oxford, where working men were imbued with a bourgeois education, there was a strike against the curriculum; the principal sided syndically with the men and the new Central Labour College, famously rich with anarcho-syndicalist thought, was established in London in 1909. Noah Ablett and Noah Rees from Wales were among the leaders, and they and others – W. F. Hay, William Mainwaring and even the leading Wobbly, Big Bill Haywood – were involved in the events of the first major conflict of the new violent period, when the Rhondda pits of the Cambrian Combine went on strike in 1910–11.[6] The old give and take of negotiations was gone; direct action was vigorous, as scabs were attacked and an attempt was made to blow up a coal-owner's house. Miners repulsed from an assault on a pithead looted Tonypandy shops, with some discrimination and some contact with older ritual: men paraded in finery from the shop of a draper who was also a magistrate.

There were certainly anarcho-syndicalists, conscious of their role and the possibilities of the situation, among the leaders of the Cambrian Combine dispute, as Chris Williams has discussed.[7] The strike was eventually defeated, but now the driving concept was that this was one battle, not the whole war:

radical strategy was at work, not piecemeal settlement, as in the past. An 'Unofficial Reform Committee' was set up and, after a series of collaborations and consultations that are evidently anarcho-syndicalist in mode, it produced the famous pamphlet *The Miners' Next Step*.[8] Appearing just before Christmas 1911, it sold amazingly well. Noah Ablett, described by Dai Smith as 'the main inspiration of what has been called "Welsh syndicalism" ',[9] was a major influence. While the pamphlet has been called 'the syndicalists' manifesto',[10] as it attacks the idea of leadership and insists on continued local workers' control, it also envisages the use of political persuasion – taboo to the most puristically local syndicalists. In part the result of having various authors and in part the result of its being a practical fighting document, this has enabled some historians to avoid giving the document its full anarcho-syndicalist value,[11] but there was no doubt at the time: right-wing politicians and editorialists vilified the pamphlet, and the real threat of anarcho-syndicalism in Britain can be judged from its antagonists: Ramsay MacDonald, Beatrice and Sidney Webb and Bertrand Russell all wrote books describing and implicitly attacking syndicalism between 1912 and 1918.[12] If the great and good of Labour distanced themselves carefully, there were plenty of right-wing opponents who lost no time in attacking what the gentry wing, represented by Sir Arthur Clay, Bt., saw as 'the extent of its danger',[13] while the intellectual faction, Adam Kirkaldy, Professor of Finance at Birmingham, spoke in quasi-gentry mode about the 'impudence'[14] of anarcho-syndicalism.

As the historians note, most with some relief, anarcho-syndicalism as a force did not long survive the war. The positive example of Russian communism and the negative power of the state in the 1926 strike – itself an anarcho-syndicalist weapon and brought about by the closely related strategy of industrial unions – led most to concur that the great battle had to be fought out on a national stage, either across the revolutionary barricades or through the ballot box, two scenarios both regarded as thoroughly inappropriate by the anarcho-syndicalists. They were clearly politically defeated in Britain, as they would be in the cauldron of the Spanish Civil War, though their policies would flicker in a positive light again in the 1970s, when labour statism had again so evidently failed the working people of Britain.

The anarcho-syndicalists had most impact in south Wales: John Davies calls it 'the stronghold of the syndicalists', and the history of the South Wales Miners' Federation sees its politics into the Thirties as 'semi-syndicalist'.[15] The politics of the anarcho-syndicalists, their ideas of social and industrial organization and, most of all, their emotive democraticism, have left a mark on Welsh literature in English that is recurrent, whether positive or negative.

2. LITERARY REPRESENTATIONS OF SYNDICALISM

Representations of coal-mining and its politics, like representations of women's actual activities in Wales, had to struggle out of the deforming embrace of romance. The early Welsh novelists writing in English, Joseph Keating and 'Allen Raine', never broke through the sugary boundaries of that London-oriented genre, part of the cultural hegemony of the colonial state and inherently hostile to local resistance.[16] Though Raine went further than Keating in suggesting possibilities of communal autonomous operations, she worked in the spirit of the Welsh traditional *gwerin*, or folk, not in any mode of new resistance related to anarcho-syndicalism; Keating's few industrial novels are notable for their lack of any sense of workers' opposition to the bosses, both owners and management, who dominate the plots and the society alike. The first representation of anything like local politicized resistance is in Irene Saunderson's *A Welsh Heroine: A Romance of Colliery Life*, which, published in 1911, is clearly influenced by the events of 1910–11 and firmly presents the angry dissent of the colliers, speaking in their own aggressive and far-from-standard English and, sometimes, briefly in Welsh.[17] However, after figuring the miners' resistance of the anarcho-syndicalism-inspired period, the novel's tensions are resolved through colonial romance, as the brave collier girl, both sympathetic to and protective of the radical workers, marries the now also sympathetic English army officer, a liaison so improbable as – presumably unintendedly – to cast an inherently anarchist mockery over the idea of a coherent and peaceful British state.

A subtler version of this representation and rejection of the anarcho-syndicalist resistance of the south Welsh miners is found in Rhys Davies's *A Time to Laugh* (1937).[18] Davies, London littérateur as he was, nevertheless remained in touch with his Welsh roots and did sympathize with some forms of resistance, though his distanced and naively essentialist position led him to condense anti-mine-owner aggression with historical princely opposition to the English Crown – this is an improbable and inherently romantic form of what post-colonialists call nativism.[19] Davies wrote very negatively of the miners involved in the looting at Tonypandy in his non-fiction account *My Wales*, and it is not surprising that this stance has been criticized.[20] In the novel the looting miners are described as having 'foam at their lips' and looking 'like swarms of rats' (pp. 1, 3). But the scene is not as negative as the *My Wales* version: the police also act 'vengefully', the foam is 'red-flecked' with the miners' own blood and it is 'the shopkeeping wives' who see the miners as rats. As the novel progresses, a cell of radical miners is represented with some sympathy: their attitudes and actions all reject the bland leadership of the 'milk and water Miners' Federation' (p. 89) and these sequences present as clear a view of anarcho-syndicalists at work as exists in Welsh fiction. Melville Walters is their leader, and they have been active among the strikers. They do not loot themselves or encourage it: what they want is 'a demonstration of physical power and solidarity . . . a warning' (p. 13; ellipses in text). They are self-conscious agitators, and Melville's 'subversive ideas' (p. 23) have led to his being sacked regularly. As soldiers arrive, the band ambush a detachment of cavalry and drive them off with stones; they are all arrested and jailed for up to nine months. When released they meet as an 'unofficial' committee of the Federation – a clear reference to the progressive and radical groups, anarcho-syndicalist in orientation, who were active around 1910 and 1911 and drafted *The Miners' Next Step*. Michael J. Dixon comments that Dr Morris's attitudes early in the novel, especially to the Sliding Scale 'place him firmly in the syndicalist camp'.[21]

Having represented this position, the novel moves away from it in various ways, partly by using the doctor – an outsider – as the principal point of view; his long-running affair and eventual marriage with Melville's sister also dilute the politics with romance. The final sequences of industrial action see the miners operating under the federation, not in radical groups, though it is a federation that has clearly been stimulated by the anarcho-syndicalist agitators. Davies's essentialist idea of across-time Welsh resistance comes through at times – some of the radicals looked as if they were 'replenished in some ancient strength of the earth' (p. 234) – and there is a deliberate historical blurring: these Tonypandy-like events take place a good ten years earlier. Nevertheless, it is unusual for Davies to be as politically specific as he is in the opening half of *A Time to Laugh*. It is more characteristic of his distanced position, as in *Jubilee Blues*, the third part of his coal-mining trilogy, to use a woman as the point of view of industrial trouble, there focusing on the 1920s. But his treatment of Melville Walters and his radical group must derive both from his own occasionally roused sense of political realities in Wales and from the substantial impact that the anarcho-syndicalists had in the Wales of Davies's youth.

A much more rigorous approach to miners' politics was to be the overt position of a major writer of Welsh industrial fiction, Lewis Jones. A member of the Communist Party by 1925, and also a tirelessly active radical leader, he developed his occasional journalism and sketch-writing into two major novels. He died just before finishing the second, and a third, in which the Welsh veterans of Spain were to be involved in the battle for a workers' state in Britain, was never started. In general scheme the novels seem like standard, even proletcult, socialist realism. *Cwmardy* (1937)[22] tells how a community is radicalized, through the eyes and through the actions of a young leader and his supporters; *We Live* (1939)[23] tells the larger story of these activities, including action for Spain, and ends with a romantically presented people's march – Jones died before writing this, though he had apparently made notes about it, and he might well have treated it in a more nuanced, even ironized, way.[24]

The reputation of the novels is as a major Marxist contribution from Britain to international industrial fiction. But communism was not the only force at work. As Dai Smith comments in his introduction to the 1978 reprint of *Cwmardy*:

> Like so many other South Walian thinkers in the first half of the twentieth century, Lewis Jones was marked by the vigorous democracy evident in *The Miners' Next Step* and by that anarcho-syndicalism which, in its instant promise, framed so well the aspirations of a society as bewilderingly new as any found by an Andalucian peasant enticed to Barcelona.[25]

Big Jim Roberts is strong, loyal, engaging and foolish, the archetype of the exploitable worker; his son Len, less strong and much more thoughtful, grows up to be a leftist, learning from the books lent by friends and also from his instincts. In a crucial scene Len becomes the men's battlefield leader. The colliers are unwilling to work under a dangerous roof until shoring timbers are brought in; the fireman wants no delay in the production of coal and begins to bully and manipulate the men:

> Len saw through the fireman's attempt to split the ranks, and knew they were all in a tight corner. Capitulation at this moment would leave them no alternative but to go back to the untimbered face, hoping for the best, until timber came. And for this he was not prepared. On the other hand if they refused there was nothing for it but to leave the pit for good.
>
> He looked around the perturbed men before him. They were all thinking hard and hoping someone would tell them what to do. Len glanced at the fireman and saw the triumphant smirk on his face, and for some reason or other the sneer gave him the counter-move to the fireman's threat. Turning sharply, he shouted: 'Go round the other barries, Will, and tell the men to come down by here. Tell them there be a dispute on and that Shenkin have ordered us out because we 'on't work without timber.' (pp. 136–7)

The fireman, and the owners, have to back down. The same kind of instinctive leadership comes to Len in a meeting when he suddenly speaks, nervously at first, but then confidently outlines a good strategy. He argues for combination with the miners in other pits, but such strategic linking is not outside the essence of anarcho-syndicalism and is, at most, an instance of the closely related industrial unionism on a Welsh regional basis, not directed towards communist-style centralized state organization. A similar local radicalism is pressed home in the later part of *Cwmardy*, where Len, against a good deal of opposition, from the left as well as the forces of the state, holds to a strongly pacifist line: in Wales there were Labour party figures like Keir Hardie who committed themselves to this brave and unpopular cause, but the majority of pacifists were from the Independent Labour Party, and anarcho-syndicalists like W. F. Hay were notable among them. The position, of course, coincides with that of the Marxists in the period, soon to be espoused by the British Communist Party, but its embattled and instinctive quality in the novel is clearly consistent with anarcho-syndicalism at the time.

Len is partly taught by and partly outstrips the Cwmardy union leader, Ezra Jones. He is based on Noah Rees, one of the most active of the unofficials and certainly an anarcho-syndicalist. The novels suggest that Ezra is exhausted and uncertain in the industrial struggle, to be superseded by Len, and this would seem to be a communist line, but the lessons that Jones learnt from Rees (Smith's Introduction calls him his 'mentor') about decisive, instinctive, local action seem to have strongly influenced his fiction and indeed his life, as in the famous incident at the Kremlin when only Jones remained seated when Stalin entered the room.

We Live has been thought a more rigorously party-line tract, notably by the communist critic Carole Snee, who prefers it on those grounds to *Cwmardy*, which she criticizes as having bourgeois traces (though she does not detect anarcho-syndicalism).[26] This reading of the novel derives principally from the naively upbeat 'people's march' ending and the recurrent scenes at CP meetings. In fact, the mix of official party material and the insistent validating of anarcho-syndicalist actions is just like that in the earlier novel, even a little more notable. Direct action is praised in *We Live*. Just as Len in *Cwmardy* led a small group to attack a generator building, so in a major scene his fiancée, Mary, leads the women in a sudden seizure of the unemployment board office: she decides that they will do this even though, as a male communist says, 'The committee never decided it' (p. 245). The women burst in and make the terrified official agree to stop making cuts in the dole. They put into practice just what Len, with no respect for centralized party discipline, describes: 'It's here they make us suffer, and it's here we've got to fight them and the suffering they inflict on our people' (p. 246). It is in the same spirit of localized resistance that Len suggests the colliers should stay down the pit. Historically, the stay-down strikes, starting at Nine Mile Point in 1935, were part of the battle to re-empower the miners' federation, and were largely successful in that cause, but Jones shows a feeble federation trying to get the miners back to the surface. The nature of the stay-down strikes and the feeling they aroused clearly draw on the emotional power of the local direct action of the anarcho-syndicalists, and the novel presents the action in terms of an embattled community fighting back: 'The noise of the challenge struck the air like the detonation of artillery and swept down the valley, bringing men and women to their doors and into the streets, which they hurriedly left as they made their way to the pit' (p. 265).

If the action looks back in this way to earlier mass radicalism, the party meetings in *We Live* are themselves more equivocal than many readers seem to have thought. It is clear that Harry Morgan, party secretary, is represented as something of a self-serving apparatchik: it is he who insists to Mary that 'You can't be a Communist outside the Party' (p. 173) and it is evident that his choice of Len to go to Spain is based on jealousy. The title of the chapter that recounts this event, 'A Party Decision', reads somewhat ironically in the light of Morgan's manipulations, and Len himself, like Lewis Jones, remains committed more to the emotional immediacy of resistance than to the elaborate and centralized authority of Communist Party decision-making – a point finally obscured by the officialese of the popular front march that concludes the novel, but, as noted above, is not from Jones's own hand.

3. REMEMBERING ANARCHO-SYNDICALISM

Lewis Jones's feeling for the value of the anarcho-syndicalist position was imbued by his time at the Central Labour College and his familiarity with Noah Rees and other radical leaders, and remained strong enough to colour, even to challenge, his loyalty to Communist Party thinking. It is hardly surprising that his contemporary, Gwyn Thomas, who never took on CP discipline but shared the passionate hostility to coal capitalism and the dedication to the values constructed by the people of the coalfield, should also show in his fiction a distinct fondness for moments of direct local action and a hostility to distant structures of authority, whether religious, political or colonial, or the many forms of intertwining imposition which south Wales experienced. But it is now a more reminiscent and less confident treatment of anarcho-syndicalism.

Gwyn Thomas wrote *Sorrow for Thy Sons* (1986)[27] before *Cwmardy* was published, but he knew Lewis Jones, and honoured him in the novel as

Howells, a communist speaker whose approach is notably anarcho-syndicalist: at a meeting, at first he 'was allowing the audience to do their own thinking' and finally 'Howells had left them in mid-air. He had made their minds ready for struggle' (pp. 221–2). The struggle is the anti-Means Test actions of the early 1930s, a form of communally based resistance that was, like the stay-down strikes, deeply supported by the people of south Wales, was fully in the spirit of anarcho-syndicalism and also, even in such a difficult time, was partly successful. But *Sorrow for Thy Sons* is generally imbued with the spirit of firm, even aggressive, local action to resist injustice. Alf, the central figure, unemployed miner and medium for early versions of Thomas's biting wit, realizes that a friend's wife is not collecting clothes for charity but to line her own pockets. He immediately steps in, redistributes the clothes to poor children, and withstands the wrath of the bogus saint. Not all is so noble: Thomas was always aware of how people could be degraded by their context and, on another occasion, when Alf has been given an insulting tip for shovelling in a cellarful of coal, he deliberately has sex with the miser's man-crazy but mentally retarded daughter.

No doubt this is the sort of thing that led to the novel being rejected in 1937 by Gollancz's readers for lacking 'the relief of beauty that Rhys Davies can give'.[28] While this underrates Davies's partial engagement with industrial action, as argued above, it does point to a substantial body of London-published work by Welsh writers which ignored or opposed the spirit of anarcho-syndicalism. In Jack Jones's novels of the 1930s, especially *Black Parade* (1935) and *Bidden to the Feast* (1938),[29] the tensions of industrial south Wales are both seen and resolved through the mechanism of the family – a social unit without the political edge of a union, whether anarcho-syndicalist or not, and the same is true at a slightly higher social level of Gwyn Jones's novel about the 1926 strike, *Times Like These* (1936), which was accepted by Gollancz.[30] The most conservative of all the Welsh mining novels, Richard Llewellyn's *How Green Was My Valley* (1939), actively attacked unions in favour of family nostalgia, and showed the Meredith family at the end acting as strike-breakers, to save for the owners pits and equipment that were being abandoned and damaged through the Tonypandy-like actions of radical local action by the strikers.[31]

Gwyn Thomas did not so much withdraw from a position sympathetic to anarcho-syndicalism as reshape his expression of his views. The mixture of valuing direct action and being sceptical about its success found in *Sorrow for Thy Sons* dominates Thomas's later fiction, rich with a recurrent, fugitive and often symbolic memory of direct local resistance. Thomas, for all his socialist faith, was never attracted to any form of partyism, but his work can be read as deeply critical of contemporary politics and English dominance of Wales,[32] and there is a recurrent respect for anarcho-syndicalist positions. In the novels that made him famous as a witty and whimsical writer of modern Wales, such as *The Alone to the Alone* (1947) and *The World Cannot Hear You* (1951), he offers a group, usually of four men.[33] They operate as a multiple narrative viewpoint – a very unusual form of narration indeed, anarcho-syndicalism recycled as literary form – and also intervene to try to remedy some of the worst distortions that England, coal and capitalism have imposed on the people of what Thomas liked to generalize as 'The Terraces'. This is, however, not political intervention: in *The Alone to the Alone* they try to save the beautiful but decidedly dim Eurona from the disasters of love with Rollo, a quasi-fascist bus conductor. In *The World Cannot Hear You* they attempt to protect a sad south Welsh Everyman, Omri Hemlock, from the plans for his self-improvement by a manipulative, inherently colonizing (but also Welsh) entrepreneur of people and profit. Comic, wistful, even despairing, Thomas's stories insist on the communal identity of the south Welsh, and also on their own right to try to remedy their situation, however difficult that may be. Imaging both the values and the limitations of anarcho-syndicalism as his novels do, he is fictionally realizing the shadow of resistance that the narrative quartet ironically disavowed as 'syndicalism and class spite' (see above, p. 51).

More than spite is the purpose of the syndicalists in Thomas's most overtly political novel, *All Things Betray Thee* (1949), which gives a fictional account of the resistance of the iron workers in the Merthyr region in 1831, combined with the Chartist attack on Newport in 1839.[34] Here the action is clearly anarcho-syndicalist, as groups of armed men from various villages combine, with a distinctly limited amount of overall discipline. Both the methods and the outcomes relate to the 1930s Spain that Thomas knew thoroughly, as well as to early radical Wales, and he finally insists on the tragic failure of this adventure in resistance, but also on the value it still bears as a precedent of local political self-defence. The spirit is plainly that of the future Cambrian Combine strikers: the novel finally says the resistance has created 'the promise of a new enormous music' (p. 318). Through Thomas's work it is clear that anarcho-syndicalism is still an influence in south Welsh fiction and thought, though it no longer has the triumphalism of the pamphlets or the aggressive vigour of the early representations.

A similar approach, both remembering and reshaping the appeal that south Wales found in anarcho-syndicalism, is in the novels of Menna Gallie, a writer now being republished and reassessed through the work of the feminist publishing house Honno – in itself an activity that bears clear resemblances to the ideas of anarcho-syndicalism, like many of the resistance movements of the 1960s and 1970s. Gallie came from a mining background and was a Welsh speaker, but her first novels used English-language male-oriented models – the 'educated boy' structure of *Man's Desiring* (1960), and the mining village of *Strike for a Kingdom* (1959) and *The Small Mine* (1962).[35] Yet in her two industrial novels, Gallie offers women's groups, and also groups of children, as being both defensive collectives and the basis for actions to ameliorate some of the problems faced in the communities, both in the 1926 strike and in the later nationalized period. These problems include those of gender politics, though not all the women join the female syndicate – at the end of *The Small Mine* Cynthia, her fiancé dead, leaves the valley, as Alf's educated brother Hugh did in *Sorrow for Thy Sons* – but it is clear in both cases that a socialized form of value remains still in place among the community, a diluted but still recognizable version of the syndicates of earlier times.

The idea of group resistance survived: in Ron Berry's powerfully written novels groups of men, usually young and fairly heedless, engage in communal activities and kinds of violence, though these now come closer to the desperation of individualist anarchy than to the purposive politics of syndical actions. A more positive version is in Raymond Williams's *The Volunteers* (1985).[36] Bearing some resemblance to *All Things Betray Thee*, which Williams much admired,[37] the novel, published in 1985 with Thatcherism at its zenith, imagines a near-future, near-totalitarian Britain. Resistance ought to have come from 'the volunteers' themselves, long-buried radical moles, but they, essentially a reflex of a centralized state organization, have been redirected by the system they have volunteered to resist, and it is from outside the statist volunteers' scheme that actual opposition occurs. This is partly through a group of terrorists who shoot and wound the Secretary of State for Wales in St Fagan's Castle, Cardiff, but most strikingly, and for Williams clearly most importantly, through the determined local resistance by workers at a Newport coal-depot against soldiers trying to rescue the coal for the government. Williams refers to the miners' strikes of the 1970s and 1980s, and also looks back to a whole series of Welsh radical actions. The men stay in the yard, with their 'elected representatives' (p. 36), to confront the army and the police; their instinct is sheer resistance: 'the more we fight back the more likely it is they'll have second thoughts: pull off and negotiate' (p. 41); under threat of arrest 'the men in the yard made their own decision . . . nobody ordered this; it was a collective, almost an instinctive decision' (p. 46). Williams is, no doubt consciously – his knowledge of political history was wide and subtle – casting this event in the spirit of *The Miners' Next Step*; and the action also follows the models of Len in *Cwmardy* and Mary in *We Live*: one of the coal-loaders suddenly sees a chance, finds his way into an army lorry and blocks the entrance to the yard – and is shot dead as a result. It is this which stimulates the terrorist cell – local instinctive resistance is the core to opposing the new totalitarian state.

Like others in the 1970s Williams was attracted to the rigorously and vigorously democratic politics that are best described, and well known in Wales, as anarcho-syndicalism – this was also a period when a good deal of research was done on international anarcho-syndicalism, especially on France and the USA but also, for the first time, on Britain. But because of a widespread ignorance of the Welsh material – Ian Haywood's British Council book on British working-class fiction discusses only Lewis Jones and, in one basically English novel, Raymond Williams[38] – and also because of a false impression that the Welsh material was dominantly Marxist, the substantial roles played by anarcho-syndicalist ideas in Welsh fictional self-representations have long been obscured.

While collective action can have many sources, and communal self-help can derive from many value systems around the world, it is nevertheless possible to suggest that the value of syndical community, both in its own terms and as a system of defence and resistance, is still not forgotten in Wales or its fiction. Clearly the *gwerin* ideal is still strong in Welsh-language circles – the title of the long-running television series *Pobol y Cwm*, 'People of the Valley', refers to what is effectively a rural syndicate. And that seems the focal point of value in Emyr Humphreys's powerful and searching novel series *The Land of the Living*. The bardic values of John Cilydd More, poet, nationalist and suicide, dominate the series, and though in the last volume, *Bonds of Attachment* (1991),[39] Humphreys responds warmly to the quasi-syndicalist actions of the Welsh language movement, his own pacifism and a sense of moral order withdraw approval from the physical violence of people like those in the Free Wales Army – they are killed by their own bomb. In more recent fiction the idea of a collective resistance remains potent, whether it is the desperate drug-dazed characters of Niall Griffiths's *Grits* (2000), the alienated, connection-seeking unemployed of Richard John Evans's *Entertainment* (2000) and Rachel Trezise's *In and Out of the Goldfish Bowl* (2000) or, most moving of all, and also still capable of violent action, the physically and mentally damaged people of Lewis Davies's *My Piece of Happiness* (2000) – authors discussed in more detail by Katie Gramich in this volume (see pp. 181–90).[40]

Anti-statism and local resistance have long been strong in Wales, an ensemble of regions always suspicious of a capital, whether Rome, London or Cardiff, a social culture topographically and politically reliant on the self-sufficient local community. By long tradition and collective temperament attuned to dissent and, if necessary, resistance, the Welsh were almost fated to be attracted by the values of anarcho-syndicalism. While historians have long been aware of this trend in politics, though sometimes reluctant to recognize its true force, literary critics, tending to overlook the contemporary politics of a text, have quite failed to see that this set of values, offering as they do ideas of self-government without self-indulgence, is close to the centre of the values most highly regarded in Welsh fiction, whether in English or in Welsh. Anarcho-syndicalism, it appears, is a major figure in the rich but so far little-trodden carpet of Welsh fiction.

NOTES

[1]   Gwyn Thomas, *The World Cannot Hear You* (London, 1951), p. 267.
[2]   On this see Joseph White, 'Syndicalism in a Mature Industrial Setting: the Case of Britain', in Marcel van der Linden and Wayne Thorpe (eds), *Revolutionary Syndicalism: An International Perspective* (Aldershot, 1990), pp. 101–18 (pp. 101, 110); and Robert J. Holton, 'Revolutionary Syndicalism and the British Labour Movement', in Wolfgang J. Mommsen and Hans-Gerhard Husung (eds), *The Development of Trade Unionism in Great Britain and Germany, 1880–1914* (London, 1985), pp. 266–82 (p. 269).
[3]   See the discussion of *gwerin* values in Gwyn A. Williams, *When Was Wales: A History of the Welsh* (London, 1985), pp. 237–9.
[4]   Bob Holton, *British Syndicalism 1900–1914* (London, 1976), p. 21.
[5]   D. K. Davies, 'The Influence of Syndicalism and Industrial Unions in the South Wales Coalfield', unpublished Ph.D. thesis, Cardiff, 1991.
[6]   See Holton, *British Syndicalism*, p. 80.
[7]   Chris Williams, *Capitalism, Community and Conflict: The South Wales Coalfield 1898–1917* (Cardiff, 1998), p. 17.
[8]   Anon., *The Miners' Next Step* (Tonypandy, 1912).
[9]   Dai Smith, *Wales: A Question for History* (Bridgend, 1999), p. 167.
[10] See John Davies, *A History of Wales* (London, 1993), p. 491.
[11] See, for example, Eric Hobsbawm, 'The "New Unionism" Reconsidered', in Mommsen and Husung (eds), *The Development of Trade Unionism*, pp. 13–31 (pp. 13–14, 27–8).
[12] J. R. MacDonald, *Syndicalism, A Critical Examination* (London, 1912); Beatrice and Sidney Webb, *What Syndicalism Means* (Letchworth, 1912); Bertrand Russell, *Roads to Freedom: Socialism, Anarchism, Syndicalism* (London, 1918).
[13] Sir Arthur Clay, Bt., *Syndicalism and Labour* (London 1911), p. 93.
[14] Adam Kirkaldy, *Economics and Syndicalism* (Cambridge, 1914), p. 111.
[15] Davies, *History of Wales*, p. 494; Hywel Francis and David Smith, *The Fed:*

History of the South Wales Miners in the Twentieth Century (London, 1980), p. 247.

[16] For a discussion of these authors in the context of colonial forces, see Stephen Knight, *One Hundred Years of Fiction* (Cardiff, 2004), pp. 17–30.

[17] Irene Saunderson, *A Welsh Heroine: A Romance of Colliery Life* (London, 1911).

[18] Rhys Davies, *A Time to Laugh* (London, 1937).

[19] For a discussion of Davies's treatment of Welsh industrial themes, see Stephen Knight ' "Not a place for me": Rhys Davies's Fiction and the Coal Industry', in Meic Stephens (ed.), *Rhys Davies: Decoding the Hare* (Cardiff, 2002), pp. 54–70.

[20] Rhys Davies, *My Wales* (London, 1937); Dai Smith, *Wales: A Question for History*, p. 135.

[21] Michael J. Dixon, 'The Epic Rhondda: Romanticism and Realism in the Rhondda Trilogy', in Stephens (ed.), *Rhys Davies: Decoding the Hare*, p. 46.

[22] London, 1937.

[23] London, 1939.

[24] See Dai Smith, 'Introduction' to 1978 reprint of *We Live*, unpaginated.

[25] Dai Smith, 'Introduction' to *Cwmardy*, reprint edn. (London, 1978), unpaginated.

[26] Carole Snee, 'Working-Class Literature or Political Writing', in Jon Clark et al. (eds), *Culture and Crisis in Britain in the 1930s* (London, 1979), pp. 165–91 (pp. 184–90).

[27] Gwyn Thomas, *Sorrow for Thy Sons* (London, 1986).

[28] See Dai Smith, 'Introduction' to *Sorrow for Thy Sons* (London, 1986), pp. 5–10 (p. 9).

[29] Jack Jones, *Black Parade* (London, 1935); *Bidden to the Feast* (London, 1938).

[30] Gwyn Jones, *Times Like These* (London, 1936).

[31] Richard Llewellyn, *How Green Was My Valley* (London, 1939).

[32] See Stephen Knight, 'The Voices of Glamorgan: Gwyn Thomas's Colonial Fiction', *Welsh Writing in English*, 7 (2000–1), 16–34.

[33] Gwyn Thomas, *The Alone to the Alone* (London, 1947); *The World Cannot Hear You* (London, 1951).

[34] Gwyn Thomas, *All Things Betray Thee* (London, 1986 [1949]). Further references will be to the reprinted edition and will be inserted in the text.

[35] Menna Gallie, *Man's Desiring* (London, 1960), *Strike for a Kingdom* (London, 1959; repr. Dinas Powys, 2003); *The Small Mine* (London, 1962; repr. Dinas Powys, 2000).

[36] Raymond Williams, *The Volunteers* (London, 1985).

[37] See his 'Introduction' to the 1986 reprint.

[38] Ian Haywood, *Working-Class Fiction: From Chartism to* Trainspotting (Plymouth, 1997); only Williams's *Second Generation* (London, 1964), set in Oxford, is discussed.

[39] Emyr Humphreys, *Bonds of Attachment* (London, 1991).

[40] Niall Griffiths, *Grits* (London, 2000); Richard John Evans, *Entertainment* (Bridgend, 2000); Rachel Trezise, *In and Out of the Goldfish Bowl* (Cardiff, 2000); Lewis Davies, *My Piece of Happiness* (Cardiff, 2000).

6

Ralph Bates and the Representation
of the Spanish Anarchists in
Lean Men and *The Olive Field*

RAIMUND SCHÄFFNER

The Spanish Civil War has rightly been called the meeting point and battle-ground of all the significant political movements and ideologies of the twentieth century. It is, therefore, hardly surprising that it has aroused acrimonious controversies and intense passions, politicized the world of art and literature, and inspired a wealth of monographs, biographies, memoirs and literary works, most of them riddled with their authors' political and ideological persuasions. The majority of the artists, writers and intellectuals who have taken a stand have portrayed the Civil War as a Manichaean contest between democracy and fascism, as an exemplary political conflict between civilization and barbarism, social progress and reaction, as 'a war of light against darkness'.[1] For many years, it was common practice to dismiss the anti-authoritarian legacy of Spanish history and systematically efface the anarchist component in the Civil War or, at least, treat anarchism disparagingly and malign the anarchists as weapon-carrying bandits, counter-revolutionary traitors, violence-prone criminals, and cowards.

There were, however, a few dissident voices. Responding to a poll held by *Left Review*,[2] both Ethel Mannin and Aldous Huxley took sides with the anarchists, praising their emphasis on individuality, personal dignity, liberty and humanity, and extolling their decentralist and federalist tendencies as well as their scorn for materialism. In his eyewitness testimony of the Spanish Civil War, *The Spanish Cockpit* (1937), Franz Borkenau gave a frank assessment of Republican politics, and a year later George Orwell followed in similar vein. In his highly controversial autobiographical account, *Homage to Catalonia* (1938), he demolishes liberal and Marxist myths by refuting simplistic views of the Civil War as a struggle between the forces of good and evil. Orwell lays bare the social and political divisions that permeated the left and accuses the communists of having betrayed the revolution. In more recent years, anarchist, independent Marxist and non-aligned historians have provided ample evidence to substantiate a different interpretation of the Spanish Civil War.[3] They have foregrounded the concurrent social revolution carried out by the anarchists in 1936, drawn attention to the internecine struggles among the rival factions of the left and exposed the counter-revolutionary Stalinist politics of the Partido Communista de España (PCE).

Until fairly recently, literary-critical studies of the Thirties were dominated by the work of the small group of canonical writers known as the 'Auden Generation'. But recently this narrow perspective has been widened considerably, and the literature of the 'Red Decade' has been thoroughly reassessed. As a result, many novelists and poets have been recovered from neglect and oblivion, among them Ralph Bates (1899–2000), an outstanding communist propagandist, journalist and novelist, who went to Spain in 1923 and became involved in the working-class movement, until he finally left the country for good in 1937. Bates wrote two novels, *Lean Men* (1934) and *The Olive Field* (1936),[4] which are set in the years preceding the revolutionary events and deal with the increasing polarization both between left and right and within the left.

In this article, I shall examine the way Bates represents anarchism and the anarchists, who formed the largest group of the left. The few critical works that deal with his novels have not accorded this issue the attention it merits. Rather than offering a comprehensive reading of the texts, I intend to explore selected thematic aspects, situating them in their historical context. I wish to begin by considering the origin and nature of Spanish anarchism, then investigate its relationship to the Church and to religion, and finally look closely at the conflict between the collectivist and communist currents of anarchist thought, with particular focus on their revolutionary theory and practice.

'Anarchism seeks to recreate society, and the history of anarchism inevitably concerns dreams, struggle, and defeat.'[5] Nowhere have these words been nearer the truth than in Spain, where anarchism constituted the predominant influence in the social and labour movement. Although often forced to go underground, it expanded rapidly among agricultural workers and smallholders in the rural areas in Andalusia and Levante, and among industrial workers in the mining districts of Catalonia and Oviedo and in the urban areas of Barcelona, Valencia and Madrid. From its inception, Spanish anarchism was part of a larger international movement. Its ideological roots lie in Bakunin's anti-authoritarian, revolutionary collectivism. When the Italian Giuseppe Fanelli arrived in Spain in 1868 to convert the local and regional workers' federations to anarchism, the social, economic and political situation provided a fertile ground for the dissemination of anarchist doctrines. In the early nineteenth century, the introduction of capitalist legal and social relationships had destroyed the long-standing cooperative and collectivist traditions of life in the pueblo. The main institutions upholding the new social order – the State, the Guardia Civil and the Church – had long been the target for the unmitigated hatred of the dispossessed and politically repressed population. One reason for the enthusiastic reception of anarchist ideas was the ideological affinity between anarchism and the indigenous tradition of federalism. Anarchist theorists incorporated the communal heritage into their vision of a free society based on self-governing, independent communes, and gave a revolutionary thrust to the reformist federalist ideas promoted by Pierre-Joseph Proudhon and Francisco Pí y Margall, while at the same time recognizing industrialization and technological advance as vehicles of, and necessary requirements for, human liberation and social and economic progress.

Despite the essential contribution of anarchism to the modernization of Spanish society, and despite its antireligious and anticlerical bent, conservative, liberal and Marxist historians have consistently conceptualized Spanish anarchism in atavistic and religious terms. Gerald Brenan describes it as 'an expression of nostalgia for the past' and an attempt to reconstruct the primitive collectivist commune.[6] Following this line of argument, the Marxist social historian Eric Hobsbawm defines anarchism as a political movement belonging to the pre-industrial period of transition from feudalism to capitalism.[7] And James Joll argues that: 'much anarchist thinking seems to be based on a romantic, backward-looking vision of an idealized past society of artisans and peasants, and on a total rejection of the realities of twentieth-century social and economic organization.'[8] The use of religion as an analytical tool goes back to Constancio Bernaldo de Quirós y Pérez, who, in his *Bandolerismo y delincuencia subversiva en baja Andalucía* (1913), calls anarchism 'a secular religion, based upon an apocalyptic belief in an unrealizable egalitarian society',[9] and was then taken up and popularized by Juan Díaz del Moral in his influential social-psychological study, *Historia de las agitaciones campesinas andaluzas* (1929). This millenarian approach, viewing anarchism as a pre-modern, pre-political, incoherent, quasi-religious movement, dominated English academic research into Spanish anarchism until the 1960s.[10] Trying to account for the radicalism of

Spanish anarchism, Brenan and, later, George Woodcock and James Joll, in their popular and widely read histories of anarchism, attach great importance to national and cultural characteristics which, they claim, predispose the Spaniards to all forms of fanaticism and extremism. In the works of Brenan and Raymond Carr this stereotyping takes on a racist tone. Brenan traces the deeper layers of Spanish thought and feeling to their Oriental origin,[11] and Carr classifies the Spanish anarchists as racially inferior Moorish fatalists.[12]

More recently, the millenarian argument has been challenged and refuted by a growing number of historians with divergent political affiliations.[13] While acknowledging the intricate relationship between Spanish anarchism and religion and assigning it a millenarian bent, they caution against overemphasizing moral-religious aspects, regarding this as a distortion of its theory and practice. Seeing anarchism as 'a rational, not a millenarian response to a specific social configuration',[14] they point out that, as opposed to millenarianism, anarchism has a secular philosophy of history, a rational and systematic framework of political, social and economic analysis, and a coherent theory of revolution. Anarchists refuse to draw up detailed schemes of a future society and, eschewing any idealization of prophetic, messianic saviours, believe in the capability of human beings to bring about social change. Finally, these historians criticize colleagues who use an oversimplifying religious model of pursuing political ends, for the use of the terms 'religious' and 'millenarian' associates anarchism with mysticism and ineffectual utopianism, and thus dismisses its doctrines and goals as unrealistic and unattainable. As Kaplan concisely puts it: 'In a secular age, the taint of religion is the taint of irrationality.'[15]

Ralph Bates clearly follows the path opened up by Moral. In *Lean Men*, he identifies anarchism as a primarily agrarian movement of peasants and artisans, a theory 'suited to the simpler and more personal problems of the countryside'.[16] Explaining its success in the industrial urban centres, he argues that the majority of industrial workers were recruited from the agrarian south and remained deeply traditional in their habits of mind and behaviour. The central character, Francis Charing, puts the popularity of anarchism in Andalusia down to the fact that, of all socialist movements, anarchism was first to appear on the scene and channelled the masses' millenarian fervour and instinctive spirit of revolt into a revolutionary doctrine almost religious in its emotional, rather than rational, appeal (p. 205).

In *The Olive Field*, the communist Justo Robledo repeatedly discredits anarchism as a kind of new religion without theological doctrines: 'philosophically Anarchism is nothing more than a Christianity without God'; thereby implying that it replaced Christian belief as a response to the Spaniards' search for a unifying idea.[17] In his story, 'Compañero Sagasta Burns a Church', Bates reiterates this argument, sketching a frame of mind and psychological disposition that Moral and Joll also detected in apocalyptic-chiliastic sects of medieval and early modern times:

> the psychology of anarchism is religious. Its tragic courage, its total selfless-ness, its sense of drama, its worship of Action, its fanatical belief in the Myth [. . .], its *burning*, I say burning mystical love for its leaders, its unquestioning obedience, its subtle and amazing intuition, all this, it is evident, discloses anarchism to be a religion.[18]

Nevertheless, Bates's anarchists profess strong anticlerical and antireligious leanings. In order to understand the tremendous violence of the outrages against the Church, it is necessary to bear in mind both the profound influence Catholicism exerted on Spanish society and culture and the intense atheism of the anarchist movement, which categorically rejects religion and the state as incarnations of the authoritarian principle. The fact that even Mudarra, the fierce iconoclast, cannot help being enchanted by statues and images of saints, and the examples of the revolutionaries Masera and Gerard underline the forceful influence and cultural hegemony of Catholicism, which is also manifest in the anarchists' use of religious diction and metaphors as a means for articulating atheist and social revolutionary ideas.

The close historical link between State and Church, the most apparent indication of which was the Inquisition, is a major issue in the novels under consideration, where religion has clear class connotations. In the sixteenth and seventeenth centuries, the Spanish Church showed an interest in social and political issues more profound than in any other European country. Then a process of moral and intellectual degeneration set in and, after its expropriation in the early nineteenth century, the Church abandoned its traditional role as champion of the poor and joined forces with the landed oligarchy, industrial capitalists and the army, turning religion into an instrument of controlling and oppressing the masses. In *The Olive Field* Bates describes these reactionary forces as 'natural allies' (p. 177), and in the relationship between Father Soriano and the local landlord, Don Fadrique, he demonstrates how the political, social and clerical elites and their interests interlock. In return for its monopoly on religion and its privileged position in morals and education, the Church legitimizes and enforces the acceptance of the socio-economic status quo by promoting a belief in the hereafter and preaching a slavish morality, with its stress on authority, obedience, submission, humility and piety.

Consequently, the clergy is vehemently opposed to any attempt at modernizing the political, social, economic and religious structures of Spanish society. However, the Church not only serves as a morally and intellectually corrupt stronghold of political and social reaction and an impediment to progress; it also neglects its spiritual tasks and its role as an instrument of salvation. Having perverted their own religious ideals of brotherhood, human solidarity and charity, the parasitic, greedy clergy's practice is completely inconsistent with their moral and ethical pretensions. Soriano is preoccupied with courting the rich landowners and invests all his energy in promoting his own egotistical interests and career, maintaining his social privileges and extending his temporal power. In *Lean Men*, Catholic nurses ignore the needs and suffering of anarchist and atheist patients. The conditions have reached so deplorable a state that even the moderate doctor Mariscal believes 'that the destruction of the power of the Church has become a national necessity' (p. 77).

Since the early nineteenth century, anticlerical liberals and socialists had repeatedly tried to reduce and/or break the power and influence of Catholicism. Although the Church's cultural hegemony among industrial and agricultural workers and intellectuals had been slipping continuously for several decades, Manuel Azaña's optimism in announcing in the Cortes on 13 October 1931 that Spain was no longer Catholic was largely unfounded. The first government of the Second Republic closed convents and state schools, which were dominated by the Church, disbanded the immensely powerful and wealthy Jesuit Order, ended the subvention of the priests, introduced civil marriage and divorce, and planned a uniform state system of secular education, in which members of religious congregations were banned from teaching.[19] This policy of secularization caused the Church, which controlled a large part of the Spanish capital, and its political arm, the Confederación Española de Derechas Autónomas (CEDA) and, later, the semi-Fascist Acción Popular, led by José María Gil Robles, to side with the Army. It came as no surprise when the clergy openly endorsed, legitimized and theologically sanctioned the Fascist coup against the Republic. In the *Joint Letter of the Spanish Bishops to the Bishops of the World*, of 1 July 1937, the Spanish episcopacy declared the Civil War a crusade against atheism and materialism, a struggle between good and evil, a conflict between Catholic, patriotic forces and anti-Spanish, anti-Christian elements. Franco was glorified and mystified as a Messiah, as a saviour of the nation and of Christian civilization.

In *Lean Men* and *The Olive Field* Bates displays a pragmatic attitude towards the Church. He depicts religious buildings violently attacked by the anarchists as symbols of the detested regime and, calling to mind the

Montjuich Affair of 7 June 1896,[20] describes vividly the disturbance of religious festivities, the breaking of religious taboos and the performance of blasphemous acts. While showing the motives behind these actions, he discards them as fanatic outbursts of irrational instincts, a millenarian fervour and moral indignation rather than as the result of reasoning, and therefore, in *The Olive Field*, he calls them 'silly' (p. 173). In *Lean Men* Francis Charing, the non-aligned socialist García and Robledo criticize the legislative measures the Republican Government introduced in order to weaken the Church's hold on society as being tactically unsound. Instead of precipitate action that enables the enemy to rally round the propagandist defence of religion and the nation, they advocate educational work, aiming at a long-term change of consciousness, infusing into the masses the ideals of humanity, universal culture, equality and social justice (see p. 226). In 'Compañero Sagasta Burns a Church', which was written under the impact of the Fascist rebellion, Bates is less hostile to the anarchist church-burners. He confesses that he will neither condone nor condemn the forms which anticlericalism has taken, and describes the precautions the anarchists take in order to avoid damage being done to the neighbouring houses.

Another subject Bates discusses in some detail concerns the anarchist conceptions of revolutionary tactics and strategy. After years of fluctuating fortune and bitter factional quarrelling, cycles of economic depression and political persecution, failed strikes and uprisings, the upsurge of revolutionary syndicalism in France increased the influence of the anarcho-syndicalists in the labour movement and promoted the formation of the Confederación Nacional del Trabajo (CNT) in 1910. With the CNT's emergence, Spanish anarchism turned into a powerful mass movement, continuously gaining in strength. Its programme was designed to merge long-range anarchist-communist aims, more immediate syndicalist demands for an amelioration of working conditions and higher wages, and syndicalist forms of organization and struggle. Nevertheless, the relationship between syndicalism and anarchism remained an intricate one. The history of the CNT was characterized by permanent dissension between two fundamental currents that centred on tactical and strategical questions and had their origins in the 1880s and 1890s, when collectivists and anarcho-communists struggled for hegemony in the anarchist movement. In the 1920s, reformist syndicalists, led by Salvador Seguí and Angel Pestaña, spoke out for cooperation with Republican parties and the State in order to secure reforms that they believed to be in the interests of the workers. To counter their growing influence and to prevent the workers from turning towards the socialists and communists, anarchist militants in 1927 founded the Federación Anarquista Ibérica (FAI). Strongly situated in the anti-political revolutionary tradition, they saw themselves as guardians of anarchist theory and practice, and defined the FAI's task as combating revisionism within the CNT and reaffirming the CNT's commitment to anarchist principles and ideals. The conflict escalated and finally led to a split in the CNT at the 1931 National Congress. Although the FAI was undoubtedly the dominant ideological influence in the CNT during the Second Republic, it would be misleading to describe their relationship in terms of a dictatorship by the FAI, as the moderate wing of the CNT and many commentators, including Bates, insinuate (see *Lean Men*, pp. 209, 368, 523–4). Murray Bookchin has shown that this is a gross misinterpretation of reality, grounded in ideological prejudice, ignorance or sheer malice rather than in historical evidence.[21]

In *The Olive Field*, repudiating the communist theory of the state expounded by Robledo, Aquiló formulates the anarchist position, which Bates dismisses outright as a 'confused hail of words' (p. 12). Starting from the premise that all power corrupts and is reactionary by nature, the anarchist doctor denounces the state as an instrument of domination, oppression and exploitation. In line with Bakunin's and Kropotkin's writings on its historical development and against Rousseauist, Hegelian and Marxist theories, Aquiló sees the state not only as a negation of individual and social liberty, but also as an impediment to the cultural development of humankind and as one of the principal causes of social and moral evils. Far from defending it as a vehicle of revolutionary change, he calls for its abolition as a precondition for the realization of a free, equal and just society. Consistent with their total opposition to the state, anarchists reject political parties and all participation in the political process, and, like the CNT and the FAI in *Lean Men*, urge their followers to abstain from voting.[22] Their alternative to the takeover of the state is the social revolution, a social and cultural process that involves a fundamental transformation of all economic, social and political structures, and of human relationships. Instead of political activity they champion different forms of direct action, which, under the slogan 'Propaganda by the Deed' (ranging from economic forms of struggle and insurrections to individual acts of terror), earned anarchism its popular image as an incarnation of violence and destruction. A closer look at anarchist publications demonstrates, however, that things were far more complex than the identification of anarchism with terrorism suggests. Like their counterparts in the Marxist camp, the leading figures of the anarchist movement considered violence to be integral to the revolutionary process, but insisted that it should be directed against economic and political targets, not against individuals. Repelled by individual acts of terrorism, the benefit of which they doubted on moral and tactical grounds, they regarded strikes, sabotage, civil disobedience and similar forms of collective action as legitimate means of revolt against inhuman conditions, but, in conformity with the anarchist principle that ends cannot be divorced from means, rejected them as a way of establishing a better world.

These debates, controversies and developments are reflected in the two novels under scrutiny here. Bates holds the FAI up to opprobrium and presents it as the agent of disharmony and the conspiratorial centre of mindless terrorism and violent disorder. In *Lean Men* he demonizes the FAI as 'evil teachers who deluded the workers with impossible doctrines' (p. 209), and denigrates its supporters as demagogues, crazy companions of the Deed and insane, bloodthirsty criminals making 'wild demands' (p. 366). Sarria's description is typical of this kind of stereotypical characterization of anarchists:

> The orator, black-shirted and white-faced, was intoxicated with doctrine and emotion, they could make little sense of his utterances. He seemed to vocalize all the wild rumours, all the animal fears and enthusiasms that surged in the collective mentality before him. It really seemed to Francis that Sarria was some kind of loudspeaker for the confused and conflicting hysteria that the last few days had raised. Conscious control of words and thoughts seemed to have disappeared from his speech, he was behaving as the leader of a frustrated wolf-pack might behave. At one minute he would be screaming praises of the 'Sacred Revolution', at the next wailing over the loss of brave compañeros, and then without preparation he would fling some impossible proposal before the crowd. (p. 311)

This is in stark contrast to his 'Compañero Sagasta Burns a Church' where, in a totally different social and political context, Bates admiringly calls the FAI militants 'fine fellows . . . aware of their moral superiority' (p. 681).

In *Lean Men*, in particular, Bates gives considerable space to the question of *pistolerismo*. In Spain, militants advocated the use of violence against the large landowners as early as the 1880s, when a secret society called *La Mano Negra* (whose existence has never been proved) was accused of all sorts of crimes, including murders and attacks on property. When in the 1920s employers hired professional gunmen (*pistoleros*) to kill members of anarcho-syndicalist groups, the anarchists reacted by assassinating representatives of the economic, political, military and clerical establishment. This destructive and violent element of Spanish anarchism is represented in *The Olive Field* by Aquiló. When he praises a *pistolero* – whom Robledo characterizes as an ordinary bandit and gunman, a common thief and murderer – as 'the ideal revolutionary' and 'the true type of the free man' (p. 17), the communist accuses the anarchist of cultivating the myth of the anarchist assassin. In both *Lean Men* and *The Olive Field*, anarchists generally are described as enjoying the flourish of the pistol and the knife, which they prefer to reason and persuasion in political meetings and discussions. Arguments are usually settled by resort to violence. Bates further weakens Aquiló's political stance by undermining his moral integrity, which was a matter of great importance to the Spanish anarchists, with their emphasis on the values of dignity, pride and self-respect. Referring to an episode reminiscent of Bakunin's *Confession*,[23] Robledo charges Aquiló with cowardice and a betrayal of his political principles:

> And you, Señor Aquiló, when you were in prison for inciting some little village flare-up, you wrote to the Civil Governor pleading for pardon. You were repentant, you had been misled, and so forth. You wrote three letters, one to the Bourbon himself, anything to crawl out of prison while there were three dead men in . . . (p. 17)

Bates does not attach too much importance to the issues of political abstention and individual violence, and focuses on collective forms of direct action, such as occupations, demonstrations, riots, insurrections and strikes, launched by the FAI in the hope of igniting the masses and bringing on the revolution. While Sarria, Aquiló and other FAI activists are caricatured as blind and hateful fanatics, Mudarra is conceived in a more complex and ambivalent manner. Father Martínez sees in him not only a sacrilegious iconoclast, but also a very likeable man. He personifies the *obrero consciente*, and, like Francis Charing and Bates himself, 'Mudarra, the finest guitarist in Los Olivares, is an example of the artist as a man of action'.[24] Transcending the traditional domain of social revolutionary practice, anarchism put great emphasis on cultural and artistic activities in the struggle for social emancipation. Art and literature were seen as a significant means in the process of achieving the ideal of the *hombre completo*.

Mudarra complies with the demands classical anarchist theorists made on conscious, devoted vanguardists. Believing strongly in the justice and triumph of the anarchist cause that furnishes his life with meaning and purpose, he serves the movement with great enthusiasm, extreme energy, heroic bravery, utmost determination, revolutionary fervour and unquestioning dedication to the anarchist precepts. Equally rejecting class collaboration, parliamentary politics and trade-union bureaucracies, he keeps close contact with the people and defines his role as that of a catalyst who strengthens and channels revolutionary instincts and energies, foments rebellion and incites uprisings, hoping to trigger off the social revolution.

Mudarra is identified with the insurrectionist approach to revolution. Convinced that revolutions are to be achieved primarily not by propaganda and education, but through practical action, he incarnates Bakunin's philosophy of action and cult of spontaneity, revolutionary will and instinctive rebellion. An act of sabotage fills him with 'the joy of unfettered defiant Action' (p. 156). Like other FAI militants in the two novels, he ignores the consequences of his deeds, detests theorizing and places action above ideas, impulse above reason, as in his sacrilegious, iconoclastic attacks on religious institutions. Bates definitely exaggerates this anti-intellectual edge, but both the FAI and the CNT were primarily movements of practice: they laid great stress on the virtues of action and shunned the theoretical aspects of revolutionary work.

Mudarra is also associated with the myth of violence as a strategy for bringing about a transformation of social and economic conditions. He acquires self-identity and human dignity in acts of revolutionary violence. While Bates's politico-ideological mouthpiece and alter ego, Francis Charing, and Caro have strong ethical reservations against using violence personally[25] and, believing that it tends to breed new violence, question its practical and political benefit, Mudarra has no such scruples and ignores a potential conflict between the humanitarian morality of anarchism and the inhuman necessity of killing people. In accordance with Christopher Caudwell, who, in 'Pacifism and violence',[26] rejects this 'pacifist argument' against the use of violence in the revolution, Mudarra is prepared to make use of all possible means to realize his political and moral aims: he accepts the 'guilt in the necessary murder', and ascribes to it cathartic and therapeutic, morally elevating and liberating effects. In this context, the regular pruning and grafting of the olive trees is highly significant. These techniques of cultivation involve wounding and bleeding and can be interpreted as a symbol both for the tonic properties of violence as employed in armed revolutions and for the inseparability of pain from pleasure.[27] Mudarra's position has close affinities with that formulated by Georges Sorel in his influential and highly controversial work, *Réflexions sur la violence*, which was first published in 1906, at the height of French syndicalism, as a series of articles for *Le mouvement socialiste*. Denouncing pacifism and humanitarianism, Sorel differentiates his conception of proletarian, unselfish, heroic violence from state force, and glorifies proletarian violence as an act of revolt and a manifestation of individual and collective will that does not aim at acquiring power or conquering the state, but at destroying hierarchies, social, economic and political structures. In contrast, state or bourgeois force serves to control and repress oppositional movements and to secure and promote the power and privileges of the possessing class.

Whereas *The Olive Field* is ambiguous in terms of characterization, on the level of plot Bates's message is unequivocal. He depicts several rebellions in such a way as to illustrate the shortcomings of anarchist theory and practice and, simultaneously, affirm the Marxist doctrine of revolution and class struggle as the only practical way of achieving social change. In the first part of *The Olive Field*, the action culminates in an insurrection by landless labourers and smallholders in the Andalusian village of Los Olivares. The land question had long been a crucial theme in Spanish politics and was 'by far the most pressing social question facing the Republic'.[28] When the socialists and republicans inaugurated land reforms in order to alleviate the distress of the masses, these piecemeal measures were not only resisted by the landowners, the middle class and the Guardia Civil, who considered they went too far, but also alienated the rural working class, whose aspirations and hopes for genuine social and economic reform and a fundamental land redistribution were frustrated. In *The Olive Field*, a severe drought and a hailstorm ruin the crop, causing unemployment and wage cuts and thus exacerbating the workers' dire poverty and suffering. In this explosive mixture of long-standing discontent and sudden material ruin caused by natural and economic factors, the popular rage and revolutionary fervour vent themselves in lootings, demonstrations, strikes and spontaneous riots. Bates shows this anarchist conception of revolution to be impractical: there is a lack of planning, organization and support and, consequently, none of the riots and strikes achieves its aims. It is left to Caro to realize that revolution cannot be incited the anarchist way, and so he leaves the FAI to join the Marxists. Like Francis Charing and Robledo, he decries the FAI for making workers participate in useless and abortive riots and strikes that lack efficiency and waste revolutionary energies. Concluding that unprepared, unguided action is inevitably doomed to failure, they stress the necessity of a disciplined party to educate and direct the masses, who have not yet reached the state of political and social awareness necessary for successful social transformation.[29]

To underline this position, in the final third of *The Olive Field* Bates fictionalizes the Asturian insurrection of 1934, which in a number of ways foreshadowed the Civil War. After moving to the northern region of Asturias, where mines, docks and factories are smouldering with revolt, both Caro and Mudarra become involved in the political events, which were partly the spontaneous product of the rank and file's radicalization and partly planned by the socialists as part of a nationwide rising to overthrow the government. Mudarra proves his military prowess on behalf of the FAI. Caro joins both the communist group and the mining syndicate affiliated to the CNT, which in Asturias was controlled by the reformist Treintistas and cooperated with the socialist Unión General de Trabajadores (UGT), the strongest section of the labour movement in this province. The reunion of Mudarra and Caro in the struggle illustrates Bates's appeal to form a united front of the left. The Asturian uprising, however, was crushed because it lacked support outside the region and the left was riven by dissent. After two weeks, during which they 'abolished the political authority of the state and the economic and social authority of the bourgeoisie',[30] the insurrectionaries were defeated by the army, which largely consisted of Foreign Legion and Moorish troops – a circumstance that for many anarchists was conducive to racism. In the ensuing reign of terror, thousands were arrested, incarcerated, tortured and executed. Mudarra's imprisonment, torture and murder symbolize the futility of the anarchist strategy. Caro proclaims his political faith and determination to continue working for the revolution, and, together with Lucía, returns to Los Olivares. This ending is not convincing, since, as Klaus points out, it is inconsistent with Caro's ideological and political development.[31]

Bates's attitude towards the Spanish anarchists and his treatment of anarchism in his novels is more ambivalent and complex than that of other Marxist writers. Assessing his political beliefs, Munton and Young state: 'In general he was not influenced by Marxism, but found William Morris, Keir Hardie and even Prince Kropotkin, the anarchist theorist, more congenial.'[32] Close examination of *Lean Men* and *The Olive Field* has shown that this claim is a sweeping simplification that needs to be qualified. Bates displays strong artistic and ethical motives, characteristic of William Morris and Keir Hardie, as well as a genuine distrust of abstract theories and power, but ultimately he regards Marxism as a theory and practice superior to anarchism, which, as he urges in an article for *Time and Tide*, 'with its theoretical objection to the existence of a State and its incapacity for organization can obviously never be the instrument of revolution'.[33] In *Lean Men* Bates rejects anarchism as a 'nebulous vapidity' (p. 198), as an irrational and emotional creed that does not offer a coherent alternative social system and that, due to its stress on individualism, prevents the kind of collective action he considers necessary to bring down the existing order. This does not prevent him from including the anarchists in the revolutionary camp and, indeed, his demand for non-sectarianism is a distinguishing feature of the two novels. Bates harshly condemns the Stalinist policy of the popular front, which he soon after came to embrace, but sixty years later, with the benefit of hindsight, in an interview with the German *Tageszeitung*, again repudiated:

> We lost the war because of the Popular Front. It is an instrument to win elections, but it cannot govern. Distribution of land, expropriation of factories and all that was not possible. The Popular Front confined itself to resisting Franco, but it could not decide to arm the people. That would have been the way to win the war.[34]

Placing the cause of proletarian revolution above the party line,[35] both Francis Charing and Caro champion a united front of the left, comprising communists of all persuasions, socialists and anarchists, who, despite their theoretical and strategical shortcomings, are held in high esteem for their personal qualities of courage, altruism, dedication, enthusiasm, fighting strength and sense of justice. The narrator of 'Compañero Sagasta Burns a Church' summarizes Bates's view: 'Anarchism is impossible, [. . .] it is noble, just and beautiful, but unrealisable' (pp. 683–4). This is a far cry from the typical Marxist denunciation of anarchism, but, as an appraisal of anarchist theory and practice, it is, nevertheless, deeply flawed.

NOTES

[1]   Stephen Spender, *The Thirties and After: Poetry, Politics, People (1933–75)* (London, 1978), p. 18.

[2]   *Authors Take Sides on the Spanish War* (London, 1937).

[3]   Pierre Broué and Émile Témime, *The Revolution and the Civil War in Spain* (London, 1972); Murray Bookchin, *The Spanish Anarchists: The Heroic Years 1868–1936* (New York, 1977); Burnett Bolloten, *The Spanish Revolution: The Left and the Struggle for Power during the Civil War* (Chapel Hill, 1979); George Esenwein and Adrian Shubert, *Spain at War: The Spanish Civil War in Context, 1931–1939* (London, 1995); Robert Alexander, *The Anarchists in the Spanish Civil War*, 2 vols (London, 1999).

[4]   Bates did not write a novel or a book-length study on the Civil War, but only a few documentary sketches. In a letter to H. Gustav Klaus, Bates comments that he planned to write a sequel to *The Olive Field* taking up later events, but was prevented from doing so by the outbreak of the Civil War; see H. Gustav Klaus, *The Literature of Labour: Two Hundred Years of Working-Class Writing* (Brighton, 1985), p. 198, n. 10. For biographical information, see H. Gustav Klaus, 'Homage to Catalonia: The Fiction of Ralph Bates', *London Magazine*, 28 (1989), 45–56. A full bibliography of Bates's writings is provided by Alan Munton and Alan Young, *Seven Writers of the English Left: A Bibliography of Literature and Politics, 1916–1980* (New York, 1981), pp. 83–115.

5   Jerome R. Mintz, *The Anarchists of Casas Viejas* (Bloomington, 1994), p. 1.

6   Gerald Brenan, *The Spanish Labyrinth: An Account of the Political and Social
     Background of the Civil War* (Cambridge, 2000 [1943]), p. 188.

7   E. J. Hobsbawm, *Primitive Rebels: Studies in Archaic Forms of Social
     Movement in the 19th and 20th Centuries* (Manchester, 1959).

8   James Joll, *The Anarchists* (London, 1964), p. 277.

9   Temma Kaplan, *Anarchists of Andalusia (1869–1903)* (Princeton, NJ, 1977),
     p. 207.

10   Brenan, *The Spanish Labyrinth*, pp. viii, 75, 157, 188ff., 192; Joll, *The
     Anarchists*, pp. 11–13, 241; George Woodcock, *Anarchism: A History of
     Libertarian Ideas and Movements* (Harmondsworth, 1963), pp. 299–334;
     Hobsbawm, *Primitive Rebels*, pp. 84–5; Franz Borkenau, *The Spanish Cockpit:
     An Eye-Witness Account of the Political and Social Conflicts of the Spanish
     Civil War* (London, 1986 [1937]), p. 298; Stanley G. Payne, *The Spanish
     Revolution* (London, 1970); Robert W. Kern, *Red Years/Black Years: A
     Political History of Spanish Anarchism (1911–1937)* (Philadelphia, 1978).

11   Brenan, *The Spanish Labyrinth*, p. xviii.

12   Raymond Carr, *The Civil War in Spain* (London, 1966), p. 445.

13   Bookchin, *The Spanish Anarchists*, p. 59; Kaplan, *Anarchists of Andalusia*,
     pp. 11, 210–12; Mintz, *The Anarchists of Casas Viejas*, pp. 5–6; Peter Marshall,
     Demanding the Impossible: A History of Anarchism (London, 1992), p. 454;
     George Esenwein, *Anarchist Ideology and the Working-Class Movement in
     Spain, 1868–1898* (Berkeley, 1989), pp. 1–4.

14   Kaplan, *Anarchists of Andalusia*, p. 11.

15   Ibid., p. 211.

16   Ralph Bates, *Lean Men: An Episode in a Life* (London, 1934), p. 378; further
     references are inserted in the text.

17   Ralph Bates, *The Olive Field*, with new Introduction by Valentine Cunningham
     (London, 1986 [1936]), p. 74; further references are inserted in the text.

18   Ralph Bates, 'Compañero Sagasta Burns a Church', *Left Review*, II (1936),
     681–7 (685); further references are inserted in the text. For Joll's view, see *The
     Anarchists*, pp. 17–39.

19   See Ralph Bates, 'The Church in Spain', *Time and Tide*, 15 (1934), 1649–52.

20   During the religious celebration of Corpus Christi, a bomb was thrown at the
     procession led by the leading figures of the Church hierarchy and the military,
     killing ordinary people. For the event, the reprisals, the trials and the repercus-
     sions for the anarchist movement, see Esenwein, *Anarchist Ideology*, pp. 191–202.

21   Bookchin, *The Spanish Anarchists*, p. 242.

22   In the 1936 general election, the CNT gave up its anti-parliamentary, anti-statist
     stand, which had been its *raison d'être*, collaborated with other unions and
     political parties, and joined the Catalan government. This involvement in par-
     liamentary politics meant that the CNT reinforced the very institutions they had
     denounced in the past, and abandoned the social revolution.

23   In his *Confession*, written in 1851 during imprisonment in the Peter and Paul
     fortress (first published in 1921), Bakunin calls himself a repentant sinner, a

criminal who does not deserve forgiveness. Scholars disagree on whether this was a cunning ruse, as sympathizers assert, or an outright betrayal of his beliefs, as his enemies claim. In a secret message of 1854, given to his sister Tatjana, Bakunin again proclaims his anarchist beliefs.

[24] Peter Hazeldine, 'Socialism and Realism: *The Olive Field*', *PN Review*, 14 (1988), 39–42 (41).

[25] After having killed an anarchist assailant in self-defence, Francis Charing, ridden by doubts and feelings of guilt, agonizes over this act of 'necessary murder' (*Lean Men*, pp. 454–7). And, at the end of the novel, he finds himself in a moral dilemma when the only way to escape imprisonment appears to be the murder of his guard (p. 554). The theme of 'necessary murder' – the term is a quotation from W. H. Auden's poem 'Spain' (1937) – is again discussed in Bates's story 'Comrade Vila' (1936), where the killing of fascists is considered as 'legitimate and no "necessary murder" involving individual or collective guilt'. See Hanna Behrend, 'Methods, Means and Meaning – Ways of Reading Ralph Bates' Short Stories', in Hanna Behrend et al. (eds), *Working-Class Literature in Britain and Ireland in the 19th and 20th Century. Part I* (Berlin, 1985), pp. 91–100 (96). See also Klaus, 'Homage to Catalonia', pp. 51–2.

[26] *Studies in a Dying Culture* (London, 1947), p. 120.

[27] See Hazeldine, 'Socialism and Realism', p. 40.

[28] Esenwein and Shubert, *Spain at War*, p. 78.

[29] See Bates, *Lean Men*, p. 368, and *The Olive Field*, p. 16.

[30] Adrian Shubert, 'The Epic Failure: the Asturian Revolution of October 1934', in Paul Preston (ed.), *Revolution and War in Spain 1931–1939* (London, 1985), p. 115.

[31] See Klaus, *The Literature of Labour*, pp. 113–14.

[32] Munton and Young, *Seven Writers of the English Left*, p. 84.

[33] Ralph Bates, 'The Failure of the Spanish Revolution', *Time and Tide*, 15 (1934), 1245–6 (1246).

[34] *Tageszeitung*, 3 July 1996, 16 (my translation – R. S.).

[35] This interpretation is shared by H. Gustav Klaus, *Caudwell im Kontext: Zu einigen repräsentativen Literaturformen der dreißiger Jahre* (Frankfurt, 1978), p. 105, and Klaus, *The Literature of Labour*, p. 113. In contrast, Allen, *Tradition and Dream*, pp. 253–4, Stanley Weintraub, *The Last Great Cause: The Intellectuals and the Spanish Civil War* (London, 1965), pp. 291ff., and Hazeldine, 'Socialism and Realism', p. 41, regard Caro as an obedient follower of the party line.

7

Ethel Mannin's Fiction and the Influence of Emma Goldman

KATHLEEN BELL

1. MANNIN AND GOLDMAN

Foyle's Literary Luncheons may seem the acme of middle-class respectability. Perhaps the price is responsible (not available to the poor), perhaps the time of day (not feasible for manual workers) or perhaps the word 'luncheon' itself (the meal which the working class in Britain ate in the middle of the day was 'dinner'). Nonetheless, on 1 March 1933 a Foyle's Literary Luncheon took place, attended by six hundred people, at which Emma Goldman took as her topic 'An Anarchist Looks at Life'. Rebecca West seconded the vote of thanks proposed by Paul Robeson, who also sang. Before the speeches, letters from Havelock Ellis and Ethel Mannin were read, regretfully declining the invitation to lunch but expressing admiration for Emma Goldman.[1] Mannin's letter also requested a copy of Goldman's autobiography and preceded their first meeting in the following month.

Ethel Mannin, now out of print, was well known in the inter-war period; she continued to publish and her books continued to be reprinted until the 1970s. She came into contact with major literary and political figures, discussed them in her autobiographies and joined them in political activities. She contributed to the pamphlet *Authors Take Sides on the Spanish War*[2] and spoke at political meetings. Any history of literature must take into account the impact barely remembered authors had on the writing and intellectual climate of their time. Gender politics – especially questioning marriage – was a significant feature of political debate in the 1930s, from the point of view of the reading public. Left-wing writings – particularly those by women – often engage with questions of sexuality and marriage as part of a political investigation of society.[3] Goldman, West and Mannin were three women who openly opposed the sanctity of marriage as well as engaging in political debate. While their arguments came under attack, they could also attract large audiences.

Foyle's luncheon also offers a reminder that middlebrow authors and readers were not necessarily political conservatives but might be at least curious about a range of political perspectives. Conventionally formal novels may provide a safe arena for political debate, but this safety and the comfort in which they can be read may suit them to a questioning approach to politics and society.

The works of Ethel Mannin are rooted in their time and make no great claims to be lasting works of literature; Mannin was mistrustful of literary status, although she might have enjoyed it. Nonetheless, they are part of the literary history of the mid-twentieth century and recall a strand of it too easily forgotten, rooted in a critique of gender relations, opposed to capitalism and setting forward an anarchist agenda.

Ethel Mannin was already a notable figure on the London literary scene when, in 1933, she first encountered Emma Goldman; each had read the other's autobiography. Mannin was in her thirties and Goldman in her early sixties. Mannin evidently hoped their acquaintance would develop into friendship; however, the two women did not meet again until 1937, drawn together by similar interests in the Spanish Civil War. Mannin was a member of the Independent Labour Party and a supporter of the POUM, while Goldman supported the anarchist CNT-FAI. The women were also linked in disillusionment with the Soviet Union; having initially praised the Russian Revolution, Mannin's visit, described in her 1936 travel book, *South to Samarkand*,[4] led to doubts. Some conclusions mirrored Emma Goldman's earlier experiences, outlined in *My Disillusionment in Russia* (1924). In *Women and the Revolution* (1938),[5] she wrote that Russia

> has failed to achieve a classless society because of the forces of bureaucracy – the development through Stalinism of those tendencies which Lenin himself feared, as we have seen – and a new bourgeoisie of better-paid and privileged workers is arising as a result of this bureaucracy. The dictatorship of the proletariat is being succeeded – if indeed it was ever fully established, which is doubtful – by a dictatorship of bureaucrats headed by a dangerous megalomaniac whose one ambition now seems to be [to] execute or imprison all who did outstanding work in the making of the original Revolution.

At first Mannin was more positive than Goldman about the Russian Revolution's initial impact, identifying it as a major cause of improvement in women's lives, but the book, despite its epigraph from Lenin, indicates a shift in Mannin's views, and by the end of the year Ethel Mannin's sympathies were overwhelmingly anarchist.

Like Emma Goldman, Mannin was notorious for breaking with sexual conventions and standard moral views. She was open about her first affair at the age of nineteen, which resulted from curiosity rather than love. This was followed by an unsuccessful marriage to another man; Mannin separated from her husband and, embarking on a series of affairs, lived as the single parent of a small daughter, who attended Summerhill, a school run on libertarian principles by A. S. Neill. By the end of the 1930s she had been divorced for adultery (at her request) so that she could marry Reginald Reynolds, whose health was poor.[6] This marriage was a legal convenience; Mannin did not believe in marriage and, although she loved her husband, did not live with him. Despite openness about her sexual history, Mannin did not go into details about her affairs or even describe her feelings closely. Without being prudish about sex, she was deeply unwilling to expose herself emotionally. This restraint may point to a source of conflict between Mannin and Goldman, derived from attitudes rather than a political perspective.

Mannin's writing about Goldman suggests a desire to fit Goldman into a predetermined heroic mould, followed by discomfort when this is unsuccessful. Mannin seems to have been obsessed with Goldman, frequently returning to her in her writing as if wishing to understand her fully. Goldman appears as a figure in Ethel Mannin's novels, most fully in the 1941 novel *Red Rose*, a mildly fictionalized account of Goldman's life begun almost immediately after her death in the preceding year, and she is the subject of discussion in both Mannin's political books and autobiography. This process begins in *Women and the Revolution*, which combines a critique of capitalist society in relation to women with accounts of women's involvement in past and present revolutionary activity (drawing on Goldman's knowledge of the Spanish *Mujeres Libres* movement, but also including fascist revolutions) and concluding with an outline of what life in a communist society might offer to women. Emma Goldman's is among the brief biographies included and this, read in conjunction with the dedicatory letter, suggests hints of uncertainty, even in Mannin's earliest descriptions of Goldman. Most of the accounts of revolutionary women, with the exception of the chapter on fascist 'revolutions', which points to the limitations fascism places on women, are written in purple prose, with an emphasis, where possible, on the physical beauty of the female revolutionaries. On a single page Alexandra Ismailovich's face is described as 'the face of a girl with fine eyes, high forehead, dark swept-back hair, generous mouth, a beautiful face', while Vera Figner is initially 'a mere girl [with] a sensitive, beautiful face, rounded, unlined' before her imprisonment while, twenty-two years later, on her release from gaol she has 'a face still beautiful, but the dark hair has become grey, and the face has the drawn look of great suffering imposed on a sensitive nature' (p. 116). By comparison with this, Emma Goldman may well have been disappointed in the culminating description of her physical appearance:

> Red Emma! A four-square, thick-set, domineering little woman, square-jawed, disconcertingly forthright, irascible, and as relentless in her demands on herself as on others where the revolutionary cause is concerned, and behind that forbidding exterior, a martyr burnt up with the flame of her passion for human liberty, a soldier who will die fighting; a warm and gentle woman who has known the love of men, who loves children, who has known many and enriching friendships, warmly and quickly responsive to love and affection, sympathetic to the troubles of her friends, loving beauty and peace, though there has been so little time for either in her crowded life; a truly great woman, a great Person, judged by any standard. Her heart might break; over Berkman, the martyrdom of his fourteen years' imprisonment, the tragedy of his death; over Russia; over Spain; but her spirit, never! Her whole life is an example of unfaltering courage and unswerving faith, in the face of persecution and bitter disappointment. (p. 140)

The passage moves from disappointment in Emma Goldman's appearance and character through a determined assertion of her greatness to the excuses that might be advanced on her behalf. She was, of course, the only revolutionary woman in the book with whom Mannin was actually acquainted, and it seems possible that Mannin's idea of what such a woman should be like was incompatible with a real human being. In *Bread and Roses*, her anarchist outline for a utopian society, Mannin insists 'there are no ugly women in Utopia . . . they all have a natural grace', almost suggesting that beauty or ugliness should be taken as an indicator of character.[7] Mannin's later accounts of Emma Goldman are less polite. In her 1959 memoir, *Brief Voice: A Writer's Story*, Goldman is described as 'a hideously ugly little old woman, being as wide as she was high', 'rude and aggressive' with a 'harsh, twanging, American-Russian-Jewish voice',[8] while in *Rebels' Ride: A Consideration of the Revolt of the Individual* Goldman is described as a 'domineering, self-assertive, aggressive foreigner'.[9]

Mannin made a more extensive attempt to understand the character of Emma Goldman in *Red Rose*, published the year after Goldman's death in

1940. The novel declares in its subtitle that it is based on the life of 'Red Emma' – wisely, since borrowings from Goldman's autobiography are almost word for word at times. This may be a justifiable liberty, since Mannin also explains that Goldman herself had recommended a novelistic treatment of her life. Mannin herself makes an appearance in the novel as Mary Thane, a character she introduced in her 1929 novel *Crescendo*,[10] and with whom she was happy to be identified. Mannin's main concern is with Goldman the woman, attempting in particular to understand her relationship with Alexander Berkman. In the introduction it becomes apparent that, despite her arguments elsewhere to the contrary, Mannin finds herself unable to define as love a free union which permits sexual relationships with others, asking in the Preface 'how could she have loved anyone else so passionately whilst her precious Sasha was in prison?' Taken in conjunction with her earlier statement that Emma's love for Sasha did not last but only their comradeship,[11] it seems likely that the concerns expressed as those of her readers are, in fact, Mannin's own. While Emma Goldman was undoubtedly a major influence in Mannin's espousal of anarchist doctrines in the late 1930s and early 1940s, Goldman herself remained a problem for Mannin.

In some ways, *Red Rose* appears perverse; Goldman's politics and most dramatic gestures are reduced so that political involvement is little more than a backdrop to a series of personal experiences and love affairs. There is no reference to the debates at the 1907 Anarchist conference in Amsterdam or even of the speeches that preceded Goldman's arrest. A similar restraint is imposed by omitting one of the most colourful episodes of Goldman's life: the occasion on which she horsewhipped Johann Most on stage in front of an audience. Given the reliance on *Living My Life*, these are evidently deliberate omissions and not the result of ignorance. The introduction to *Red Rose* asserts that Goldman 'insisted in her relations with people, particularly her lovers, that the woman was of secondary importance to the revolutionary' (p. 10). The novel seems unwilling to accept this insistence; in *Red Rose* political urgency is the insufficiently examined motive force for most of the characters. The emotions are often accorded precedence over the political beliefs and actions to which they give rise.

Taken with *Women and the Revolution*, *Red Rose* points to the way Mannin viewed women's involvement in political struggle. Emma Goldman is not depicted as logically or intellectually convinced of her political beliefs; instead, she is emotionally and passionately committed. In this, the treatment of Goldman is typical of the women discussed in *Women and the Revolution*. The qualities valued include 'flame-like devotion', service, selflessness and courage.[12] While these were undoubtedly valued in male revolutionaries, too, since revolutionary political change seemed to require selfless devotion to a cause, Mannin's emphasis upon them seems to imply that, for women in particular, emotional commitment – ideally allied with a beautiful appearance – should be preferred to intellectual conviction. This is borne out by Mannin's concern elsewhere to elevate what is natural and instinctive. While many of Ethel Mannin's political concerns for women are rightly placed in a feminist agenda, Mannin was not a conventional feminist. In *Bread and Roses* she writes that she was convinced that women should not assert 'intellectual equality with men' because 'psychologically as well as physiologically men and women are different' and 'in general women are not mechanically minded or scientifically minded' while 'in general men do better creative work . . . and always will do' (p. 152). She also insisted that 'Nature has so arranged it that women's primary creative work is the production of children' and that women are 'subject to the periodic instability – nervous and emotional – involved in the possession of a womb' (pp. 152–3). However, she called for women's equal status with men and opposed artificial barriers to prevent women from taking work for which they were qualified. She disliked the drudgery of domestic work (especially performed by servants) and supported women's right to contraception and abortion on demand. In addition, her concern with the primacy of the emotions and instincts might therefore seem to suggest (although Mannin's opposition to 'dreary sex rivalry' (p. 153) prevents her from saying as much) that masculine intellect is not necessarily the best guide to 'the good life' and that female instincts, geared to motherhood and the beautiful home – however impeded by the possession of a womb – might be a more effective basis for political action. Certainly, many heroes of Mannin's novels suffer from damaging and destructive limitations.[13]

The elevation of the natural and instinctive seems a key part of Mannin's conversion from ILP socialism to anarchism, resolving some of the tension between the individual and the state in her earlier books. By 1940 Mannin was asserting that: 'Out of all the "dark", chaotic confusion of D. H. Lawrence's tirades against "sex in the head" there emerges the basic wisdom of the superiority of the emotions over the intellect as a guide to the Good Life.'[14] This in turn was linked with a belief that:

> Humanity's one hope is the remarriage of a living Christianity with its primitive partner, free communism (not to be confused with Stalinism), the freedom and equality of a classless society with goods in common and distribution to each according to his need, in the manner of the early Christians. (p. 168)

This sense that the emotions – given by nature and good if unfettered by society – give rise to political commitment and action may explain some of the odd transitions which take place in Mannin's fictions. For instance, at the conclusion of the 1935 (pre-anarchist) novel *Cactus*, the voice of the dead German soldier Karl – a keen militarist and German supremacist – represents the Spirit of Revolt, addressing his English fiancée, urging her from beyond the grave to oppose imperialism and espouse revolution.[15] While there is no logic in the character of the living Karl to lead to this conclusion, perhaps the reader is meant to believe that the force of passion not only survives beyond death but also rids the surviving spirit of the neuroses and confusions which lead to a false ideology. Startlingly this novel, with its evident opposition to war as well as 'war-lords', was reprinted by Penguin in 1941 despite wartime censorship and paper shortages. Presumably Mannin's popularity with readers continued despite her anarchism and pacifism, or even because of them.

Neurosis is often allied to class critique in Mannin's novels. Her most excoriating criticism is reserved for conventional, middle-class women, characterized in *Women and the Revolution* as 'Mrs Middleclass-Bore'. For instance, she opposes alimony on the ground that there is nothing wrong in a middle-class woman undertaking menial work:

> if there is nothing wrong in Gladys Brown working in a factory why is there anything wrong in Mrs Middleclass-Bore doing similar work? [. . .] the fact that [Gladys Brown] began at sixteen what Mrs Middleclass-Bore is perhaps not called upon to begin till she is thirty-six or forty-six, merely shows how much luckier it is to be born into the comfortable middle class – and how unfair to be born into the working class. (p. 217)

This class critique – with an anarchist slant – is evident in *Rose and Sylvie*,[16] which tells the story of two girls, a working-class servant and a younger, upper middle-class girl in the household where she works. Each is attracted to the other's beauty, character and different class experience, and during their childhood they have no problem in remaining friends. Their friendship is forbidden and they run away to the seaside. They are caught; Sylvie is sent to a Swiss finishing school while Rose is cured from her mild neuroses about sex and childbirth and enabled to achieve full womanhood after magistrates have sent her to an institution which combines the methods of Homer Lane and A. S. Neill. In the epilogue, the grown-up Sylvie – over-cultured and not wishing to have children – encounters a happily married Rose, pregnant and surrounded by children, who has become an ideal peasant

woman. Sylvie is repelled by Rose's naturalness and attempts to recover
from her discomfort by giving Rose a ten-shilling note – which Rose's husband
returns. This episode, in which money is used as an inadequate repayment
for social unease, may have its root in another episode which disturbed
Mannin – Goldman's marriage of convenience to the anarchist miner James
Colton, after which she gave him ten shillings to go to the cinema. (Mannin
discusses this episode more than once; it evidently troubled her.) This conclusion to *Rose and Sylvie* suggests that there is an instinctive sense of
equality between individuals but that their ability to communicate with one
another is repressed by education and society.

This may derive from the concept of revolution Goldman advanced in her
afterword to *My Disillusionment in Russia* (1924). Goldman criticized the
Russian Revolution for suppressing the 'sense of justice and equality, the
love of liberty and of human brotherhood', using the phrase 'Man's instinctive sense of equity' and condemning the Communist state for its 'fearful
perversion of fundamental values'. She called instead for a revolution which
would liberate and regenerate individuals in their relationships to one another:

> No revolution can ever succeed as a factor of liberation unless the MEANS
> used to further it be identical in spirit and tendency with the PURPOSES to be
> achieved. Revolution is the negating of the existing, a violent protest against
> man's inhumanity to man with all the thousand and one slaveries it involves. It
> is the destroyer of dominant values upon which a complex system of injustice,
> oppression and wrong has been built up by ignorance and brutality. It is the
> herald of NEW VALUES, ushering in a transformation of the basic relations of
> man to man, and of man to society. It is not a mere reformer, patching up
> some social values; not a mere changer of forms and institutions; not only a re-
> distributor of social well-being. It is that, yet much more. It is, first and foremost,
> the TRANSVALUATOR, the bearer of *new* values. It is the great TEACHER of
> the NEW ETHICS, inspiring man with a new concept of life and its manifestation
> in social relationships. It is the mental and spiritual regenerator.[17]

It is this view of Goldman's with which Mannin seems most in sympathy.[18]
Both see the new values which revolution will herald deriving from qualities
and instincts already inherent in human beings. They call on women, in
particular, to make the revolution in their souls and work with men against
the common enemy – capitalism and the state.

Mannin's belief in the natural and instinctive affects her views on literature
and the arts in general. Her respectable working-class background seems to
have given her a detestation of many bourgeois shibboleths, as her attacks
on 'Mrs Middleclass-Bore' indicate. Her 1930 account of her parents contrasts

them with people 'who spell art with a capital A or beauty with a capital B' and identifies them as 'people who do not fit any of the class distinctions', 'real people' whose 'common denominator is their authenticity; they are philistines, and proud of it'. Authenticity – explicitly aligned here with a natural confidence in the body and 'the simple, unselfconscious decency and dignity of the animals'[19] – is opposed to an intellectual attitude to art. In *Bread and Roses*, drawing on Herbert Read's echo of Eric Gill in crying 'to hell with culture', Mannin insists that art too, ideally, is 'something natural' (p. 88), integrated with society rather than separate from it and derived from authentic selfhood. In utopia, she asserts:

> The artist is free to say [. . .] whatever he feels impelled to say; he may feel compelled to express some comment on society, satirical or critical as he sees it; he may feel that he has some spiritual message to convey, some illumination to offer; he may be solely concerned with self-expression, the expression of something deep in himself, or the expression solely of his creative impulse. (p. 92)

Urging that artists should not be treated as a privileged class, as in the USSR, her concern is not merely for the finished artistic creation but also for the impulse that prompted it. However, discussing 'propaganda', she considers what constitutes a 'well-made' work of art, insisting that in the present society the good artist is one whose moral and criticism of society is 'implicit in the work itself'. In a utopian society, however, poetry, literature and drama exist 'sometimes purely for delight, sometimes for the illumination of life – but never [. . .] degraded to the purpose of propaganda' (p. 91). For Mannin, therefore, propaganda within art was a sad necessity of pre-utopian times, and should appear subordinated to the novel, for fear of damaging its artistic wholeness. It is unclear how this fits with the integration of art into life, since the purposes of delight and illumination would seem to suggest that artists have some kind of specialist function of a pseudo-priestly kind, which might seem to separate them from their fellow humans.

2. MANNIN'S NOVELS AND ANARCHISM

From the perspective of the twenty-first century, many of Ethel Mannin's views and beliefs seem surprising or even foolish. Nonetheless her novels do raise questions about society and the state and continue to address serious political debates. Some of her novels, adopted by the Book Club during the Second World War, use a time of crisis to question the present and hint at the possibility of a different kind of society. *Captain Moonlight* (1942) has a historical setting, ending at the time of the Captain Swing riots in England. It tells the story of a prosperous farmer's son, Jesse Hallward, who is not clever like his younger brother, is instinctively opposed to boundaries and borders and on the side of poachers against gamekeepers. This makes him sympathize with the poor and incurs the brutal wrath of his conventional and religious father:

> Jesse felt that he understood. A fence made you want to trespass, for one thing; and since hunger and dispossession had come to the valley men who had lived honestly enough before begun poaching; who could blame them? Only those who could not imagine what it felt like to be hungry and dispossessed. [. . .] He had an instinctive sympathy with rioters and poachers and men against the law. It was something his father had driven into his blood at the end of a leather belt.[20]

His instincts, combined with the brutality of social oppression, draw him into sympathy with rebels and outsiders and he comes to long for social change. At home, Jesse's sympathies lie with his sister, Jessica. She, like him, is an instinctive rebel but struggles for a while to conform before eloping with a gypsy (helped by her brother) and dying in childbirth at the age of sixteen. Subsequently Jesse, believing he has killed Sally, his promiscuous and dishonest mistress who wants to trap him into marriage (contrasted with two other women: the good prostitute Lucy and the virtuous Mary), escapes to Ireland, where he marries and finds happiness and relative freedom. Towards the end of the novel Jesse returns to England, where he helps his brother to come to terms with his rebellious farm-labourers and is pursued, on suspicion of Sally's murder, before returning to Ireland. Here, it is implied, he will find happiness and relative freedom for a while. However, the episodes in Ireland remind the reader that their extreme poverty will leave Jesse and his family vulnerable when the great potato famine begins.

Mannin's choice of gypsies and Irish peasants as her representatives of freedom may seem highly conventional. They may have been attractive to Mannin because of the contrast they presented to her own experience of working-class life, allowing them to present a desirable, but not too well known, otherness. She does, however, point to the limitations within their lives; they are simply the best that can be achieved. Her gypsies and Irish peasants stand for the authentic world, and have fixed gender roles – something Mannin believed would occur naturally in most instances in an ideal society. Moreover, she suggests that Irish peasants possess the 'natural dignity of animals', echoing a phrase used earlier of her parents. While Mannin treats gypsies sentimentally, her assertion of the value of gypsy culture can be contrasted with the contemporaneous attempted extermination of Europe's gypsies by Nazis – an atrocity which still receives little attention in histories of the Second World War. Similarly, Mannin's celebration of Ireland and reminder of oppression in Ireland was published at a time when Ireland's neutrality was the subject of wide criticism.

There is something startling in Mannin's depiction of Jesse Hallward's reaction to the English countryside on his return from Ireland. After an initial sense that the scene of cornfields is 'so steeped in peace that it was difficult to imagine the unrest everywhere', his view of the landscape undergoes a critical change:

> He was struck for the first time by the gentleness of the English scene, the gentle undulation of the corn and meadow-lands, the gentle swell of the hills, in such striking contrast to the wild bare hills and stony wastes to which he had grown accustomed. It was smug-looking country, he found himself thinking; it so obviously belonged to landed gentry, with its stately parks and its carefully fenced game preserves. And he longed for the sight of floods of grey water heaving against brown rocks covered with golden seaweed, and teeming grey rains beating down upon grey stone, and cloud reflected in brackish bog pools, and the blessed smell of a turf fire. [. . .] All that was wild and free was home. Here he was nothing but a hunted hare with a pack at his heels. (pp. 239–40)

This experience is plainly one the character might undergo as he changes his allegiance from England and his first home to Ireland and the home of his wife and children. It may also reflect Mannin's own longing for her second home in Ireland, which she could not visit in wartime. But it is also a startling and radical rejection of the view of England, so common in wartime, which treated the landscape itself as the threatened repository of all that is good.[21]

Mannin's 1944 novel, *Proud Heaven*, also adopted by the Book Club, is different in its methods. In some surprising ways it anticipates *Brideshead Revisited*: its focus is on a friendship between two men which begins at Oxford; it is concerned with the fate of a stately home (in this case called Mullions) and it shifts to the way in which the narrator becomes concerned in his friend's family and affair.[22] At the core of the novel is the romance between Lucian Allington, an ideal upper-class man, and Lily Groves, from a working-class family, who becomes a famous violinist under the name Barbara Mulgrave. The story is told by Lucian's friend, Robert Charles, who meets Lily and falls in love with her after Lucian's death. Experience from reading other literary texts would seem to suggest that Robert Charles must in some way be an unreliable or morally dubious narrator, but the reader is asked to take him as totally reliable, even after he deliberately leaves Lucian's widow and her lover to their deaths. He seems to be largely a male version of the Ethel Mannin character, Mary Thane – a man of working-class background used as the voice of intelligence and truth.

The plot chronicles Lucian Allington's attempt to reform politics, acting through existing institutions, such as the League of Nations. He is an intellectual (as is Robert Charles) and writes influential books. The failure of his marriage is symbolized by the birth of a stillborn child. Towards the end of his life, Lucian meets Lily Groves, who has achieved fame through a combination of natural genius and very hard work. They fall in love and eventually their love is consummated. After Lucian's death, Lily gives birth to a son. Lucian's widow dies with her lover and Robert helps Lily to buy Mullions, where she will live with her son and her parents. Robert and Lily contemplate a relationship, but a ghostly intervention by Lucian tells them the love Lucian and Lily shared is such that she should not contemplate any other relationship. Lucian's engagement in the world of politics enables Mannin, through her narrator, to act as political commentator. Lucian is as good as is possible for an upper-class intellectual, but the narrator is aware of his prejudices and able to point out the basis of anarchism in Lucian's thinking, for instance in relation to the General Strike. He also points out to the reader the flaws in Lucian's character, stemming from the contradiction between his aristocratic prejudices and political conclusions:

> He sought to reconcile within himself forces which were in fact irreconcilable – his innate belief in a natural aristocracy, born to lead and to rule, and the logical conclusions of his impatience of politicians, which led to a stateless society in which there was no place for leadership, and in which, figuratively speaking, the 'rabble' seized Mullions and lived out its squalid and swarming life in those gracious rooms, degrading all that beauty and dignity to no more than a warren for a species of human rabbit [. . .] the rabbity rabble with its blasphemously materialist conceptions of the Good Life, its devastating utilitarianism [. . .] (p. 42)

As Mannin herself demands, the focus on politics appears to arise naturally from character and plot at this point. By the early focus on two intellectual men she sets up the possibility of political debate and commentary in a way she found difficult with female protagonists. However, with the introduction of Lily Groves, whose existence is revealed only after the account of Lucian's death, a solution to Lucian's contradictions (and hence political problems) is indicated. Lily's approach to music is expressed in terms of feeling and passion, although Mannin also stresses the amount of work and luck a working-class genius would need to achieve her ambition. Her parents experience art as part of life and Lily confirms the rightness of their attitude:

> Neither [Mr] nor Mrs Groves went to concerts; such an idea could never have occurred to them; they just liked music when they came across it – a street barrel-organ, or someone playing and singing in a music-hall programme, or at 'the panto' to which, annually, they took the children, or during the course of 'a bit of a do' – a birthday party, or a wedding – at the house of a friend or relative, or even, in Mrs Groves's case, church music: 'And they were right,' said [Lily], 'music – all art – should be a part of daily life, not something kept apart, to be solemnly "gone to" in a concert-hall or museum or gallery.' (p. 74)

These follow the views expressed in the non-fiction work of the same period, *Bread and Roses*, so can be taken as Mannin's own. Lily's love affair with Lucian seems to suggest a transforming unity across class divisions, which is intended as a model for the future; perhaps readers are supposed to detect a religious allusion in their son's interest in carpentry. Towards the end of the final chapter Mullions, which Mannin now proclaims through her narrator is 'the heart of England' (p. 188), has been taken over by members of the working classes so that Lucian's child can grow up there, suggesting that nature and instinct provided by the working class may synthesize with intellect to provide a model community (except that Lucian is dead and the focus will pass to his heirs). The novel ends, however, in 1943, with Mullions commandeered by the military; its peace is destroyed, its trees felled, its gates melted for arms and its windows 'mostly broken' (p. 185). Robert addresses the dead Lucian and effectively tells him that his time has passed, urging a more thorough reassessment of society. Surprisingly for wartime, this is rooted in a mistrust of plans for peace and the effects of victory:

> The common people of the world, not the politicians and the intellectuals and the professional revolutionaries, but the toiling masses – these are the people who can save the peace, salvage civilisation, save mankind in spite of its Gadarene descent. They, ultimately, are the natural aristocracy, for blood, in the last analysis, is red, not blue . . . Your artist and intellectual is at a discount; he is a luxury – like Mullions . . . So you are better out of it, Lucian; there would be nothing for you now but the Ivory Tower, and the drawbridge permanently up. (pp. 187–8)

Having hinted at the possibility of a synthesis – the happy romantic ending as a model of the good society – its feasibility is withdrawn, on the grounds that society cannot yet accommodate even the idea of this happy ending.

In both *Captain Moonlight* and *Proud Heaven* we have a closure which offers hope but which also evades the desire for satisfaction. In *Captain Moonlight* Jesse is free and reunited with his Irish wife, filled with new tenderness for her, but a final reference to the effects of privation and anxiety on her appearance (p. 248) leads the reader to anticipate the forthcoming famine. Moreover, Jesse's wife may offer peace but she is not the only woman he has loved; his great passion was for Mary, who was too proud to marry him and instead became his brother's wife. The conclusion therefore is presented as no more than the best in unsatisfactory circumstances. Meanwhile *Proud Heaven* offers death as the only satisfactory outcome for his hero, whose time has either passed or is not yet come.

Perhaps the dissatisfaction they create is the most significant aspect of Mannin's writing – the point at which her political beliefs counter the expectations we have of the genre. It is impossible to tell how much Mannin's anarchist beliefs, as expressed in her fiction, influenced her readers but, at the least, they indicated an arena for imaginative political engagement.

NOTES

1   The full proceedings of this luncheon can be found on the Berkeley website at *http://sunsite.berkeley.edu/Goldman/Writings/Speeches/foyles.html*.

2   This 1937 pamphlet, calling on the writers and poets of Britain to state which side they took on the Spanish War, elicited a range of replies from a large number of writers. Mannin used the opportunity to affirm her support for the anarcho-syndicalist CNT-FAI as opposed to USSR communism.

3   As Janet Montefiore has argued, this is particularly prevalent in historical novels. Examples include Sylvia Townsend Warner's *Summer Will Show* (London, 1936), in which the heroine falls in love with her husband's mistress, supports the Paris Commune and reads the newly printed *Communist Manifesto*, and Naomi Mitchison's *Blood of the Martyrs* (London, 1939), which uses the setting of Nero's Rome to explore questions of male homosexuality, rape, prostitution and free love in relation to class oppression and the resistance of the powerless. Other texts, for example by Lewis Jones and George Orwell, are more conservative in their treatment of gender relations while radical in other respects.

4   London, 1936.

5   Ethel Mannin, *Women and the Revolution* (London, 1938), p. 294. Further references to this book are inserted in the text.

[6]   Reginald Reynolds, a pacifist follower of Gandhi, is another notable figure in the politics of the period. Incidentally, he detested Emma Goldman.

[7]   *Bread and Roses: An Utopian Survey and Blueprint* (London, 1944), p. 154. Further references to this book are inserted in the text.

[8]   London, 1959, p. 15.

[9]   London, 1964, p. 120.

[10] London, 1929.

[11] Ethel Mannin, *Red Rose* (London, 1941), pp. 14, 10.

[12] The examples come from the account of Jessy Helfman, see *Women and the Revolution*, pp. 100–1.

[13] For instance, the hero of *Crescendo* murders a woman before committing suicide. However, it may be helpful to recall the degree to which the psychologically damaged hero was a convention in inter-war fiction.

[14] Ethel Mannin, *Christianity – or Chaos? A Re-Statement of Religion* (London, 1941), p. 166. Further references to this book are inserted in the text.

[15] Ethel Mannin, *Cactus* (London, 1941 [1935]), p. 219.

[16] Ethel Mannin, *Rose and Sylvie* (London, 1938).

[17] Emma Goldman, Afterword to *My Disillusionment in Russia* (New York, 1924); included in Alix Kate Shulman (ed.), *Red Emma Speaks: An Emma Goldman Reader* (Amherst, 1998), pp. 400–2.

[18] For instance, she quotes extensively from this and related passages in *Christianity – or Chaos?*, p. 232.

[19] Ethel Mannin, *Confessions and Impressions* (London, 1930), p. 14.

[20] Ethel Mannin, *Captain Moonlight* (London, 1943), p. 12. Further references to this book are inserted in the text.

[21] As demonstrated by the popular song 'There'll always be an England/ While there's a country lane . . .' (Ross Parker and Hugh Charles) sung by Vera Lynn during the Second World War. Its sentimentality merges the English landscape with both Empire and freedom.

[22] I would not dream of suggesting that Evelyn Waugh read Ethel Mannin. The similarity may, however, point to a model for fiction that Waugh adopted.

8

Herbert Read and the
Anarchist Aesthetic

PAUL GIBBARD

When in his final years Herbert Read came to reflect on the body of writings he had produced, he observed that readers sometimes overlooked the anarchist convictions on which these writings were founded. One of his most influential books, *Education through Art* (1943), was, as he put it, 'deeply anarchistic in its orientation', and yet, for all the interest it generated, there had been scarcely any public recognition of its political basis.[1] Read traced his conversion to the anarchist cause back to his teenage years, and argued that though he might have displayed a brief interest in other political movements he had always remained true to certain fundamental anarchist ideas. In *Poetry and Anarchism* (1938), published when he was in his forties, Read makes a clear assertion of his anarchist faith, but recognizes that:

> To declare for a doctrine so remote as anarchism at this stage of history will be regarded by some critics as a sign of intellectual bankruptcy; by others as a sort of treason, a desertion of the democratic front at the most acute moment of its crisis; by still others as merely poetic nonsense.[2]

If he does not always label his writings on art and literature with an explicit 'anarchist' tag – perhaps partly out of fear of limiting his readership – we may nevertheless identify the anarchist principles that underpin them. Read is an innovatory art critic, and it is possible to lose sight of the distinctly anarchist character of his theorizings in the complex use he makes of ideas borrowed from such realms as psychology or Marxist dialectics. If we relate his ideas of art to the tradition of the anarchist aesthetic,[3] his anarchist vision of art emerges more clearly – both where it coincides with the views of earlier anarchists, and where it departs from them in new directions.

While Read worked in a variety of fields over the course of his life (as, for example, an army officer, a commentator on literature and art, an anarchist propagandist and an arts administrator), he maintained that his primary calling was that of the poet. In his autobiographical work, *Annals of Innocence and Experience* (1940), he records that he first 'became conscious of the art of poetry' in his seventeenth year, that is, in around 1909 or 1910.[4] He published his first collection of poems, *Songs of Chaos*, in 1915, and continued to produce volumes of poetry at intervals throughout his life. The awakening of his poetic sense in his teens was closely followed by the awakening of his political sense. If he had for a time in his youth instinctively adopted the sort of Tory opinions professed by his father (who had been a yeoman farmer), in 1911 he was converted to the anarchist cause by the arguments he encountered in Carpenter's *Non-Governmental Society*.[5] He studied the works of classical anarchist thinkers, such as Proudhon, Bakunin and Kropotkin, and of other radical writers such as Nietzsche, Ibsen and Tolstoy. The developments in his poetic sensibility and his political sensibility were closely related. At the heart of anarchism lies a notion of individual freedom, and this notion also lay at the heart of Read's conception of the poet. As he recounts in the *Annals*:

> It is possible to conceive of poetry as an established form, and of the poet's duty as merely to add to the general fund. That is the classical conception of the poet. But my conception was, and still is, of poetry as a unique experience: the individual, with his particular moods, emotions, thoughts, trying to express himself integrally, in his own choice of words.[6]

As a young poet Read sought to free himself from verse forms which constrained personal expression, and in this quest weighed up the examples of the past. He rejected what he saw as the self-conscious archaism in Tennyson's poetry in favour of Blake's apocalyptic visions. If he admired Yeats, he distrusted the nostalgic spirit of the 'Celtic twilight'. He developed a particular liking for Browning, whose 'technique . . . was free: a reaction against the Parnassian polish of Tennyson and Arnold'.[7] As Read attempted to formulate a new philosophy of poetry he found himself to be in sympathy with the principles then being set out by a group of contemporary poets, the Imagists. In the preface to the anthology *Some Imagist Poets* (1915), which included contributions from Richard Aldington, H.D., F. S. Flint and D. H. Lawrence, the Imagists demanded that poetry should be clear, hard-edged and concentrated, and that it should 'present an image', that is, that it should deal in exact particularities rather than vague or abstract generalities. The preface is animated by a spirit of freedom and a disdain for old poetic habits. The aim of the Imagists is:

> To create new rhythms – as the expression of new moods – and not to copy old rhythms, which merely echo old moods. We do not insist upon 'free-verse' as the only method of writing poetry. We fight for it as a principle of liberty. We believe that the individuality of the poet may often be better expressed in free-verse than in conventional forms. In poetry a new cadence means a new idea.[8]

The preface also demands 'absolute freedom of subject matter' for poets, and states a passionate belief in 'the artistic value of modern life'.[9] The credo of the Imagists greatly influenced Read, and he quotes from it at length in the *Annals*. The axioms he sets down three years later in *Art and Letters* partly derive from the Imagists, and many of his early poems, in collections such as *Eclogues* (1919), *Collected Poems* (1926) and *Poems 1914–1934* (1935), bear an obvious Imagist stamp. A poem such as 'Night', from the first of these collections, clearly conforms to Imagist principles:

> The dark steep roofs chisel
> The infinity of the sky:
>
> But the white moonlit gables
> Resemble
> Still hands at prayer.[10]

This sort of poem stands in contrast with some in his first collection, *Songs of Chaos* (1915), in which he had not yet managed to break free from constraining influences. The songs of chaos are characterized by conventional rhyme-schemes and metres, with some poems striving for an effect of childish naivety, and one aiming at social criticism. The poems of Read's subsequent collections are much more experimental in form, and mark a deliberate attempt to break with older established poetic forms. As the Imagists make clear, however, the principle of freedom of which they speak is something more than poetic: it extends to the social sphere, and is bound up with an affirmation of individuality. The joint interest which Read develops in artistic and political freedom was not uncommon around this era. Many artists who demanded freedom in the artistic sphere saw freedom in the political sphere as its logical corollary, and so adopted the anarchist credo. Read's concern with individual freedom in both art and society emerges, veiled slightly perhaps, in several of his subsequent works, in which he describes the struggles of romanticism with the constraining influence of classicism, imagination with reason, and personality with character. It is only in the volume *Poetry and Anarchism* of 1938 that he returns explicitly to questions of anarchist and artistic freedom.

One of the fundamental ideas of anarchism is a rejection of the notion of the state. Commentators accused Read of a lack of consistency in relation to this idea. While Read accepted that he had 'temporised with other measures of political action' than anarchism,[11] he believed that it was 'perfectly possible, even normal, to live a life of contradictions'.[12] His acceptance of a knighthood in 1953 attracted the scorn of many anarchists; but in the early 1930s he had displayed a brief sympathy for authoritarian principles.[13] After taking an interest in guild socialism for part of the First World War, Read's attention was attracted to the Russian form of socialism by the success of the Bolshevik Revolution. This was an authoritarian rather than libertarian form of socialism, which placed the state firmly at its centre. His interest in the Russian model should, however, be set against certain declarations he made during the period. In a letter written to a friend in April 1918, for example, he spoke in favour of a 'revolt of the individual against the association which involves him in activities which do not interest him; a jumping to the ultimate anarchy which I have always seen as the ideal of all who value beauty and intensity of life'.[14] This affirmation of individualism is mirrored in comments he makes in his war memoir, *In Retreat*, published in 1926:

> The war seemed to annihilate all sense of individuality. The mass of it was so immense that oneself as a separate unit could not rationally exist. But there is a sense in which the death of individuality means the birth of personality . . . And so in the presence of danger, and in the immediate expectation of death, one can forget the body and its fears, and exist wholly as a mind.[15]

Even under the most bitter conditions, Read suggests, a fundamental sense of individuality manages to flourish. This is one aspect of his anarchist faith which seems to have endured at some level, even when he contemplated authoritarian Russia with interest. In any case, as he took pains to point out, Russian socialism was not ultimately at odds with anarchism: it was the fate of the state – at least according to Marx's prediction – to 'wither away', and leave a society which had much in common with that advocated by the anarchist communists.

In *Poetry and Anarchism* the lines of Read's early thinking about freedom in poetry and politics converge. For Read the poet's attempt to express his individuality had involved a breaking free from constraining forms, which bore a parallel with the individual's quest to gain freedom from constraining forms in society. However, Read now goes a step further and claims that the poet's task is not merely to break down old poetic forms, but to break down social forms as well. He argues:

> there is nothing I so instinctively avoid as a static system of ideas. I realise that form, pattern, and order are essential attributes of existence; but in themselves they are the attributes of death. To make life, to insure progress, to create interest and vividness, it is necessary to break form, to distort pattern, to change the nature of our civilisation. In order to create it is necessary to destroy; and the agent of destruction in society is the poet. I believe that the poet is necessarily an anarchist, and that he must oppose all organised conceptions of the state, not only those which we inherit from the past, but equally those which are imposed on people in the name of the future.[16]

Read identifies here a specific social purpose for the anarchist artist. The implicit relationship between art and anarchism – touched on in certain earlier writings – is made explicit. In tracing out a specific task for anarchist art Read consciously enters a debate which anarchists and artists had been conducting over a considerable period.

The major anarchist theorists of the previous one hundred and fifty or so years had all addressed the question of art in their writings. Artists, attracted to anarchism, also spelt out the relations they perceived between their art and their political views. In his *Enquiry Concerning Political Justice*, William Godwin, a novelist and playwright as well as an anarchist philosopher, emphasized that artists in an anarchist society should embody principles of freedom and independence in the practice of their art.[17] Freedom was not simply a political principle, but a principle which permeated all facets of life. In arguing for the creative freedom of the anarchist artist, Godwin was supported by the later writings of Bakunin. Bakunin identified a natural 'revolutionary potential' in art. He believed that tyranny flourished where the individual was neglected in favour of abstract ideas – art, however, operating through a process of individualization, had the power to combat tyranny by recalling 'to our mind the living, real individualities'.[18] According to Bakunin, the artist, in operating freely, naturally created anarchist art. The freedom which Godwin and Bakunin allot the anarchist artist, however, was rejected by Proudhon, who argued that anarchist artists must shape their work to serve an overtly social purpose. He demanded that artists incorporate the 'ideal' into their work with the aim of improving the nature of society. Kropotkin followed Proudhon in insisting that anarchist art must serve a specific social function. There is a fundamental division, then, between those anarchists who believe that the artist is constrained to produce an art that has an overt social purpose, and those who believe instead that the artist should operate with perfect freedom.

The question of a propagandist or a free anarchist art divides not only the anarchist theorists, but also the anarchist artists. While probably a majority of anarchist artists defend their artistic freedom against propagandist demands, a significant group, which includes a major figure such as Tolstoy, are prepared to submit to the constraint of producing overtly social art. Artists such as Wilde, Paul Signac and certain symbolist poets favour an art that is free, but maintain that their art may nevertheless contain a revolutionary dimension. These artists subscribe to the classical anarchist conception of individual freedom, in which freedom is considered to be not simply an absence of constraint, but to have a positive quality – it is a condition in which the individual is fully able to realize his or her authentic self. As Wilde puts it: 'for the full development of Life to its highest mode of perfection . . . [w]hat is needed is Individualism.'[19] These artists consider that free art fosters this form of self-realization, and so contributes to the anarchist goal. While Read subscribes to the anarchist idea of positive freedom,[20] and also develops a complex theory of artistic personality, he does not initially seem to link personality, freedom and artistic creation together in a distinctly anarchist way. Making use of Freudian theory, Read locates the source of artistic creation in the unconscious; its images may, or may not (as in Read's experiments with automatic writing), be mediated by the personality. In turning to the notion of the unconscious, Read seems to leave little place for traditional anarchist notions of self-development or self-realization through art. However, this element does gradually emerge in his writings, and achieves perhaps its fullest expression in his theory of education through art.

Read often seems to approach anarchism from the perspective of an artist rather than from that of a social theorist. In his youth he seems to have perceived a similarity between the poetic freedom he advocated and anarchist freedom; in *Poetry and Anarchism* he seems to reject authoritarian socialism, not so much because it restricts the freedom of the mass of the people, but because it restricts the freedom of artists. Read views as intolerable the Russian government's demand that artists conform to the doctrine of 'social realism'. The art produced under these requirements is doomed to failure, according to Read, because it falls into mere 'rhetorical realism, devoid of invention, deficient in imagination, renouncing subtlety and emphasising the obvious'.[21] Constraints of the type imposed by the doctrine of social realism can never lead to the production of great art, and Read sets about demonstrating 'the positive connection between art and individual freedom'.[22] For Read, great art depends on a process of the unhindered organic development of the artist's personality. And then, as Read explains:

> The moments of creation are still and magical, a trance or reverie in which the artist holds communion with forces which lie below the habitual level of thought and emotion. This is what the man of action, the politician and fanatic, cannot appreciate. They bully and shout at the artist and force him into the hubbub of practical activities, where he can only produce mechanically to an intellectually predetermined pattern. Art cannot be produced under such conditions, but only a dry and ineffectual semblance of it. Compelled to produce under such conditions, the more sensitive artist will despair.[23]

It is clear, then, that Read would reject any calls for anarchist artists to produce a particular kind of art to promote the anarchist cause. Given, however, that Read views the poet as capable of contributing to the struggle against the state, the question then arises as to the implicit method by which Read perceives art as fulfilling an anarchist function.

In developing his anarchist theory of art, Read takes into account the artistic views of several major anarchist theorists. He cites with approval Bakunin's observation about art's capacity for battling the tyranny of intellectual 'abstraction'.[24] Unsurprisingly, however, Read rejects the anarchist idea of art set out by Tolstoy in *What is Art?*[25] In this composition of his final period, when he professes a form of pacifist Christian anarchism, Tolstoy propounds his view that art must serve a direct moral and social function. He considers that the aim of art is to establish a 'brotherly union among men', and that art functions by evoking shared feeling.[26] To this end Tolstoy believes all art should be simple and easily intelligible, and condemns the greater part of western literature – including many of his earlier works – in favour of Bible stories, fables and folk-tales. While Kropotkin endorses Tolstoy's social aim, Read objects to it. For one thing, he dislikes Tolstoy's claim that 'universal art . . . has an internal criterion – religious perception', rather than an external, that is aesthetic, criterion. And Read goes on to place Tolstoy in the same class as the social realists, who diminish art by seeking to employ it in the service of a moral idea.[27]

Kropotkin was the anarchist theorist from whom Read adapted the major lines of his anarchist theory. He particularly admired the way in which

Kropotkin had formulated his anarchist doctrine in accordance with modern scientific principles, and had shown how mutual aid acted as a factor in evolution. Read's version of anarchism was very close to the anarchist communism of Kropotkin, whose theory, Read believed, only needed updating to take account of the recent progress of industrialization. For this reason Read recommended the use of anarcho-syndicalist methods in the aim of bringing about an anarchist communist society. Read published a collection of Kropotkin's writings with the Freedom Press in 1942.[28] It is perhaps significant, and betrays Read's perspective on anarchism, that the final excerpt in the volume is entitled 'Art and Society'. In this passage, taken from *The Conquest of Bread*, Kropotkin argues that art should be the expression of individuals who are closely integrated with society. This was possible in the past. The Greek sculptor, for example, sought to express 'the spirit and heart of the city', while those who worked on the medieval churches took inspiration from and spoke directly to the people. The problem for the modern artist is that 'the united city has ceased to exist; there is no more communion of ideas'.[29] Read is perfectly in accord with Kropotkin on this point. The modern artist of exceptional sensibility stands, according to Read, 'in psychological opposition to the crowd – to the people, that is to say, in all their aspects of normality and mass action'. This is an unfortunate state of affairs, for, as Read goes on to explain: 'As poets and painters we are futile until we can build on the basis of a unified commonality.'[30]

But if Read agrees with Kropotkin's diagnosis, he does not accept the remedy Kropotkin proposes. Kropotkin calls on artists to place their art and their ideas 'at the service of the revolution', for it is only in the future anarchist society that artists will be able to flourish again.[31] Kropotkin follows Tolstoy and Proudhon in constraining the artist to produce a social form of art. While Read gladly produces overtly social art when the impulse takes him – 'A Song for the Spanish Anarchists' is an obvious example – he absolutely rejects the element of constraint which such theorists impose. On this point Read is therefore obliged to diverge from the anarchist theorist he most admires.

Anarchist artists and writers, including the neo-impressionist Paul Signac and the symbolist Francis Vielé-Griffin, maintain that it is possible to produce art which has no obvious propagandist content, and yet which fulfils an anarchist function. Taking issue with the Proudhonian requirement of social art, Signac explains how truthful art serves to illuminate flaws in the existing society and so undermine it:

It would be a mistake – committed all too often by the best-intentioned revolutionaries like Proudhon – to make it a standard demand that works of art have a precise socialist thrust, for that thrust will appear strongly and more eloquently in the pure aesthetes, revolutionaries by temperament, who leave the beaten path to paint what they see, as they feel it, and who very often unconsciously deal a solid blow of the pick to the old social edifice that, worm-eaten, cracks and crumbles like an old deconsecrated cathedral.[32]

On occasion Read suggests that art is more concerned with beauty than with truth. And if he favours imaginative expression over a realist notion of truthful expression, he nevertheless comes to define art as 'a mode . . . of envisaging the individual's perception of some aspect of universal truth'.[33] The notion of certain anarchist artists that a 'pure' form of art can nevertheless reveal truth about the nature of society – and thereby undermine existing structures – is one which Read approaches in an oblique manner.

In 'The Nature of Revolutionary Art' Read allots to art two possible revolutionary functions, one destructive, the other constructive. These functions must be viewed in the context of Read's idea of the historical development of art. Every artwork, according to Read, is constituted of two elements, a formal element and a variable element. The formal element – and this is a crucial foundation of Read's theory of art[34] – is related to physical structures in nature, and appeals psychologically to the viewer through its basic qualities of rhythm, harmony, proportion and so on. Its appeal is archetypal and unchanging through time. The variable element is constituted by such matters as the style and mannerisms which clothe the underlying form and reflect the epoch and inclinations of the artist. There is a sense then in which art 'is not static; it is continually changing', and for this reason – to the extent that it exposes stagnation in society – is 'essentially revolutionary'.[35] When art does become static, however, as in the case of bourgeois realist art or conventional academic art, it is up to the artist to break down forms by means of his own work. Read, writing in the middle part of the twentieth century, sees surrealist art and abstract art as fulfilling this revolutionary function – the surrealists, negatively, in assailing bourgeois art and breaking down the barrier between reality and the dreamworld; the abstract artists, positively, by conserving eternal artistic values of rhythm and proportion in their purest form, in preparation for the reconstruction of society.[36] In *Poetry and Anarchism* Read restates this argument in a slightly different manner, and in doing so draws near to Signac's view: 'The importance of contemporary art is purely negative', Read argues, 'it aims at a dissolution of conventional notions of reality. It clears the deck for the collective art of the future.'[37] If at times in this debate Read seems to use the notion of the 'revolutionary' in a narrow artistic sense rather than in a broader social sense, nevertheless his adherence to the notion of art as destructive of established versions of reality places him in accord with an important strand of the anarchist aesthetic.

Anarchism in Read's terms is a doctrine of both individualism and collectivity. Anarchist artists who emphasize the individualistic quality of their work sometimes find it difficult to relate their work to the question of solidarity. Wilde does so by proposing that the individualist artist provides a model of self-realization, which can be followed, in a modified form, by every member of society. The poet Adolphe Retté describes symbolism as an art of solidarity because it unites individualists in an anarchist association.[38] Making use of ideas elaborated by Freud and Jung, Read offers a further suggestion. In certain of his earlier works, Read traces the origin of artistic inspiration to the Freudian unconscious or to the preconscious state of mind; later, Read amplifies his view of inspiration by reference to Jung's notion of the collective unconscious. As the collective unconscious derives from ancestral memory, and is common to all people, it offers the anarchists, according to Read, a basis for hope: 'What is common to the psychic structure of mankind', he argues, 'is the only foundation for a community of behaviour and aspiration.'[39] Artists who are able to tap into the universal archetypes of the unconscious produce by definition a type of 'collective' art. This is one suggestion by Read for a way in which individual art may take on a broader social quality – and it offers one means of reconciling artistic freedom with the notion of an art of solidarity.

Another artistic problem addressed by Read in his writings concerns the status of mass-produced goods in modern society. Can such items, he asks, satisfying as they do a utilitarian function, possess the essential qualities of art? This raises the further question for us as to whether, if that is the case, Read characterizes such art in anarchistic terms. Many anarchist thinkers rejected increasing industrialization in favour of a return to a rural society. One social theorist who had considered the role of the machine in society, the anarchist sympathizer William Morris, attracts Read's attention – but on examination offers little, as Morris 'did not believe that industrial design or anything else could be transformed without a transformation of society'.[40] In *Art and Industry* (1934) Read tackles the aesthetic problems posed by mechanized production. Comparing the qualities of handmade, utilitarian goods with those mass-produced by machine, Read argues that the latter may, like the former, possess aesthetic qualities, but that they will 'appeal to the aesthetic sensibility as abstract art'. That is to say, they will appeal through their formal qualities, rather than through humanistic, emotional qualities.[41] The same organic principles by which Read judges 'high' abstract art – criteria of proportion, harmony and so on – can be applied to mass-produced items. Whether such items may be classed as anarchist art is not a question that Read poses explicitly in this work, although he does insist that the problem of industrial design is, with the question of a 'just and unjust social structure . . . one and the same problem'.[42] In this area, however, he does offer several interesting suggestions. He argues that designers should attempt to 'order materials till they combine the highest degree of practical economy with the greatest sense of spiritual freedom'.[43] The users of such goods should, furthermore, according to Read, be educated in the aesthetic appreciation of design. To the extent that Read describes such art as free and as capable of speaking to the people, it can be seen as bearing something of an anarchist slant.

In a number of his writings Read addresses the question of the form that art should take in the anarchist society of the future. He believes that outdated modes of art will be left behind, and envisages, as does Kropotkin, that the artist will adopt a new position, integrated with society. Abandoning the constraints of the patronage system or the market-place, the artist will achieve this integration if he is able to assume the position simply of another type of worker in society. As work becomes less brutish, and leisure hours longer, every worker also has the potential to become an artist. Art for Read will remain an individualistic pursuit, and every type of art developed in this future society will constitute a legitimate expression of the artist's personality. This is not to say that Read contemplates abandoning his critical sense – there will still be good and bad art, judged according to the appropriate aesthetic standards. But as freedom increases, and man moves closer to harmony with natural law (a process foreshadowed – if in the realm of fantasy – in the third part of Read's novel *The Green Child*[44]), art will achieve great improvements and draw ever nearer to perfect expression.

The principal means by which Read aims to bring about the anarchist revolution is through art. If he identifies a revolutionary potential in art's ability to dissolve established notions of reality, he perceives an even greater revolutionary potential in the process of educating children through art. Many anarchists, including Godwin, Kropotkin and Paul Goodman, have advocated a liberating education, aimed at drawing out the interests and natural abilities of children – none of the anarchists, however, places such an emphasis on the role of art. Read's is a form of education that develops free expression, spontaneity and a sense of mutuality, and fosters the 'integral personality', in contrast to education schemes in which rational systems dominate. His method makes use of psychology and in particular of the Jungian notion of the collective unconscious. Crucial in Read's theory of education is art's relation to the organic forms of nature. Education provides the child with 'concrete sensual awareness of the harmony and rhythm which enter into the constitution of all living bodies and plants, which is the formal basis of all works of art, to the end that the child, in its life and activities, shall partake of the same organic grace and beauty'. In this way the child develops an 'instinctive knowledge of the universe and a habit or behaviour in harmony with nature'.[45] It is in this idea that Read exposes an important anarchist aspect of his educational theory. The classical anarchists maintain that a moral law inheres in nature, and the child in Read's scheme acquires this morality through his artistic education. The natural moral law is a fundamental aspect of anarchist theory, in that it offers the basis for order in society, an order that comes from within (in that humanity is part of nature) rather than coercively from without. Read's anarchist theory of education, then, is partly a fusion of two ideas – his own theory, according to which art reflects the natural order, with the classical anarchist idea of natural law, on which the ordered anarchist society is founded. It is possible then to trace out the way in which the education of a child through art is linked to the foundation of the future anarchist society.

In his introduction to his selection of Kropotkin's writings, Read praises Kropotkin for formulating anarchist theory in modern scientific terms. By closely observing society Kropotkin identified principles in action – such as mutual aid – which could play an important role in the development of a future anarchist society. In a sense, Read pursues a parallel aim. By studying art in society, Read detaches principles – such as the tendency in art towards organic form – which will be important not only for art in the future, but also in the formation of an anarchist society. In his discussions of anarchist aesthetics his preference emerges for a free art which nevertheless fulfils a social function. In relating organic form in art to natural law, he is able to declare that in education through art: 'our ethics are aesthetics'.[46] The identity could also be put thus: his aesthetics are ethics. This anarchistic moral aspect of art provides the justification for one of Read's boldest claims – and, in these terms, the artist indeed becomes an anarchist.

NOTES

1   Herbert Read, 'My Anarchism', in *The Cult of Sincerity* (London, 1968), p. 76.
2   Herbert Read, *Poetry and Anarchism* (London, 1938), p. 7.

3   On this topic see, for example, André Reszler, *L'Esthétique anarchiste* (Paris, 1973) and Michael Scrivener, 'The Anarchist Aesthetic', *Black Rose*, 6 (1979), 7–21.

4   Herbert Read, *Annals of Innocence and Experience* (London, 1940), p. 77.

5   Edward Carpenter, *Non-Governmental Society* (London, 1911).

6   Read, *Annals*, p. 82.

7   Ibid., p. 95.

8   Cited in ibid., pp. 97–8.

9   Cited in ibid., p. 98.

10   Herbert Read, *Collected Poems* (London, 1966), p. 25.

11   Read, *Poetry and Anarchism*, p. 7.

12   Cited in George Woodcock, *Herbert Read: The Stream and the Stone* (London, 1972), p. 12.

13   See David Goodway, 'The Politics of Herbert Read', in *Herbert Read Re-Assessed* (Liverpool, 1996), pp. 177–95.

14   Cited by George Woodcock, 'The Philosopher of Freedom', in Robin Skelton (ed.), *Herbert Read: A Memorial Symposium* (London, 1970), p. 74.

15   Herbert Read, *In Retreat* (London, 1926), p. 50.

16   Read, *Poetry and Anarchism*, p. 8.

17   William Godwin, *An Enquiry Concerning Political Justice* (London, 1793).

18   Mikhail Bakunin, *Selected Writings*, ed. by Robin Skelton, trans. by Arthur Lehning (London, 1973), p. 160.

19   Oscar Wilde, *The Complete Works of Oscar Wilde* (Glasgow, 1994), p. 1175.

20   See Woodcock, *Herbert Read*, p. 249.

21   Read, *Poetry and Anarchism*, p. 15.

22   Ibid., p. 15.

23   Ibid., p. 17.

24   Read, 'My Anarchism', p. 81.

25   Leo Tolstoy, *What is Art*, trans. by A. Maude (London, 1930 [1899]).

26   Ibid., p. 268.

27   Herbert Read, 'Art and the People', in *A Coat of Many Colours* (London, 1945), pp. 27–9.

28   Peter Kropotkin, *The Conquest of Bread* (London, 1972), p. 134.

29   Herbert Read, *Art and Society* (London, 1956 [1936]), p. 71.

30   Read, *Poetry and Anarchism*, p. 38.

31   Peter Kropotkin, *An Appeal to the Young*, trans. by H. M. Hyndman (London, 1889), p. 12.

32   Un Impressioniste Camarade [Paul Signac], 'Impressionistes et revolution-naires', *La Révolte*, 13–19 June 1891, p. 4.

33   Read, *Art and Society*, p. 1.

34   Read, *Poetry and Anarchism*, p. 28.

35   Herbert Read, 'The Nature of Revolutionary Art', in Michael Paraskos (ed.), *To Hell with Culture, and Other Essays on Art and Society* (London, 2002), p. 128.

36   Read, *Poetry and Anarchism*, p. 29.

37   Ibid., p. 29.

38   Adolphe Retté, 'Tribune libre', *La Plume*, 1 August 1961, p. 194.

39   Herbert Read, *Education through Art* (London, 1961), p. 194.

40   Herbert Read, *Art and Industry: The Principles of Industrial Design* (London, 1961 [1934]), p. 10.

41   Ibid., p. 57.

42   Ibid., p. 198.

43   Ibid., p. 63.

44   Herbert Read, *The Green Child* (London, 1934).

45   Read, *Education through Art*, pp. 63, 70.

46   Ibid., p. 276.

9

Aldous Huxley and Alex Comfort: A Comparison[1]

DAVID GOODWAY

At first sight Aldous Huxley and Alex Comfort may seem mismatched, a grossly unequal pairing: Huxley one of the most admired and widely read novelists of the first half of the twentieth century and Comfort a mere sexologist. Yet, although the brilliant dystopian *Brave New World* continues to impress, Huxley's brittle, nihilistic and very knowing novels of the 1920s – *Crome Yellow, Antic Hay, Those Barren Leaves, Point Counter Point* – whose influence was acknowledged by many younger writers, from Evelyn Waugh to Angus Wilson, hold up much less well. The *Guardian* recently went so far as to commemorate his birthday by citing three damning comments – from Edmund Wilson, Bertrand Russell and George Orwell – but nothing, significantly, in favour.[2] In contrast, Comfort's achievements as a pioneering scientist and acclaimed creative writer have been obscured by the phenomenal worldwide sales of *The Joy of Sex* (1972); and a reassessment of his best novels – *The Power House* (1944) and *On This Side Nothing* (1949) – and most distinctive poetry – *The Signal to Engage* (1947) and *And All But He Departed* (1951) – is much overdue.

Huxley and Comfort also have a great deal in common. They were both polymaths. They had a background and/or interests in biology and medicine. They both became active pacifists and stalwarts of the Peace Pledge Union (PPU). For both it was their pacifism that led them to anarchism. Although neither were socialists, both were influential in the development of a new anarchism of the late twentieth century, grounded not in class conflict and economics, but in biology, psychology, ecology and alternative technology. Both men had a more than usual interest in sexuality (or certainly were not afraid to express it). Both emigrated to California, where each was to write on mystical and religious experience. And although they belonged to different generations, Huxley being born in 1894 and Comfort in 1920, Huxley's years as a pacifist and libertarian, from 1935 to his death in 1963, easily envelop Comfort's most creative and active period as an imaginative and political writer.

Aldous Huxley was born into what Noel Annan has influentially analysed as 'the intellectual aristocracy'. His grandfather, the biologist Thomas Henry Huxley, was 'Darwin's bulldog'; and his father Leonard, Charles Darwin's godson and T. H. Huxley's biographer, was to become in the early twentieth century editor of *Cornhill Magazine*, albeit long after its Victorian prime. On his mother's side, one great-uncle was the poet and critic Matthew Arnold, another great-uncle, W. E. Forster, the Liberal politician responsible for the Education Act of 1870; his great-grandfather was Dr Thomas Arnold of Rugby and his aunt Mrs Humphrey Ward, author of *Robert Elsmere* and other popular novels. By marrying the historian George Macaulay Trevelyan, his cousin, Janet Ward, linked the Arnolds and Huxleys to the even more impressive cousinage of Trevelyans and Macaulays; and when his half-brother, the physiologist and Nobel Prize winner Andrew Huxley, married Jocelyn Pease, great-great-granddaughter of Darwin's brother-in-law, the Huxleys became connected with the Peases, Wedgwoods and Darwins.[3]

In contrast, Comfort's parents came from working-class families, yet they were upwardly mobile: they both took degrees at Birkbeck, his father becoming Assistant Education Officer at the London County Council, and they sent their son, as a day-boy, to a public school, Highgate.[4]

Huxley, naturally, went to Eton, although as a King's Scholar; but in 1911 he went down with keratitis, an inflammation of the cornea, which caused near-blindness. After eighteen months, during which he taught himself Braille, his sight began to return, yet it remained severely impaired for the remainder of his life. He had wanted to become a doctor, but this was prohibited by his defective eyesight, and it was to read English that he went up to Balliol College, Oxford, in 1913, remarkably only a year late. He left Oxford with a First, spent eighteen months as a schoolmaster at Eton, and escaped in 1919 to London and literary and other journalism, initially working as assistant editor to John Middleton Murry on the *Athenaeum*.[5]

Comfort went up in 1938 to Trinity College, Cambridge, on a classics scholarship, but he, unlike Huxley, was able to read medicine. He proceeded to qualify as a doctor at the London Hospital, again on a scholarship, graduated in 1944 and worked for a year as Resident Medical Officer at the Royal Waterloo Hospital, London, picking up a Diploma in Child Health and thereby his psychological training. By this time he had published a travel book, three novels, two plays and three collections of poetry. His first three books appeared with Chapman and Hall, where Arthur Waugh, Evelyn's father, was his publisher, and then he moved to Routledge, where Herbert Read became his admiring friend. At the same age, twenty-five, Huxley had three volumes of verse to his name.

Comfort returned in 1945 to the London Hospital as a Demonstrator, and then Lecturer, in Physiology. He now built on his boyhood hobby of conchology and in 1949 was awarded a London Ph.D. in biochemistry for his research into the nature of molluscan shell pigments. His twofold background in medicine and biology enabled him to be appointed in 1952 as Nuffield Research Fellow in the Biology of Senescence, in the Department of Zoology, University College London. The 1950s saw Comfort's main effort concentrated on the biology of ageing: he was the founder of gerontology in Britain, publishing the standard textbook on the subject, *The Biology of Senescence*, in 1956. Although ill-health had prevented Huxley from pursuing a medical career, his family was steeped in biology, zoology and physiology. His elder brother, Julian, to whom he remained close, was also a distinguished zoologist, and he maintained his interest in biology and medicine, with an especial relish for alternative medicine, throughout his life.

Comfort's pacifism resulted from reading First World War reminiscences as a schoolboy and in this he was following a general trend. On the other hand, he held to his pacifism, unlike most of the Thirties pacifists, throughout (and beyond) the Second World War. He became moreover 'an aggressive anti-militarist', in his self-description, this coming to a head, while still a medical student, in the campaign against indiscriminate bombing. Early in 1944 he drafted a declaration protesting against the Allied bombings and organized the signing of the petition by 'writers, artists and musicians', among them Herbert Read, Benjamin Britten, Peter Pears, Clifford Curzon, Laurence Housman, Denton Welch, Julian Symons and George Woodcock. In consequence he was officially blacklisted by the BBC.[6]

This aggressive pacifism, emphasizing individual responsibility and direct action, is one of the threads running through Comfort's at first sight disparate career. His analysis of, and opposition to, the total war of 1939–45, was extended seamlessly to nuclear weapons: he wrote 'The atomic bomb is not different in kind or in result from the other weapons and methods of war which characterize contemporary society'[7] and continued:

> We have just witnessed an act of criminal lunacy which must be without parallel in recorded history. A city of 300,000 people has been suddenly and deliberately

obliterated . . . by the English and American Governments. It is difficult to express in coherent language the contempt and shame which we feel . . . The only remedy which is possible to us, if we are to remain human beings and not be lepers in the eyes of every decent person and every period of history, is the condign punishment of the men responsible. Not one political leader who has tolerated this filthy thing, or the indiscriminate bombardment of Germany which preceded it, should be permitted to escape the consequence of what he has done . . . It is high time we tried our own war criminals . . .[8]

It was in this way that he greeted the dropping of the atomic bomb on Hiroshima. For twenty years he was a foremost campaigner against war and the preparations for war: as a speaker and pamphleteer for the Peace Pledge Union (PPU); as a sponsor of the Direct Action Committee (against Nuclear War) and its precursors; as an activist in the Campaign for Nuclear Disarmament (CND); and as a member of the Committee of 100 (he was one of the 'names', including Bertrand Russell, imprisoned in September 1961 for calling for the Trafalgar Square sit-down). Comfort remained a member of both the PPU and CND, maintaining his subscriptions during his eleven years' stay in the USA.

Comfort's thoroughgoing pacifism (he opposed all war in the modern period) is not, very unusually, combined with a Gandhian advocacy of non-violence. 'I do not believe that it is evil to fight', he explained in 1946. 'We have to fight obedience in this generation as the French maquisards fought it, with the reservation that terrorism, while it is understandable, is not an effective instrument of combating tyranny.'[9] The French Maquis provided Comfort during the Second World War with a major inspiration, affording him a model of popular resistance, by individuals not in association with any state. This is exemplified especially – indeed anticipated – in *The Power House*, praised by V. S. Pritchett as a 'powerful, bitter, and Romantic novel' and 'an immensely exciting narrative', 'to be read . . . by all who are interested in the talents of the future'.[10]

Huxley's radicalism was to emerge considerably later in his life than Comfort's. While an undergraduate he had become a Fabian; and as a visitor to Philip and Lady Ottoline Morrell's Garsington Manor, six miles outside Oxford, well described as 'the headquarters of intellectual opposition' to the First World War, he imbibed a pacifism,[11] although only lukewarmly, since he had a clerical job at the Air Board before his spell of teaching at Eton.

Both his socialism and tepid pacifism were sharply dropped after 1918 as he began to espouse an aristocratic authoritarianism, under the spell first of H. L. Mencken, the American journalist and iconoclastic critic of mass democracy, and then, from the mid-Twenties, of Vilfredo Pareto, the great sociologist, one of the half-dozen progenitors of the discipline, but also a putative precursor of Italian Fascism with his unsentimental dissection of parliamentary democracy and theory of the circulation of elites.[12] In contrast to 'the bedraggled and rather whorish old slut', which is how, in language almost worthy of Ezra Pound, he was in 1931 to describe modern democracy, Huxley advocated 'the creation and maintenance of a ruling aristocracy of mind', the right to vote being 'made contingent on the ability to pass a fairly stiff intelligence test' and nobody being allowed to stand for parliament 'who had not shown himself [*sic*] at least capable of entering the higher grades of the civil service . . .'. He was therefore proposing a system that would enable his family and other members of Britain's traditional 'intellectual aristocracy' to take command of the state, convinced that such a system 'would not in any degree endanger the cause of humanitarianism'.[13] Yet he was also an enthusiastic eugenicist, going so far as to advocate the compulsory sterilization of 'the feeble-minded' or 'half-wits' as late as 1934–5.[14]

This is the Huxley who wrote *Brave New World*, in which, faced with contemporary trends in the Soviet Union, yet much more in the United States, his concern is not for the dehumanized masses but for the handful of dissatisfied intellectuals, such as Bernard Marx and Helmholtz Watson. It comes as even more of a jolt to realize that Huxley, who in the late 1920s had become a close friend of Lawrence and, indeed, published his edition of *The Letters of D. H. Lawrence* seven months after the appearance of *Brave New World*, considered existence in the Indian pueblo as little more acceptable than that in his New World Order.

During 1934–5 Huxley underwent a far-reaching personal crisis, indeed a breakdown, from which he emerged a humanistic and libertarian pacifist. He was rescued from his crisis by three gurus: F. M. Alexander, the Australian teacher of the 'Alexander technique', the mysterious Dr J. E. R. McDonagh, who believed that many – even most – disorders are caused by the poisoning of the intestines, and Gerald Heard, who converted him to pacifism. It was Heard's prior interest in the Revd H. R. L. (Dick) Sheppard's Peace Movement, launched in July 1935, that enabled him to inform Sheppard on 31 October 1935 that 'Aldous Huxley has joined the move'.[15] Between them Heard, Alexander, McDonagh and pacifism made a new man of Huxley, mentally, physically and spiritually. As Maria Huxley told her husband's American publisher, but almost certainly overestimating the influence of just one of the factors, as early as February 1936:

the old enemy of insomnia is checked and by the man Alexander . . . He certainly has made a new and unrecognizable person of Aldous, not physically only but mentally and therefore morally. Or rather, he has brought out, actively, all we, Aldous's best friends, know never came out either in the novels or with strangers.[16]

Huxley flung himself into the hard work of pacifist activism; and it was entirely consistent that, when the Sheppard Peace Movement evolved into the Peace Pledge Union in May 1936, he became one of the 'Sponsors' who constituted the collective leadership, continuing as an Honorary Sponsor of the PPU throughout the years of his American residence. While 1935 was a second bookless year, the writer's block was now breached. *Eyeless in Gaza* was at last completed in March 1936 and published in June. This long, fine and very absorbing novel was received poorly and has never been given its due. The new Huxley was now on public display and admirers of the cynical fiction of the 1920s did not take to a work committed to his conversion to pacifism and meditation.[17] *Ends and Means*, his most ambitious pacifist work, begun in Europe and completed in the United States, was brought out in November. The greatest insight of *Ends and Means* is that society must be radically re-constructed through decentralization: in effect, through the abolition of power, though this is not a term he employs. The necessity for decentralization be-comes a principal theme in all his subsequent writing on politics and society.[18]

Around the time that he was writing *Ends and Means* Huxley was asked the celebrated questions: 'Are you for, or against, the legal Government and the People of Republican Spain? Are you for, or against, Franco and Fascism?' He replied: 'My sympathies are, of course, with the Government side, especially the Anarchists; for Anarchism seems to me much more likely to lead to desirable social change than highly centralized, dictatorial Communism.'[19] Of the 149 writers who responded, only Huxley, Ethel Mannin and, very ellip-tically, Herbert Read mentioned the anarchists positively. When Emma Goldman returned from Spain to form the English section of the Solidaridad Internacional Antifascista (SIA) Huxley was, therefore, one of the people asked to become sponsors: 'I was delighted to see that you are so close to the ideas that I have fought for all my life. It is so rarely that one finds in England men or women dedicated to a truly libertarian ideal'.[20] But in April 1937 Aldous and Maria Huxley and their son Matthew, together with Gerald Heard and his lover Christopher Wood, had sailed for the USA, where Huxley and Heard were proposing to proselytize for pacifism. They had intended to return but did not, settling instead in California. Huxley thus replied:

The events of the last few years have made it clear, so far as I am concerned, that the libertarian ideal for which you have fought so long is the only satisfactory and even the only *realistic* political creed for anyone who is not a conservative reactionary.

With regard to the SIA, I am enclosing a small contribution to its funds. Being absent from England I think it best not to become a sponsor of the organization, inasmuch I shall be unable to do anything to help and I don't think it's satisfactory to be just a sleeping partner.[21]

Goldman proceeded to ask Huxley for a statement to be read at a 'literary and musical evening' to raise funds for the SIA.[22] His reply was very far from what she anticipated:

To my mind, the urgent problem at the moment is to find a satisfactory technique for giving practical realization to the ideal of philosophic anarchism. If we are to have decentralization, if we are to have genuine self-government, if we are to be free from the tyranny of political and big-business bosses, then we must find some satisfactory method by which people can become economically independent, at any rate in large measure. I am trying to collect relevant information on this subject and I am convinced that the technique for realizing the libertarian ideal in practice could be formulated and would work perfectly well, if intelligent people were to desire this consummation and were to set their minds to it. Much is to be learned from the theoretical and practical work of Ralph Borsodi while certain contemporary trends of invention – Kettering's work on small Diesel power plants for domestic purposes, Abbott's [*sic*] work on a machine for making direct use of solar energy – point clearly to the possibility of realizing that economic independence which must be the material basis of a libertarian society. Borsodi has demonstrated that about two-thirds of all production can actually be carried out more economically in small domestic or co-operative units than in large, highly centralized, mass-producing units. But so obsessed are modern men by the idea of centralization and mass production that they can think in no other terms. I feel strongly that this purely practical, material side of anarchism is the side that, in the immediate future, requires the most intensive study, together with practical application wherever possible.[23]

Goldman was aghast. She knew none of the names cited by Huxley and wrote desperately to Rudolf Rocker (in Crompond, New York State). Rocker was well acquainted only with Borsodi's ideas – indeed he had corresponded with Alexander Berkman about them – but did know about Kettering and, although he had not heard of Abbot, was familiar with the principle of utilizing solar (and tidal) energy.[24]

It is these ideas that William Propter expounds in *After Many a Summer* (1939) – Huxley's first book since *Ends and Means* – citing Borsodi's discovery (but without naming him) and arguing that Jeffersonian democracy was, and has to be, grounded on an independence from government and big business.[25] He had built a

> system of trough-shaped reflectors, the tubes of oil heated to a temperature of four or five hundred degrees Fahrenheit; the boiler for raising steam, if you wanted to run a low-pressure engine; the cooking-range and water-heater, if you were using it only for domestic purposes

and commented: 'I've had two-horse power, eight hours a day . . . Not bad considering we're still in January. We'll have her working overtime all summer.' This is 'a gadget that Abbot of the Smithsonian has been working on for some time . . . A thing for making use of solar energy' and is to run an electric generator. Charles Greeley Abbot, a leading astrophysicist and secretary of the Smithsonian Institution, had published his pioneering *The Sun and the Welfare of Man* in 1929.[26] Propter's aspiration is to establish 'a full-fledged community working under the new conditions' and *in extenso* he points out:

> Take a township of a thousand inhabitants; give it three or four thousand acres of land and a good system of producers' and consumers' co-operatives: it could feed itself completely; it could supply about two-thirds of its other needs on the spot; and it could produce a surplus to exchange for such things as it couldn't produce itself. You could cover the State [of California] with such townships.[27]

The first time that Huxley expressed Propter's analysis and remedy in non-fictional publication was as late as 1946 (in the USA), in *Science, Liberty and Peace*:

> What is needed is a restatement of the Emersonian doctrine of self-reliance – a restatement, not abstract and general, but fully documented with an account of all the presently available techniques for achieving independence within a localized, co-operative community.[28]

Huxley's preoccupation with mysticism had asserted itself, down to a renewed concern with human and social problems from the later 1940s,[29] and *The Perennial Philosophy* (1945) was to be his substantial work of synthesis. It was not the fully documented account of all the techniques, including alternative technology, for achieving independence in a cooperative community, which

he had appeared to be contemplating in his letters of spring 1938 to Emma
Goldman and Julian Huxley, when he was gathering information with respect
to the practical realization of 'philosophic anarchism'.[30] That could have been a
book of major importance, a mid-twentieth-century updating of Kropotkin's
Fields, Factories and Workshops. As Rocker had commented to Goldman:

> A man like him can be of enormous use to our cause. Human liberation will
> probably come to us from a wholly different direction than we have usually
> assumed up until now. What we need are spirits without dogma . . . people with
> gifts for observation and deep ethical consciousness.[31]

Yet what there is of Huxley's libertarian thinking is impressive enough, since
it is an anticipation of the new kind of anarchism which has emerged so
strongly and influentially, particularly in Britain and the USA, since the
1960s. Huxley and Lewis Mumford, starting before the Second World War,
can be considered as forerunners of this 'new anarchism'. Comfort and Paul
Goodman were the pioneers in the 1940s and 1950s. Colin Ward and Murray
Bookchin, in their very different ways, exemplify this new anarchism of the late
twentieth century, with its emphasis on biology, ecology, anthropology, alternative technology: as opposed to (in Comfort's words) 'Engels and economics'.

For Comfort 'the tenets which . . . make up the political expression of
pacifism' are threefold:

> that every appeal to organized force, by its inevitable degeneration into irre-
> sponsibility, is a counter-revolutionary process, and tends to produce tyranny;
> that the only effective answer to total regimentation is total disobedience; and
> that there is nothing which is more disastrous than contemporary war – nothing
> which can make war a 'lesser evil'.

He therefore came to believe that 'pacifism rests solely upon the historical
theory of anarchism'; and he was calling himself an anarchist by 1942–3.[32]
He declared:

> I write as an anarchist, that is, as one who rejects the conception of power in society
> as a force which is both anti-social and unsound in terms of general biological
> principle. If I have any metaphysical and ethical rule on which to base my ideas,
> it is that of human solidarity and mutual aid against a hostile environment . . .[33]

His political theory is simple, but highly individual and original. The existing
situation is one of social barbarism or irresponsible society, dependent on

obedience. Civilization can be defended – or expanded – only by individual resistance, by the individual exercising responsibility through disobedience.

As a doctor and a biologist it is science which comes first for him, not anarchism:

> I recognize two obligations – to do nothing to increase the total of human suffering, and to leave nothing undone which diminishes it. For that reason I personally think I should split my time between letters and applied science, and do . . . I feel that art is concerned to state the problem, and science and direct action (not 'politics' but mutual aid) to solve it in so far as it can be solved.[34]

What kind of science can 'solve' 'the problem'? The relevant sciences, for Comfort, are biological, medical and social – the life sciences, we might say. During a key period in his thinking – which produced his classic contribution to anarchist thought, *Authority and Delinquency in the Modern State: A Criminological Approach to the Problem of Power* (1950) – it was social psychology and sociology which he judged most relevant. So he could write:

> The task of the 'revolutionary', the individual committed to the purposive changing of the pattern of society towards the life-centred values, can now no longer be treated as a task of political intrigue. It is a branch of medicine – its main weapons are study and conciliation upon one hand, and readiness to disobey, based upon combined love and self-interest, upon the other.[35]

In a lecture to the Anarchist Summer School of 1950 Comfort made yet another of his striking statements:

> Personally, I would like to see more of us, those who can, taking training in social sciences or engaging in research in this field . . . I want to see something done which has not been done before – a concerted, unbiased, and properly documented attempt to disseminate accurate teaching of the results of modern child - psychiatry, social psychology and political psychology to the general public on the same scale as we have in the past tried to disseminate revolutionary propaganda.[36]

Colin Ward, writing as 'John Ellerby', has acknowledged that such advice was influential in the genesis of the applied, pragmatic anarchism manifested in his editorship of *Anarchy* in the 1960s and his later writings.[37]

In 1951 Comfort was proposing some kind of collective Anarchist Encyclopaedia. If collaborators were not forthcoming, confident like Huxley in his polymathy, he told Read:

I shall have to do the requisite reading and concoct the whole thing myself, but it would need a book of the general stature of *Das Kapital*, and I need to be exiled to find time to write it. I'm satisfied it has to be done, with psychology replacing Engels and economics.[38]

The last remark relates to a remarkable but brief *New Statesman* article of three years earlier:

The changes in our patterns of living have gone so far since Marx and Engels that some of their comment on historical forces looks as archaic as a full-bottomed wig. To the economic factors of the Industrial Revolution, which began the present process, we have to add innumerable new factors, previously overlooked. To Marxism we have to add social anthropology, and we revise in adding.[39]

Huxley similarly complained that 'almost all history . . . has been written in terms of politics and economics', believing that 'the fundamentals of human existence' were physiology and psychology.[40] Comfort comprehensively rejects not only Marxism but also the quasi-Marxist 'class-struggle' anarchism of anarchism's late-nineteenth- and early-twentieth-century heyday. He himself had never embraced either, for he was never, at any point, a socialist – and neither was Huxley, other than for his brief, unimportant Fabianism. As Comfort wrote during the Second World War: 'The war is not between classes. The war is at root between individuals and barbarian society.'[41]

The 1960s were a transitional decade for Comfort. *Barbarism and Sexual Freedom*, his Freedom Press book of 1948, had been the starting-point for *Sexual Behaviour in Society* (1950), which was revised as *Sex in Society* (1963). Then, in 1962, came a formative experience when he was invited to visit India at the suggestion of his former colleague, the geneticist J. B. S. Haldane. A 'translation' from the Sanskrit of the medieval erotological classic, *The Koka Shastra*, immediately resulted, in 1964. Comfort's own manuals, *The Joy of Sex: A Gourmet Guide to Lovemaking* and *More Joy: A Lovemaking Companion to The Joy of Sex*, which he wrote as a medical biologist, followed in 1972 and 1973 respectively. Their combined sales of twelve million (as of 1993) have resulted in him now being best known as their author.

Huxley's novels, early and late, are pervaded with distaste for the physical world, a disgust above all with sex, despite his persistent fascination with it and, as we now know, his considerable appetite for heterosexual but emotionless affairs, in which the bisexual Maria indulged him.[42] In *Island* (1962), though,

Will Farnaby escapes from the alienation and guilt of London infidelity and discovers a world in which – as for Comfort – sex is liberated, joyful and loving. Huxley's long-deliberated depiction of the good society is the first fully realized libertarian utopia since Morris's *News from Nowhere*, although Ursula Le Guin's *The Dispossessed* was soon to follow in 1975. It was a book which meant a great deal to Huxley, who regarded it as a serious contribution to social thought. He viewed it as 'a kind of pragmatic dream . . . And yet, if we weren't all so busy trying to do something else, we *could* . . . make this world a place fit for fully human beings to live in.'[43] The critics were divided, and those who did not like the book were exceedingly hostile.[44] His brother Julian recalled that Huxley was 'saddened and upset by the incomprehension of so many of the reviewers, who treated it as a not very successful work of fiction, and science fiction at that'; and his second wife, Laura, records that he was

> appalled . . . that what he wrote in *Island* was not taken seriously . . . each one of the ways of living he described in *Island* was not a product of his fantasy, but something that had been tried in one place or another, some of them in our own everyday life.[45]

In contrast, Comfort's *Tetrarch* (1980), though quasi-utopian and wholly Blakean – the daily greeting in the sexually fulfilled Losian world is 'Did you love well?' – was unashamedly a high-spirited fantasy novel.

Huxley's utopia is Pala, an island in the Indian Ocean. In the 1840s a Scottish doctor had been summoned by the dying Raja of Pala, whom he was able to save by inspirationally adopting James Esdaile's use of hypnosis to produce anaesthesia (a technique also employed by Comfort's Callimachus, the Greek physician to Nero, in *Imperial Patient* [1987]). Dr MacPhail and the Raja proceeded to reform Palanese society and improve its agriculture by utilizing the best both of western science and rationalism and of eastern religion and culture. A century later Pala is still a monarchy and has a government and parliament but it is also, and more importantly, a federation of self-governing units, whether economic, geographical or professional. We are told that the Palanese 'found it quite easy to pass from mutual aid in a village community to streamlined co-operative techniques for buying and selling and profit-sharing and financing'.[46] The tyranny of the traditional family, nuclear as well as extended, has been overcome by building on the Palanese foundations of 'Buddhist ethics and primitive village communism', and Mutual Adoption Clubs integrate each individual into a vast extended family of between fifteen and twenty-five couples and all *their* relatives.

Sexuality is not merely free and guiltless but fundamental to the Mahayana Buddhism of the Palanese: *maithuna* is the yoga of love – 'When you do *maithuna*, profane love *is* sacred love' – and therefore lovemaking is a form of enlightenment and contemplation. This entails that *maithuna* is part of the school curriculum (pp. 77–82). The soma of *Brave New World* has become the consciousness-heightening *moksha*-medicine, producing 'boundless compassion, fathomless mystery . . . meaning . . . [and] inexpressible joy' (p. 143). There is no army. The island has avoided industrialization by always choosing to adapt its economy and technology to human beings, not the human beings to 'somebody else's economy and technology' (p. 146). There is no division of labour between mental and manual workers: each professor or government official enjoys a couple of hours of daily agricultural labour. The teaching of and research into the sciences of life and mind – biology, ecology, psychology – are emphasized at the expense of physics and chemistry. Ecology is central to the social and global perspectives of the Palanese:

> Never give children a chance of imagining that anything exists in isolation. Make it plain from the very first that all living is relationship . . . 'Do as you would be done by' applies to our dealings with all kinds of life in every part of the world. We shall be permitted to live on this planet only for as long as we treat all nature with compassion and intelligence. Elementary ecology leads straight to elementary Buddhism. (pp. 219–20)

Here, belatedly, is Huxley's vision of the practical realization of 'philosophic anarchism'. And he needed to resort to the east, like Comfort, for the example of a free, unembarrassed and socially central sexuality.

Ten years after Huxley's death in Los Angeles, Comfort arrived in Santa Barbara to work at a radical think-tank, the Centre for the Study of Democratic Institutions, in 1973. The Centre folded the following year, but he remained in California, holding a series of posts in psychiatry and pathology at Stanford University, the University of California School of Medicine (Irvine), Brentwood Veterans' Hospital (Los Angeles) and the University of California, Los Angeles, and publishing *I and That: Notes on the Biology of Religion* in 1979 and the related *Reality and Empathy* five years later. In 1985 he retired and returned to live in England, where he was to die in 2000.

Huxley's two brief accounts of his experiments with mescalin, *The Doors of Perception* (1954) and *Heaven and Hell* (1956), have been widely read, *The Doors of Perception* and *Brave New World* being indeed his most influential books; but Comfort never shared Huxley's interest in drugs. Otherwise it is the similarities that are striking, similarities which link the personalities and careers of two maverick, very atypical Englishmen.

NOTES

1   I am most grateful to John Doheny for his comments on this essay.
2   'Déjà vu', *Guardian*, 26 July 2003.
3   N. G. Annan, 'The Intellectual Aristocracy', in J. H. Plumb (ed.), *Studies in Social History: A Tribute to G. M. Trevelyan* (London, 1955), pp. 254–66; Ronald W. Clark, *The Huxleys* (London, 1968), pp. 338–9, 376–7.
4   The details of Comfort's life in this article are dependent on either the only book so far written about him, Arthur E. Salmon, *Alex Comfort* (Boston, MA, 1978), or correspondence and conversations with the present writer. See also 'Introduction' to *Against Power and Death: The Anarchist Articles and Pamphlets of Alex Comfort*, ed. by David Goodway (London, 1994).
5   Except where otherwise attributed, Huxley's biographical details are drawn throughout from Sybille Bedford, *Aldous Huxley: A Biography*, 2 vols (London, 1973–4).
6   Alex Comfort, *Art and Social Responsibility: Lectures on the Ideology of Romanticism* (London, 1946), frontispiece; and (for details of the petition) Alex Comfort Papers, University College London, Box 6, File 2.
7   Comfort, *Against Power and Death*, p. 49.
8   Ibid., pp. 48–9.
9   Ibid., p. 80.
10 Comfort Papers, clippings books, transcript of BBC broadcast, 26 June 1944.
11 Paul Delany, *D. H. Lawrence's Nightmare: The Writer and His Circle in the Years of the Great War* (Hassocks, 1979), p. 68.
12 David Bradshaw (ed.), *The Hidden Huxley: Contempt and Compassion for the Masses 1920–36* (London, 1994), pp. ix–xiii.
13 Aldous Huxley, *Music at Night: And Other Essays including 'Vulgarity in Literature'* (London, 1986 [1943]), p. 109; Aldous Huxley, *Proper Studies: The Proper Study of Mankind is Man* (London, 1949 [1927]), pp. 157, 162.
14 David Bradshaw, 'Huxley's Slump: Planning, Eugenics, and the "Ultimate Need" of Stability', in John Batchelor (ed.), *The Art of Literary Biography* (Oxford, 1995), pp. 163–8; Bradshaw, *Hidden Huxley*, pp. xii–xv, 147–58, 173–4.
15 David Bradshaw, 'The Flight from Gaza: Aldous Huxley's Involvement with the Peace Pledge Union in the Context of his Overall Intellectual Development', in Bernfried Nugel (ed.), *Now More than Ever: Proceedings of the Aldous Huxley Centenary Symposium, Münster 1994* (Frankfurt am Main, 1995), pp. 9–27 (p. 12). For Sheppard's Movement, see Martin Ceadel, *Pacifism in Britain, 1914–1945: The Defining of a Faith* (Oxford, 1980), pp. 173–92.
16 Grover Smith (ed.), *Letters of Aldous Huxley* (London, 1969) (hereafter *Letters*), p. 400.
17 For the contemporary disappointment and resentment experienced by Sybille Bedford and George Woodcock (although they both came to revise their assessments), see Bedford, *Aldous Huxley*, vol. 1, pp. 323–4; George Woodcock, *Dawn and the Darkest Hour: A Study of Aldous Huxley* (London, 1972), pp. 15–16, 19, 195–206; George Woodcock, *Beyond the Blue Mountains: An Autobiography* (Markham, Ontario, 1987), pp. 214–15.

[18]   For a discussion of *Ends and Means*, see David Goodway, 'Aldous Huxley as Anarchist', in Ian Angus (ed.), *Anarcho-Modernism: Toward a New Critical Theory: In Honour of Jerry Zaslove* (Vancouver, 2001), pp. 319–21.

[19]   *Authors Take Sides on the Spanish War* (London [1937]) (reprinted in *Letters*, p. 423).

[20]   Goldman Archive, International Institute of Social History, Amsterdam, XXVII A, letter of 11 January 1938.

[21]   Goldman Archive, XXXI, letter of 28 January 1938.

[22]   Goldman Archive, VI, copy of letter of 15 February 1938.

[23]   Goldman Archive, VI, copy of letter of 15 March 1938.

[24]   Goldman Archive, XXVII A, letter from Rocker, 2 June 1938; letter to Rocker, 20 June 1938; letter to Huxley, 1 July 1938.

[25]   Aldous Huxley, *After Many a Summer* (London, 1950 [1939]), pp. 131–3, 148. Cf. *Letters*, pp. 463–4.

[26]   Huxley, *After Many a Summer*, pp. 130–1; David Porter (ed.), *Vision on Fire: Emma Goldman on the Spanish Revolution* (New Paltz, NY, 1983), p. 327.

[27]   Huxley, *After Many a Summer*, pp. 144–5, 242.

[28]   Aldous Huxley, *Science, Liberty and Peace* (London, 1947), pp. 42–3.

[29]   Cf. Bradshaw, 'The Flight from Gaza', pp. 25–6.

[30]   *Letters*, pp. 434–5, for the letter to Julian Huxley.

[31]   Goldman Archive, XXVII A, letter from Rocker, 2 June 1938.

[32]   Comfort, *Against Power and Death*, pp. 79–80.

[33]   Alex Comfort, *Barbarism and Sexual Freedom* (London, 1948), p. 3.

[34]   Comfort, *Against Power and Death*, p. 97.

[35]   Ibid., p. 154.

[36]   Alex Comfort, *Delinquency* (London, 1951), p. 13.

[37]   See, for example, 'John Ellerby', 'The Anarchism of Alex Comfort', *Anarchy*, 33 (1963), 329–39 (337).

[38]   Read Archive, University of Victoria, Victoria, BC, letter from Comfort, 27 January 1951.

[39]   Reprinted in Comfort, *Against Power and Death*, p. 106.

[40]   Aldous Huxley, *Beyond the Mexique Bay: A Traveller's Journal* (London, 1949 [1934]), p. 41. See also ibid., p. 85 et seq.

[41]   Comfort, *Art and Social Responsibility*, p. 29.

[42]   Bedford, *Aldous Huxley*, vol. 1, pp. 294–6; Nicholas Murray, *Aldous Huxley: An English Intellectual* (London, 2002), ch. 11.

[43]   *Letters*, p. 944.

[44]   David King Dunaway, *Huxley in Hollywood* (London, 1989), p. 366. See Donald Watt (ed.), *Aldous Huxley: The Critical Heritage* (London, 1975), pp. 29–30, 446–55, for some examples.

[45]   Julian Huxley (ed.), *Aldous Huxley, 1894–1963: A Memorial Volume* (London, 1965), pp. 23–4; Laura Archera Huxley, *This Timeless Moment: A Personal View of Aldous Huxley* (London, 1969), p. 308.

[46]   Aldous Huxley, *Island* (Harmondsworth, 1964), p. 150; further references are inserted in the text.

10

John Cowper Powys
and Anarchism

VICTOR GOLIGHTLY

John Cowper Powys documented the course of an extraordinary imaginative response to his time, to the wars, radical movements and revolutionary risings, victories and defeats, to the counter-revolutionary cataclysms of Stalinism and fascism, and to the moral challenges presented by scientism, social inequality, gender oppression, race hatred and the wide, appalling consequences of human cruelty. Powys (1872–1963) was a friend of Thomas Hardy (1840–1928) and a contemporary of Yeats (1865–1939), Lenin (1870–1924) and Emma Goldman (1869–1940), but he far outlived them, working on into the world of the Cold War. Besides the length of Powys's writing career, from *Odes and Other Poems* (1896) to the novel *All or Nothing* (1960), he was also extraordinary for his giantism; among his novels one can instance the Wessex epic *A Glastonbury Romance* (1932) with its 1,120 pages, or – barely shorter – the mighty *Owen Glendower* (1940). And then there is his 'vivid personality',[1] satirized by his friend Louis Marlow in his novel *The Buffoon* (1916) and reflected in the extraordinary (even notorious) way in which Powys conducted himself as an essayist, life-philosopher, autobiographer and novelist. Tellingly, he regarded Walter de la Mare as a great modern poet. His explanation of why he felt unable to review the poetry of his friend Huw Menai (who was hardly a modernist) shows that he was aware of the tension between his avant-garde social views and his anachronistic preferences in artistic form:

I am *not* good at obscure modern poetry, in these things I'm *old-fashioned*. In fact in *Poetry* I'm a Tory, whereas (tho' I am an odd Tory since my favourite poet is Walt Whitman) in philosophy & morals & social questions I'm the extreme opposite of a Tory![2]

A retrospective statement in the concluding chapter of his *Autobiography* (1934) is particularly useful for an appreciation of Powys's anarchism, and its ambivalence in relation to socialism:

> To a considerable extent, this book of mine, the 'Autobiography' of a tatter-demalion Taliessin from his third to his sixtieth year, is the history of the 'de-classing' of a 'bourgeois-born' personality, and its fluctuating and wavering approach to the Communistic system of social justice: not however to the Communistic philosophy: for I feel that the deepest thing in life is the soul's individual struggle to reach an exultant peace in relation to more cosmic forces than any social system, just or unjust, can cope with or compass.[3]

The *Autobiography* was completed as the Nazi regime was born in Germany, and at a time when the ultra-left 'Third Period' still condemned the parties of the Communist International to sectarian isolation where it did not lead to bloody defeat and repression. Powys already regarded Stalinism and fascism as appalling, but different, totalitarian regimes. He was always to be consistent in this, and if his stated view in the *Autobiography* seems to have been arrived at by intuitive insight rather than through rigorous analysis, he was, after all, a novelist and not a revolutionary tactician: 'Personally I regard Communism with a kind of puzzled awe, and Fascism with a kind of puzzled prejudice, and of the two I am far more attracted to Communism.'[4]

When Powys became aware of the strife between communists and anarchists in the Spanish Civil War, his understanding of totalitarianism became more detailed and certain but was not fundamentally changed. If he regarded Stalinism as a perversion of the ideal of socialism, he saw that fascism was different in its malevolence from the muddle that market economies normally make; it followed that even 'capitalism, bad as it may be, is more human than totalitarianism' of either kind.[5] He measured both by their dissolution of liberty and democracy, and attributed the condition of tyranny to their being ideologically driven, rather than the products of concrete historical circumstances. Ideology, in Powys's view, was the antithesis of the free imagination, the true basis of revolutionary change. As he put it in his book responding to the Second World War, *Mortal Strife* (1942), 'the tyranny of an inhuman logic lies behind the force of Germany and the force of Russia'.[6]

A fully contextualized and historicized study of the origins and development of Powys's anarchism is beyond the scope of this article, but it is clear that

Powys had made his permanent moral commitment to the abolition of class society by 1914: 'The political system of the future will be based on certain vast economic changes . . . When they come it will no longer be . . . a war between nations. It will be a war between international capital and international labour.'[7]

Emma Goldman's memoir *Living My Life* (1931) gives a glimpse of Powys in New York in 1916, at a banquet in her honour, where 'members of the professions and of various social tendencies were present', on the eve of her trial for propagandizing illegally for the use of contraception. Powys took part in 'an entertaining discussion' and he 'expressed himself as appalled by his ignorance of birth-control methods, but he insisted that while he personally was not interested in the matter, yet he belonged to the occasion because of his constitutional objection to any suppression of free expression'.

Goldman informed the audience that his participation in the event was 'by no means his first libertarian gesture', for 'he had given striking proof of his intellectual integrity some years previously in Chicago', when he had cancelled his lecture series at the Hebrew Institute 'because that institution had denied its premises' to her companion Alexander Berkman.[8] This was a sacrifice, as Powys supported himself, and his wife and son in England, by his American lecturing.

Powys dramatized his early encounter with Bolshevism in New York in his third novel, *After My Fashion* (written around 1919 but not published until 1980). The central figure, Richard Storm, finds himself in the company of 'the cynical Russian',[9] Ivan Karmakoff, 'a man of about thirty with a pointed black beard and a head of small stiff black curls'.[10] Karmakoff

soon drifted into political and economic problems; and Richard, before he quite realized what was occurring, found himself listening to a most subtle and convincing argument in favour of the dictatorship of the proletariat. As . . . [Storm] listened to one clear-cut argument after another, lucidly and modestly suggested, hinted at, made way for, rather than flung dogmatically down, he became conscious that he himself had hitherto touched the fringe of these drastic issues . . . Everything was reduced to a logical inevitable sequence of cause and effect, which could neither be hastened or retarded, but which in its own predestined hour, to the discomfiture of some, to the relief of others, would reveal a new order of society . . . Storm could detect no flaw in Karmakoff's logic, wherein all that was personal and arbitrary seemed slowly to be obliterated, as if under the power of a remorseless engine. Nature was reduced to a chemistry. Human nature became a mathematical necessity. A sublime but cheerless order, irresistible and undeviating, swallowed up in its predetermined march everything that was the accomplice of chance, the evocation of free will . . . *Art*, he thought to

himself, is anyway safe from this man's logic. There, at least, will always be a
refuge for the free creative spirit that lies behind all this cause and effect.[11]

When Powys wrote of his own social ideas in *Confessions of Two Brothers*
(1916), alongside his brother Llewelyn, he was trying to resolve the problem
of the relation of individual liberty to the administrative claims of social
justice, soon to be a question of life and death in the Russian Revolution,
and later in the Spanish Republic:

> My conscience compels me to be a Socialist, and I suppose I shall always be
> one; though none could dislike more than I the idea of being interfered with by
> a stupid set of moralistic bureaucrats.
>
> I have no prejudices in the matter of political freedom. I listen with humorous
> contempt to the inane chatter of Democratic Idealists. I would resign my political
> rights to-morrow with absolute equanimity if some great despotic commission
> of Kitcheners and Roosevelts could settle the matter of poverty once for all, and
> arrange that everybody should have the pleasures of life, and be well-fed,
> warm, and contented. I prize liberty as much as any. In fact liberty is the breath
> I must breathe. But I would willingly submit to serious curtailment of the
> invaluable thing, if by so doing I could relieve my conscience at a stroke of this
> uncomfortable background of responsibility for the abominable miseries which
> we inflict on the poor.[12]

Powys arrived at this position without accepting the dialectical method of
Marx. A close woman friend, Frances Gregg, even persuaded him that he
could offer his own philosophy of the nature of reality. In *The Complex
Vision* (1920) he attempted an ethically based alternative to Marxism for a
thoroughgoing revolutionary and libertarian socialism. Undoubtedly he was
influenced in this by the anarcho-communism of Goldman and Berkman.
Powys was not a systematic thinker like Marx, and the book is remarkable
not for rigour of argument but for densely pondered insights that anticipated
the imaginatively enacted attempts at personal liberation in his fiction. He
declared in his Prologue:

> The main purpose of the book reveals . . . the only escape from all the pain and
> misery of life which is worthy of the soul of man. And this is not so much of
> an escape from life as a transfiguring of the nature of life by means of a newly
> born attitude towards it. This attitude toward life, of which I have tried to catch
> at least the general outlines, is the attitude which the soul struggles to maintain
> by gathering together all its diffused memories of those moments when it
> entered into the eternal vision.

And I have indicated as clearly as I could how it comes about that in the sphere of practical life the only natural and consistent realization of this attitude would be the carrying into actual effect of what I call 'the idea of communism'.

This 'idea of communism', in which the human implications of the eternal vision become realized, is simply the conception of a system of human society founded upon the creative instinct, instead of upon the possessive instinct in humanity . . . such a reorganization of society upon such a basis does not imply any radical change in human nature. It only implies a liberation of a force that already exists, of the force in the human soul that is centrifugal, or outflowing, as opposed to the force that is centripetal, or indrawing. Such a force has always been active in the lives of individuals. It only remains to liberate that force until it reaches the general consciousness of the race, to make such a reconstruction of human society not only ideal, but actual and effective.[13]

In his rejection of Marx's dialectical method Powys differed from the doctrine of Bakunin and his anarchist followers, who had accepted Marx's materialist development of Hegel's legacy (whilst accusing him of authoritarianism, and disregarding his economic analysis of capitalism). Like Bakunin's, his was an ethical standpoint, a belief in the absolute right of liberty for all, but he was prepared – at times – to accept that this principle might need to be bent in the interests of finally winning the class war. Like Bakunin again, in rejecting the privileges and prejudices of his background he identified himself with the most oppressed, as and where he found them.

With no organic route to the organized working class, Powys idealized Jewish and African Americans and identified himself with 'ordinary people such as touchy dole-men, and liberty-loving tramps, and old-age pensioners, and impecunious caterers for the pleasures of the crowd, and . . . factory workers and farm-labourers'.[14] He revelled in America's racial mix and the freedom he found there from social snobbery, which was in marked contrast with early twentieth-century Britain. As Jeremy Hooker has observed, the Dorset of Powys's youth was still, when he returned in the 1930s, 'one of the most class-conscious societies within the most class-conscious country in the world'.[15] In the years of his active life in America as an itinerant lecturer, as what he called 'a sort of wandering troubadour of the Classics',[16] a particular pleasure of his endless train journeys was listening during his shave 'to the sounds of the morning tuned to the sweet-throated voices of African porters!'[17] In America, Powys says: 'I became the acknowledged enemy, and I hope I shall always remain so, of all the well-constituted and successful, as these opposed themselves to the failures and the abject and the ill-adjusted.'[18]

As a writer and social thinker, and even as a popularizer of ideas, Powys was consciously and with a sense of full responsibility working against the stream. Writing in Keidrych Rhys's magazine *Wales* in response to the question 'What is your opinion of the relationship between literature and society?', he couched his answer in explicitly Romantic and decidedly non-communitarian terms:

> I think (with Goethe) that writers are joined in the fashion of their age by their weakness and not by their strength, and if the mass-thought of the community is what the question implies, I hold as an anarchistic individualist, that the business of the writer is to oppose himself, on the strength of the wisdom of many ages and many lands and many cults, to this mass-thought evoked as it is by propaganda of the crudest kind and insulting as it is to the best tradition of the community in question, which has been created not by the 'genius of the race' but by individual and great geniuses, belonging to the race, whose imagination and insight have helped it forward, forced it to express itself and made it famous![19]

For his deep attachment to a pluralistic vision Powys declared himself indebted philosophically to William James:

> my attitude . . . is essentially agnostic and heathen & indeed *pluralistic* as opposed to *monism* of every sort, the sort of pluralism W. James wrote of – tho' they tell me Whitehead is a pluralist; but I lack the *brain* to cope with *him*! My pluralism is a temperamental intuitive preference for the Many over the One – and for a certain Anarchy in things over One Cosmos and one God & one Christ. I like absolutely free speculation in these things and *I like to question* not only the *existence* of God – the *desirability* of following Christ – the moral order, like my brother Llewelyn. *The only thing* w^h. I feel I *know* to be evil wicked and wrong is *direct mental & physical cruelty* . . .[20]

One of the values of Powys's libertarianism for his work as a novelist lay in his concern with the realities of power in everyday life, social relations and sexuality: James was by no means his only philosopher, for he wrote and lectured on Nietzsche. And it may be due to his empathetic awareness of his father's sacrifice of his sensual nature and his pleasure in sexuality, which he felt was demanded in his role of Victorian clergyman, that Powys would not accept a monolithic universe, let alone a monolithic state:

> In a Plurality of worlds there is much less scope for a single divine authority than a rounded-off *block universe* even though its margins do stretch out to infinity! The idea of a Multiverse, wherein the ultimate reality is the Many rather than the One, is a thoroughly profane and secular conception of things.[21]

Nor, for Powys, could there be a single human nature; he was a gentle, kind
man tormented by compulsive sadistic thoughts, and as a novelist he gently
made clear his sympathy for all who are sexually different or actively trans-
gressive:

> A couple of young sailors from a battle-ship in Portland Harbour drifted by . . .
> their arms affectionately thrown round each others' necks and their steps lin-
> gering and reluctant . . . these two young neophytes of life carrying off their
> feeling for each other and all the dark pressure of their unknown future with . . .
> [such a] callous air . . .[22]

If Powys was concerned with building individual inner resources in
solitude, most obviously in *The Art of Happiness* (1935), this need not
imply that he sought to draw others into political quietism. His writing was
never the basis of a political current, of course, but his explicit concerns
with the liberation of women and gay men, with vivisection – most particularly
in *Morwyn* (1937)[23] – and, after 1945, with the prospect of the destruction
of the planet by nuclear weapons, did not incite passive withdrawal from
unpleasant realities. Rather, for all their apparent eccentricity, Powys's
prescient obsessions anticipated the post-war need to revive or create movements and militant social struggles that have been associated with the New
Left, feminism, eco-politics and even, perhaps, the ferocity of the animal
liberation campaign. His association of fascism with instrumental reason
that is not socially and democratically directed, with science pursued without
conscience, was especially astute:

> It is the growth of science without a proportionate growth in human character
> that has given these Dictators their chance. If Hitler won this war he would take
> Europe and clap it upon a vivisection-table and bolt the doors of his research
> laboratory so that the screams shouldn't be heard.[24]

Powys was well informed of events in Spain during the Civil War, thanks
to letters and mailings from Emma Goldman, as David Goodway reports:

> In 1942 Powys objected to Louis Wilkinson's pro-Soviet arguments: 'O why
> haven't I old Emma at my side to *put you wise* on Stalin & the Communist
> Party! I tell you, with Emma's help for 2 years I got every week, in English, the
> Anarchist Bulletin from Catalonia . . .' (He then called himself 'a parlour-pupil
> of old Emma's Anarchism'.)[25]

According to Goodway, while Powys was an individual anarchist, he had also been an ardent supporter of the Bolsheviks for twenty years after they took power. He was finally convinced by Goldman's analysis of the Spanish struggle that the Russian Revolution had not been betrayed so much as strangled at birth. Yet he did not, even then, take an absolute position against the state as an instrument of social justice, the issue that had sundered Bakunin's anarchism from Marx's communism:

> The starting-point of Bakunin's political practice was not commitment to the proletariat in its struggle against capital, but opposition to the state as such. Bakunin only rallied to the proletarian movement when he realized that the single class with an interest in the overthrow of the modern bourgeois state was the industrial working class. This realization coincided with the first stirrings of an independent workers' movement in Italy, and Bakunin went on to establish the doctrine of anarcho-communism for which he is historically remembered as a tendency within the workers' movement.[26]

When asked to record his opinions on the goals and priorities of post-war reconstruction Powys produced a political manifesto that included a proposal for 'the nationalization of land, mines, water, electricity, railways, and above all of BANKS'.[27]

It is instructive to compare Powys, for a moment, with the novelist Victor Serge (1890–1947), an acquaintance of Goldman's. Born Victor Kibalchich, the son of Russian Populists exiled in Belgium, Serge was editor of the small weekly *Anarchie* when, in 1911, he became passively associated with the 'Bonnot gang', youthful anarchists who staged bank robberies and shoot-outs. Initial public sympathy for the 'tragic bandits' was destroyed by their increasing violence. This development of anarchist 'illegalism' also revolted Serge, but he was arrested along with the group and tried, as the intellectual instigator of their murders. Serge escaped the guillotine but was sentenced to five years in prison and spent 1913 to 1917 in solitary confinement.[28] Serge's first novel, *Men in Prison* (1930), was written from this experience. Released in 1917, and expelled from France, Serge went to Barcelona, where his views evolved from anarchist individualism to syndicalism and he took part in street-fighting in a working-class insurrection.

Powys and Serge lived in very different styles, clearly, but there are important affinities of outlook, too, for 'Serge's Marxism was fused with an anarchist's spirit' and was 'deeply humanistic, preoccupied with questions of personal development and individual freedom'. Along with other anarchists in Europe and America (including, initially, Goldman and Berkman)

Serge saw their ideals realized in the October Revolution; he took a further step and 'became a Marxist because the Bolsheviks knew what to do next, and also because he shared their ultimate vision of socialism as the means to liberate humanity'.[29] Serge would have been no more patient with Powys's irrationalism than he was with that of Breton, for a time his collaborator in the Trotskyist movement. But like Serge's, Powys's writings were a celebration of courage; he developed a philosophy of individual fortitude even in the face of pain and of the truly hopeless and desperate individual fate – his title *In Spite of* (1952) is characteristic. Powys's answer to his own physical and mental sufferings took full account of the suffering of others, an awareness heightened by the protracted death from tuberculosis of his younger brother Llewelyn in 1939.

Powys was never a combatant in war or revolution, or a labour-militant, but despite his well-documented hypersensitivity and relatively advanced age he tried to fight in the 1914–18 war. He was evidently deprived of the opportunity for comradeship (whether in arms or in movements for radical social change) by disability, for he 'twice submitted himself to medical examination as part of the normal recruiting procedure – once in America and again, in 1918, after returning to Britain'. Despite a recent 'gastroenterostomy' he was exempted from active service on the grounds of a hitherto unsuspected tubercular scar on his lungs, and he instead 'became a roving speaker under the auspices of Lloyd George's Bureau of War Aims'. Indeed, as Cedric Hentschel has observed, 'we can hardly call "escapist" ' a man who in both World Wars 'defended his country' through his writing 'with such vigour and so penetrating a grasp of the underlying factors fomenting aggression'.[30] Powys's first substantial publication was *The War and Culture* (1914), published in Britain as *The Menace of German Culture*, a 103-page 'pamphlet' that defended the war conducted by Britain, France and Russia, on cultural grounds, for an American audience that included expatriate Irish nationalists. Powys was never to repeat such a capitulation to patriotic sentiment, and the book's arguments for Irish independence and for the establishment of socialism were more consistent with his later positions. Naively, however, despite his awareness of the Empire and the squalid brutality of the Boer War, he felt that the British lacked 'the true military spirit'.[31] While he regarded racial prejudice as a powerful evil, Powys was never to lose his own attitude of racial essentialism, which he conceived and expressed as a benign celebration of (in his terms, delightful) variegation and difference. His home in later life was made in Wales, and Powys wished to embrace Welsh-language culture while rejecting nationalism; writing on this to Iorwerth C. Peate in July 1944, his anti-war and anti-state feelings were running high:

to advocate nationalism *as against reason & liberty* & all the rest, as you say, and as a gesture and a move *towards peace*, when we all know that nationalism is the chief cause of – well! *one* of the causes of! – *war* seems very odd . . . for my own part I am inclined to think that Bakunin & Kropotkin and even dear old Emma Goldman tho' *she* was a born belligerent if ever there was one! are much more favourable to Peace than *any* nationalistic government. In fact though I speak only as an ignorant layman in these things I should be tempted to say that the chief causes of war are always *governments*. Governments are so much wickeder than private people & they have to propagandize private people into their wicked schemes![32]

Goldman had ensured that Powys was immune to war-time pro-Soviet feeling of the kind that sentimentalized Stalin:

But Democracy doesn't stand or fall with Capitalism. Its enemy, *our enemy*, is *authority from above*.

Capitalism is an ugly old fowl, I fully admit it, with moulting feathers and unpleasant manure; but at any rate [unlike fascism] it makes no claim to take the place of the Holy Ghost. And since it is only a wretched makeshift and a temporary convenience and we can very well imagine democracy getting on without it, there is no reason why the thrice-blessed Golden Age that ordinary human beings so hopelessly long for, shouldn't be born of this daughter of Chaos as well as any other. It obviously can't be born in an atmosphere of dictatorship; for dictatorship is *ipso facto* a return to primitive barbarism; and the Libertarian Utopia which is the heart's desire of all ordinary people, is an evolutionary hope, not a retrograde despair.[33]

Yet, writing to Peate again, in March 1945, Powys seemed ready to countenance 'the tyranny of the new totalitarian State' if only it would bring a new social and economic system into being. He was reluctant to accept such a state, he said:

But it is destined to come I think and we libertarians were wise to try and humanize it ere *and as* it comes! But nobody will be able to stop it! And it'll be agreeable to see it sweep away Class Privilege etc etc etc. I shall enjoy *that* part of it & I'm sure you will too. Yes, I fear we shall have to pay the price; but it'll be a malicious pleasure to see the *great ones* pay it as well as the rest of us![34]

Labour's 1945 election victory was not followed by a vigorous socialist transformation, and the Cold War period brought both a huge impersonal threat of annihilation and (in the west, at any rate) unprecedented social stability. Those were barren and disorientating years for radicals, but Powys's inward defiance was particularly suited to coping with the new climate and its combination of powerlessness before the atom bomb and the new opportunities for atomized individual fulfilment. Powys's anarchism had always been deeply felt, but he had tended to express his ideals rather cautiously: 'My own private feeling . . . if I can gather up enough courage to express it, is that of all our political and economic theories the Anarchist one is the one that will eventually prevail.'[35]

Powys's caution was not without cause, as he was sued by a Glastonbury businessman who claimed, wrongly, that he was the basis of the ruthless industrialist Philip Crow in *A Glastonbury Romance*. Yet, for all their evident sincerity, isolated assertions of his ideals lacked force because they were not integrated with the surrounding work:

> And suppose, reader, that you were a Catalan Anarchist fighting inch by inch for the ideal of personal liberty against politicians, generals, bishops and landowners, capitalists and dictators, couldn't you snatch a fine weapon from Zarathustra's sayings and turn it against himself, declaring that you also had an iron determination to *create the future*, and to create it on behalf of humanity?[36]

He had never been reserved in his dislike of religious authority, and had always been prepared to risk provocative asides, such as 'Jesus Christ, the most reckless of Anarchists . . .'.[37] But state socialism no longer seemed a beguiling temptation from individual anarchism, which he expressed with a new unwavering eloquence, for instance in *The Inmates* (1952):

> Every living soul . . . has one right that none can give or take away, one right in the infinite chaos of the innumerable warring worlds among which we are born, one right and one necessity, and that is the right to be free and alone in our thoughts.[38]

And in Friar Roger Bacon's speech in *The Brazen Head* (1956): ' "As long as we are considerate to other people," he said, "and as kind and sympathetic towards them as our circumstances permit, we have all got to live to ourselves, for ourselves and by ourselves." '[39]

Indeed, John A. Brebner argued (in 1972) that one can detect 'a growing trend in Powys's later fiction', as Powys was increasingly prepared to assert his anarchism, to do so without qualification, and to consider the implications for the content and the formal structure of his work:

Myrddin Wyllt and Taliesin [in *Porius*, 1951] spoke about a similar ideology and acted in accordance with it, Owen Glendower [1941] used it as his life-spring into eternity, Uryen Quirm of *Maiden Castle* [1937], Sylvanus Cobbold of *Weymouth Sands* [1934], and Johnny Geard of the [*Glastonbury*] *Romance* [1933] made themselves its priests; nonetheless it has never been expressed in such extreme terms [as in his late novels]. In their anarchistic formulation, these ideas lead to complete dissent from and total subversion of contemporary social values.[40]

And in *Porius* Powys notably and eloquently made a 'fundamental state-ment of passive revolution'[41] in a speech given by Merddyn to his servant boy, Neb ap Digon:

Nobody in the world, nobody beyond the world, can be trusted with power, unless perhaps it be our mother the earth; but I doubt whether even she can. The Golden Age can never come again till governments and rulers and kings and emperors and priests and druids and gods and devils learn to unmake them-selves as I did, and leave men and women to themselves! And don't you be deceived, little one, by this new religion's [that is, Christianity's] talk of 'love'. I tell you wherever there is what they call 'love' there is hatred too and a lust for obedience! What the world wants is more commonsense, more kindness, more indulgence, more leaving people alone. But let them talk! This new Three-in-One with its prisons and its love and its lies will only last two thousand years. The thunderer I begot – and I'd have swallowed him if his mother hadn't given me a stone instead – lasted for ten thousand years. But none of them last forever. That's the hope of the world. The earth lasts and man lasts, and the animals and birds and fishes last, but gods and governments perish![42]

Powys had never been 'so free with open discussions of sexuality, politics, militarism, and revolution' as he was in *Porius*.[43] He was leaving behind the eldritch modernism of his novels of the 1930s and developing an early form of magic realism in space-age fables where – as Brebner observed of *The Inmates* – 'thought, the magic-catalyst, produces revolution, and revolution breeds anarchy, and anarchy breeds freedom'.[44] The oratorical flourishes and manic vigour of Powys's style had once looked like overblown romantic blemishes, in modernist texts that held in ironic tension the political extremity of views – in religion and politics, or on the nature of reality – that he dramatized in his characters' lives. Now the personal, political and stylistic excesses could be seen to be the real point of the writing, and his trait of unworldly dreaminess is given an almost psychedelic intensity in his last novel, *All or Nothing* (1960). This is knowingly set in the village of 'Dunnowair', that is, 'Dunno where'; unlike the naturalistically described and prescriptively detailed utopia of William Morris's *News from Nowhere* (1890), Powys's utopianism is in the writing, and the insistence that the imagination must break all traditional bounds. Paternal authority calls for us to accept 'the regularity with which the universe swings on its way, and the regularity with which all its offspring, generation after generation of men and women, have to accept the work and the play, the waking and sleeping, of our life upon earth'.

But patriarchy is challenged by a different, gentler, way. As the mother of John o' Dreams and Jilly Tewky, the twins at the centre of the novel, insists

> 'The secret of life, and it has been so ever since the first of our race came out of the sea, is not acceptance or submission. It is rebellion! It is adventure! And who have known that in their hearts from the beginning, but the wise women of every generation!'[45]

Powys had found a new confidence in the expression of beliefs that he had held for half a century, and was reaffirming the romantic anti-capitalism of the modernist writers and artists of his youth. He had captured that spirit in *Wolf Solent* (1929), when Wolf was confronted in his brown study by the Apparition of Modern Invention:

> He felt as though, with aeroplanes spying down upon every retreat like ubiquitous vultures, with the lanes invaded by iron-clad motors like colossal beetles, with no sea, no lake, no river free from throbbing, thudding engines, the one thing most precious of all in the world was being steadily assassinated.[46]

The character of Wolf Solent is not merely that of a lone wolf, however. He had been reflecting grimly on 'the appalling misery of so many of his fellow Londoners', recalling as their representative figure 'a man he had seen on the steps outside Waterloo Station' before starting on the journey in which he is returning to his native Dorset:

> The inert despair upon the face that this figure had turned toward him came between him now and a hillside covered with beeches . . . It was an English face; and it was also a Chinese face, a Russian face, an Indian face . . . It was just the face of a man, of a mortal man, against whom Providence had grown as malignant as a mad dog. And the woe on the face was of such a character that Wolf knew at once that no conceivable social readjustments or ameliorative revolutions could ever atone for it – could never make up for the simple irremediable fact that it had been as it had been.[47]

In 1938 Powys was able to revise this tragic conclusion, in the light of his understanding of the revolutionary struggles of Spanish anarchists and workers:

> A sympathetic and cynical person might well be pardoned for thinking that not only no ideology – for that anyway is a blood-thirsty monster – but no idea even, is worth the present sufferings of the civil population and of the refugees in Catalonia; but it does after all remain, even if the first really self-respecting and completely free life for the working people of the world were bombed into annihilation, that something more than an idea, a living experience, has come into being, to which, when humanity has disillusioned itself of these murderous and childish ideologies of efficiency, it can at last return.[48]

Personal liberation, for Powys, is a necessary act of survival, yet it is also an oxymoron. The act of revolution, the perennial seizure of full human liberation, however, is an indelible moral act, even if it has been defeated in its aims again and again. In the trials and triumph of 'communistic' freedom lies the redemption of all the millennia of human suffering.

NOTES

[1] H. P. Collins, *Old Earth Man* (London, 1974 [1966]), p. 203.
[2] 1 March 1945, in John Cowper Powys, *Letters 1937–54*, ed. by Iorwerth C. Peate (Cardiff, 1974), p. 52.
[3] John Cowper Powys, *Autobiography* (London, 1934), p. 626.
[4] Ibid., p. 584.
[5] John Cowper Powys, *Mortal Strife* (London, 1942), p. 183.
[6] Ibid., p. 9.
[7] John Cowper Powys, *The War and Culture* (London, 1975 [1914]), pp. 9–10. Quoted in Cedric Hentschel, 'The Improbable Belligerent: The Role of John Cowper Powys in Two World Wars', *The Powys Review*, 7 (1980), 14–23 (16).
[8] Emma Goldman, *Living My Life*, vol. 2 (New York, 1970 [1931]), pp. 569–70.
[9] John Cowper Powys, *After My Fashion* (London, 1980), p. 251.
[10] Ibid., p. 190.
[11] Ibid., pp. 194–5.
[12] John Cowper Powys and Llewelyn Powys, *Confessions of Two Brothers* (London, 1982 [1916]), p. 73.
[13] John Cowper Powys, *The Complex Vision* (London, 1975 [1920]), pp. xviii–xix.
[14] Powys, *Mortal Strife*, p. 182.
[15] Jeremy Hooker, *John Cowper Powys* (Cardiff, 1973), p. 65.
[16] Powys, *Autobiography*, p. 561.
[17] Ibid., p. 560.
[18] Ibid., p. 500.

[19]   John Cowper Powys, 'Answer to *Wales* Questionnaire, Summer, 1939', in *Obstinate Cymric: Essays 1935–47* (Carmarthen, 1947), pp. 133–4.

[20]   9 March 1945, Powys, *Letters 1937–54*, p. 54.

[21]   Powys, *Mortal Strife*, p. 164.

[22]   John Cowper Powys, *Weymouth Sands* (London, 1934), p. 51.

[23]   See Richard Perceval Graves, *The Brothers Powys* (Oxford, 1984 [1983]), pp. 281, 298.

[24]   Powys, *Mortal Strife*, p. 185.

[25]   David Goodway, 'The Politics of John Cowper Powys', *The Powys Review*, 15 (1984/85), 42–52 (46), quoting from *Letters of John Cowper Powys to Louis Wilkinson, 1935–1956* (1958). Goodway's study of the correspondence of John Cowper Powys and Emma Goldman is forthcoming from Cecil Woolf.

[26]   David Fernbach, Introduction, *Karl Marx: The First International and After*, Political Writings, vol. 3 (Harmondsworth, 1974), p. 45.

[27]   Powys's views on post-war reconstruction appeared in Donald Brook's *Writers' Gallery: Biographical Sketches of Britain's Greatest Writers, and their Views on Reconstruction* (London, 1944), quoted in Goodway, 'The Politics of John Cowper Powys', 50.

[28]   Susan Weissman, *Victor Serge: The Course is Set on Hope* (London, 2001), p. 18. See also Victor Serge, *Memoirs of a Revolutionary: 1901–1941*, ed. and trans. Peter Sedgwick (London, 1963).

[29]   Weissman, *Victor Serge*, p. 19. See also Paul Avrich (ed.), *The Anarchists in the Russian Revolution* (London, 1973).

[30]   Cedric Hentschel, 'The Improbable Belligerent: The Role of John Cowper Powys in Two World Wars', *The Powys Review*, 7 (1980), 14–23 (23).

[31]   Powys, *Autobiography*, p. 587.

[32]   26 July 1944, in Powys, *Letters 1937–54* (Cardiff, 1974), p. 36.

[33]   Powys, *Mortal Strife*, pp. 18–19.

[34]   9 March 1945, in Powys, *Letters 1937–54*, p. 54.

[35]   John Cowper Powys, *The Pleasures of Literature* (London, 1938), p. 341.

[36]   Ibid., pp. 566–7.

[37]   Ibid., p. 343.

[38]   John Cowper Powys, *The Inmates* (London, 1952), p. 293.

[39]   John Cowper Powys, *The Brazen Head* (London, 1956), pp. 340–1.

[40]   John A. Brebner, 'The Anarchy of the Imagination', in Belinda Humfrey (ed.), *Essays on John Cowper Powys* (Cardiff, 1972), pp. 264–83 (p. 270).

[41]   Ibid., p. 265.

[42]   John Cowper Powys, *Porius* (London, 1951), pp. 276–7.

[43]   Brebner, 'The Anarchy of the Imagination', p. 274.

[44]   Ibid., pp. 277–8.

[45]   John Cowper Powys, *All or Nothing* (London, 1973 [1960]), p. 201.

[46]   John Cowper Powys, *Wolf Solent* (London, 1929), p. 12.

[47]   Ibid., p. 12.

[48]   John Cowper Powys. 'The Real and the Ideal', *Spain and the World*, Supplement, May 1938; reprinted in *The Powys Review*, 3 (1978), 78–9 (79).

11

Litvinoff's Room: East End Anarchism

VALENTINE CUNNINGHAM

This is a kind of sketch-map of anarchism-and-culture in parts of twentieth-century Britain, especially London and the London area. At least, it is a celebration of a terrain, the streets, the quarters, the topography physical and spiritual, of an anarchized cityscape. It is an effort to plot some of the most arresting convergences of anarchism and literature, to capture something of the British anarchist imagination, the peculiarities of English anarchism's actual activities, as well as its myth, its mythicity, and also its mythmakers – from Joseph Conrad to Iain Sinclair. I am especially concerned with literary anarchism – which is not quite the same thing as (though it clearly overlaps with) the literature of anarchism. I am interested not least, then, as any literary historian must be, in the historical challenge of Conrad's *The Secret Agent* – that sneering, gibing, ironic fiction of a hostile Polish exile, which claims to know so much about anarchism in London (as *Under Western Eyes* claimed to know all about the nature of anarcho-revolutionism in Russia and among the Eastern European and Jewish exiles of Geneva) and which has succeeded in becoming for so many readers *the* story, *the* myth of anarchism and anarchists in London at the turn into the twentieth century.

What is straightaway revealed in any such plotting of English anarchism is its utter messiness: its profound looseness, both political and personal. The political thought, the people involved, the affiliations they make, defy tight boundaries. Boundaries and limits are hard to perceive, as they were, evidently, difficult to impose or keep in place. Which is not surprising, given the variety of political and ethical analysis and practice offered by the sponsors of anarchist thought – Marx, Bakunin, Proudhon, Kropotkin, William

Morris, Leo Tolstoy. The anarchist goal, the nature of anarchists' utopian visions, the clientele of so-called anarchist groups and associations, evidently comprised a shifting leftist kaleidoscope. It is hard to think of anarchism or an anarchist as just one thing. Anarchism, as I perceive it, in London at least, was like a Neighbourhood Friendship Association, a loose and often wary grouping of neighbours and neighbouring ideas, a mixed politics of the left sanctioned by the argumentative neighbourliness of the hotchpotch of ideas that went into it – a political neighbourliness mirroring, we might think, the close-packed neighbourliness of the crowded quarters of the Jewish East End of London, in which anarchist ideas and people calling themselves anarchists flourished.

It was a way of politics whose rich mixture might be thought of as summed up in the life and writing of the anarchist poet Louisa Sarah Bevington, or Mrs Ignatz Guggenheimer (1845–95). A Londoner, brought up by Quaker parents in the traditions of Quakerism's religiously inspired social radicalism, she was, like George Eliot, greatly influenced by Herbert Spencer's social-evolutionary ethicity. She knew, she was prominent among, London's radical politicals, the city's assorted post-Christians, libertarians, socialists and communists, people like William Morris and George Bernard Shaw. Her political-poetic ambience was precisely the *déraciné*, floating community of London's political and artistic exiles. The man she was briefly married to, Ignatz Guggenheimer, was an exiled German Jewish artist. In the later 1880s she took up with the ideas of the Russian exile Prince Peter Kropotkin, joining in avidly with the London anarchist movement around him. She wrote a great deal for London anarchist papers, such as *Freedom* and *Liberty*. (A letter of hers was used in order to prove that an anarchist attempt to blow up the Greenwich observatory in 1894 – the germ of *The Secret Agent* – was a police set-up.) As an atheist, she was strongly hostile to Church and Queen and Empire. She preached constantly in print against money, credit, property, law. She publicly avowed expropriationism (her *Why I Am An Expropriationist* appeared in 1894, together with William Morris's *Why I Am A Communist*, in a pamphlet series, *Why I Am . . .*, from James Tochatti's Liberty Press). She believed in peace and freedom, but accepted the need for bomb-throwing as a last resort (the early Quakerism seems to have told). You might in the end have to throw the occasional bomb in the struggle against 'poverty, parasitism, degeneration, despair and the wholesale tormenting of man by man'; thus her posthumous booklet *Anarchism and Violence*. It would have been hard for most contemporary radicals to disagree with her list of modern problems. One of her volumes was entitled *Liberty Lyrics*. No libertarian could really quarrel with what this one centrally avowed. Her kind of anarchism was, evidently, part of the broadest kind of contemporary radical church. The loose political alliance and the loosely overlapping set of radical groupings and ideologies are what it condoned and sanctioned.[1]

It was all very local, and urban, and especially, though not exclusively, an East End of London phenomenon. It was a politics of exiles and aliens, refugees, cosmopolitans, not least the 'free-thinking Jews' whom T. S. Eliot notoriously thought had no place in the ideal Christian community, at least in 'large number'.[2] It flourished among poor people in the meanest streets, the urban underworld, the place of the dark underground Other. So it has a peculiar *psychogeography* (to use a favourite word of Iain Sinclair) – one commanded by a recurrent, repeatedly returned-to set of particular streets. Cable Street, of course, where East End leftists united to fight against Mosley's fascist thugs in the early Thirties, and Sidney Street. Sidney Street, chief among the memorable political East End street-names, as Sinclair puts it in *Rodinsky's Room*, his profoundest trawl into the anarchistic depths of the East End, chief of streets because it has provided such a palimpsest of stories and is foundational to a greatly photographed, aestheticized radical history, an event unable to 'break free from the heritage album'.

> Sidney Street, to the east of the Royal London Hospital, will always be police helmets, rain capes, soldiers lying full-length on the cobbles. Bobbies with shotguns tucked under their elbows, like a fancy-dress shooting party. Bowler-hatted officials. A flat-capped mob, held back, waiting under a hissing gas standard. Smoke from the burning house. A hierarchy of hats. Winston Churchill, on a rare visit to the East End, dominated the frame by wearing a topper; assuring himself of his immortality by becoming an unforgettable image. The director of operations is also the director of the film of memory. He controls the weather, the disposition of the crowd, the lighting. This was a black-and-white event; good and evil manipulated in a class-war pantomime. An army summoned to crush a knot of dangerous aliens, bohemians, part-time artists – anarchists.[3]

Writing about this anarchized cityscape involves what is almost a mantra of the 'dark places' of the city (to use that momentous phrase from the opening of Conrad's *Heart of Darkness*, as the narrator gestures towards the City of London, 'this too was one of the dark places of the earth'). In this darkness other tongues are spoken: Yiddish, German, Russian. It's a darkness embracing secrecy and hermeticism, where the secret society, the club of aliens and the arcana of race and religion and politics blend in a kind of large underground recipe for the generation and harbouring of secret knowledge. This politics

evidently appeals to people with mystic traditions in their blood, with
Kabbalah in their bones – to Jews, of course, and other native mystagogues,
modern hermeticists who know they are inhabiting the very streets where
the uplifted rebels of the city's past read and prayed and preached – the
naked Quaker James Naylor, it might be, proclaiming the Kingdom of God
along this street in Cromwell's time, or the poet William Blake dreaming his
apocalyptic dreams down this lane and meeting the Angel Gabriel coming
round that very corner there.

Anarchized London is, then, a zone of counter-voices, of otherness, built
in conspiracy and resulting in outlawry – a large scene of romanticized
banditry, in effect, where the political work illegally (as Lenin said they
should) alongside the non-political illegals; where politically inspired crime
(acts of politically motivated expropriation, or theft, it might be) coexist
with outright, and scarcely ideologized crime; where Jack the Ripper is
remembered sentimentally alongside Peter the Painter, and Fifties mobsters
like the Kray brothers are a kind of local hero who regularly rub shoulders
with, or at least sit down in the local pub alongside, the neighbourhood anarchist poets. In other words, anarchic London, as it develops into and in the
twentieth century, is a romanticized criminal complex and space which
gives rise to political writing as such (political text, the literary grenade,
'semiotic terrorism', as the 'Neoist' Stewart Home likes to call it) but also
to a genre of fiction, a literature of political crime, which is utterly at one,
generically speaking, with the crime story, the Krimi, the thriller, the detective
novel. Anarchism *is* a crime story, or at least desires the condition of crime
story. So anarchists and anarchist sympathizers – Herbert Read, Julian
Symons, Ralph Bates, Robin Cook aka Derek Raymond – of course read
and write crime stories. And the non-anarchist novelist wanting to come to
terms with anarchism – a Conrad, a Chesterton – naturally engages with it
in the form of the thriller or crime novel.

And as time goes on, of course, literary romantic nostalgias for the politically criminal *boue* embrace a wholesale nostalgia – a yearning celebration
of what is gone by, lost lives, lost books, a politics now in ruin, a people of
the ruin, of the ruined and ruinous city. Held nostalgically in the hand of an
anarchically disposed tracer of urban pasts such as Iain Sinclair, this politics
gets to have *Ichabod*, the Hebrew word denoting an old glory now departed,
written all over it. *Ichabod* is what Sinclair finds written over the old East
End synagogue or anarchist club-room door as he searches memorializingly
among anarchism's ruinous urban traces, seeking out the ghostly presences
of a once vivid past; so that anarchism becomes knowable in our time mainly
as an affair of old memory, of mysterious disappearance, of the difficult to

fix and know, to keep in focus and to grant presence to. In other words, anarchism, at least in the English writing which celebrates it, inhabits a very modernist condition of a real-presence which is also clamantly an absence – an eloquent hollowness bordering on what Conrad in *The Secret Agent* thinks of as absurdism, even as a kind of 'fiction', what he labels a 'sham'.

How then to grasp, to focus this shiftingness, to map the varying cultural anarchism of Britain, of London, these so loose political groupings and regroupings, these temporary alliances of activists, all this coming and going of artists with anarchic intentions among the darknesses of the urban crowd? Let us start with a poetry reading: the poetry reading at the opening of the new rooms of the Institute of Contemporary Arts in London's Dover Street in December 1950. The ICA has just moved its operation to these first-floor premises in Dover Street, where it plans to put on exhibitions and to hold meetings like this one. Founded in 1947 by a group of cultural warriors, in particular the Surrealist painter Roland Penrose and the Surrealism-sympathetic anarchist poet and art historian Herbert Read, the ICA had its first headquarters in Charlotte Street. The move to the new premises is auspicious for go-ahead British art and artists. The opening is a large and excited cultural event. It is a varied and loose assembly, of course. One assumes Penrose the Surrealist is there: he was, after all, the ICA's chairman at the time. T. S. Eliot is certainly there – the Grand Old Man of English poetry – with an entourage from his firm Faber and Faber, the most important poetry publisher in Britain. Stephen Spender, most famous British leftist poet of the Thirties after W. H. Auden, is there with the Faber contingent. He is a Faber poet. Herbert Read, a prime mover of the ICA, now its President, also a Faber poet, and one-time assistant to Eliot on the *Criterion* magazine, is in the chair. Read is well known as a long-time anarchist. In his memoir *Scrapbook, 1900–1951*, which discusses the beginning years of the ICA, Roland Penrose would hail Read as 'The Angel of Anarchy'.[4] Read's writings have long professed admiration for the Spanish anarcho-syndicalists. He has published poems about them. He is the author of *Poetry and Anarchism* (1938), which was published by Eliot at Faber. ('In order to create it is necessary to destroy; and the agent of destruction in society is the poet'; anarcho-syndicalism is the only politics, the only counter to fascism and Stalinism, the tyranny of leaders and bureaucracies and all anti-libertarian forces; and so on and so forth.) The room is alive with people who think that or who have thought that, or (literary radicalism being the loose affair it is) think or have thought something like that. Many of them are artists and writers with foreign experience and background, exile types (discussion at the ICA, says Penrose in his memoir, was 'often dominated by European accents'[5]).

The young Jewish Welsh poet (and medical doctor) Dannie Abse is there – a man turned on to poetry as a boy (he was born in 1923) by reading *Poems for Spain* (published by Faber, and edited by Spender and John Lehmann), especially by John Cornford's poem 'Huesca'. Abse is a poet bred in Welsh working-class radicalism. His brother Leo, who became a Labour MP and a leading campaigner for homosexual law reform, regularly brought *Left Review* into their house. Dannie Abse read Ralph Fox and about Christopher Caudwell in *Left Review*. When he learned that they had died in Spain, he says, he imagined that they looked like Sid Hamm, a friend of the Abses, who used to give young Dannie a shilling when he came round to their house, and who was killed at Brunete. Abse had been at the memorial meeting for Sid Hamm in a little hall in Cardiff called Sunshine Hall, when grown men wept as the chairman recited 'They shall not grow old, As we that are left grow old', and a leaflet in Spanish Republican colours was handed around with Sid Hamm's photograph and the caption 'THERE CAN BE NO VICTORY WITHOUT SACRIFICE'.[6]

Abse has come to the ICA with Emanuel Litvinoff – Jewish like Abse, older, recently out of the army, a published poet too. Litvinoff is called to the podium to read. He is not a well-known poet, but he is known as a poet to leftist Jewish writers like Abse and to anarchist ones like Herbert Read (he has contributed to George Woodcock's anarchist little magazine *Now*). Which is presumably why he has been invited along and why Read invites him up.

Litvinoff is a characteristic mid-century urban working-class writer. He was born in Bethnal Green.[7] His father arrived in England from Russia in 1913, and worked in the East London garment trade, pressing trousers for a living. As a Russian immigrant he was given a choice of either going off to fight for the Tsar or being recruited for the Western Front. He went east, and he never returned to London. Emanuel was one of four brothers; he left school at the age of thirteen years and ten months and went into various jobs typical of his part of London, beginning in the fur trade. He picked up his real education by reading in the public library. He read lots of public library detective stories and poetry, and was astonished when he came across T. S. Eliot's *The Waste Land*. He also read the *Daily Worker*, the daily organ of the British Communist Party. Youthful, moody, he mooched about the East End, worked as a porter in the Smithfield meat-market, hung around in Bunhill Fields, the Dissenters' graveyard, where the tomb of John Bunyan, the literary hero of English Nonconformity, is, and the graves of the London Nonconformist satirist Daniel Defoe and the London anarchic visionary William Blake. At the age of fourteen Litvinoff had joined the Young

Communist League – he was expelled for 'Trotskyism', which seems to have been mixed up with his 'bourgeois' lust for a comrade called Hannah Fischbein.

Anarchism, Litvinoff recalls, in his lovely East End picaresque autobiography *Journey Through a Small Planet*, was in his blood, was of the very atmosphere in the streets where he lived, in the whole quarter. He never forgot childhood stories of anarchist leaflet campaigns against the imperialist First World War, of followers of Tolstoy and Kropotkin chasing army recruiters away from Bloom's corner at the end of Brick Lane – men who met to argue about the wisdom of political bombing at the Jubilee Street *Arbeter Fraint* house, the socialist/anarchist club for Jewish immigrants. In his autobiography he would go on to write marvellous, nostalgic stories about his childhood among Yiddish-speaking immigrant leftists in the broad church of radical East End politics (people like Mendel Shaffer's atheist father, who joined the Anarchists and the Communists and the Buddhists and the Socialist Zionists); stories of his own youthful scuffles with Oswald Mosley's fascists on their incursions into the East End in the early Thirties; and about his craving for the 'female nood' which took him to the art classes at the Bethnal Green Men's Institute, in company with his vegetarian friend Morry Spitzer, who worked in his his father's kosher butcher shop (an aesthetic pursuit, says Litvinoff, that was all part of being a 'boisterous guerilla'), and about his profound distress over the unwanted pregnancy of Fanya Ziegelbaum, lovely seamstress, whom he kissed under the Whitechapel railway arches (dark place of dybbuk talk and rumours about Jack the Ripper): Fanny Ziegelbaum, deserted by Herschel Rosenheim of the New York Yiddish Theatre, who was playing Hamlet at the Whitechapel Pavilion – Rosenheim, red-haired, Chicago-gangster-voiced, his Yiddish Hamlet a far cry from that of Mr Parker, Litvinoff's English teacher.

Emanuel's brother Abie, Litvinoff tells us, had become a local schoolboy hero at the age of twelve for refusing to read the part of Shylock at school, and thus getting caned six times. Emanuel himself had been caned severely for shouting 'Balls' after yet more insulting jests about his name (*Litpotskyoff, Lavatoryovsky*) from teachers. 'The Lord stood at my right hand. He anointed my head with oil.' Emanuel left the Cordwainers Technical College at the age of fourteen after a vivid moment of revelation and realization that an Italian boy, known as Okey-Pokey Leoni, who was an advocate of God and Mussolini, was a real live fascist. There was an altercation and a fight with a Gentile bully. 'Fucking Jewboy. Why don't he go back to Palestine.'

Litvinoff's early life, in other words, encapsulated a certain local history of overt political, cultural and racial resistances, all converging in a characteristic anarchic East End mix. So it was not surprising that his trilogy of novels about the Russian Revolution and its consequences should begin with *A Death Out of Season* (1973), about the most memorable East End event involving anarchists or probable anarchists, the Sidney Street siege.[8] *A Death Out of Season* is an evident replay of the anarchistic motifs of Conrad (and of the Dostoevsky who lies behind Conrad) filtered, as it were, through Graham Greene. It is a re-enactment of the story of Murontzeff/Gardstein and Peter Piatkov/Peter the Painter, and the accidental killing of policemen in the Houndsditch jewellers' robbery attempt, which leads to the terrible, over-the-top shoot-out at 100 Sidney Street, a mini-war masterminded by a police force egged on by newspaper hysteria, in which two anarchists are shot to pieces by police and soldiers using rifles, machine-guns and field artillery. The novel is a compelling re-creation of the politics of the East End and its visionary immigrants (especially Jews), the ferments at the Club in Jubilee Street and among the readers of *Arbeter Fraint*, people who of course read Tennyson and haunt bookshops like Hoffman's in Old Montague Street. Hoffman is the novel's bookish leader of the 'uprising of books' – the anarchist-leftist literary front.

A Death Out of Season is a novel with many pulls, and not least the attractions of violence and lawbreaking, which are the mark of genre fiction. For this compelling piece of political fiction is also a crime story, a story tightly wrapped up in grim detective ploys and multiple double-crossings (Peter the Painter, Rodinsky the Romanian dwarf, and so on). It offers genre attractions, then, which are part not only of East End political memory, the nostalgic recall of what happened among the immigrant ancestors in the now (1973) disappeared clubs and tailoring shops, a profound salute to Jewish memory (the anarchist Yoshka dies with *Elohim* on his lips: 'Out of the primitive depths, a voice cried *Elohim*, seeking the god in whom he had no belief. And the darkness was the beard of his father flowing down from Sinai'), but which also participate actively in wider East End criminal memory (the newspapers in the novel, for instance, are loud with claims that the Houndsditch killings of those policemen are the 'most sensational crime since Jack the Ripper'). In this written recollection of anarchists, commanded formally by generic crime-story attractions, separate and different kinds of crime and violence – and separate and different kinds of crime-writing – keep blending. This writing serves, as it were, double time; as, up to a point, and for the same formal reasons, does *The Secret Agent*.

On that early Fifties night at the Institute of Contemporary Arts, of course, Litvinoff's life-story *Journey Through a Small Planet* and his novel *A Death Out of Season*, like Litvinoff's other novels, his other texts of

Jewish-radical recall and protest, were still in the future. But on this night, Litvinoff, anarchist autodidact, budding poet, not long returned from the Second World War, in which he and his brothers had been on active service (his volume of Jewish soldier poems, *The Untried Soldier*, had appeared in 1942), would step, as it were, into the ancestral, regional (politico-psycho-geographical) role of anarcho-cultural warrior, the role family and place, local politics and history, had been preparing for him.[9]

He had come along prepared to read a poem attacking T. S. Eliot – immigrant poet of the mainstream – a poem of poor-boy, poor London, East End, Jewish (and now post-Holocaust) protest. Here is Dannie Abse's account:

'To T. S. Eliot', Emanuel began in his customary rasping accent. Herbert Read nodded with pleasure . . . But Emanuel Litvinoff continued:

> Eminence becomes you. Now when the rock is struck
> your young sardonic voice which broke on beauty
> floats amid incense and speaks oracles
> as though a god
> utters from Russell Square and condescends,
> high in the solemn cathedral of the air,
> his holy octaves to a million radios.
>
> I am not one accepted in your parish,
> Bleistein is my relative and I share
> the protozoic slime of Shylock, a page
> in Stürmer, and, underneath the cities,
> a billet somewhat lower than the rats.
> Blood in the sewers. Pieces of our flesh
> float with the ordure on the Vistula.
> You had a sermon but it was not this.
>
> It would seem, then, yours is a voice
> remote, singing another river
> and the gilded wreck of princes only
> for time's ruin. It is hard to kneel
> when knees are stiff.
>
> But London Semite Russian Pale, you will say
> Heaven is not in our voices.
> The accent, I confess, is merely human,
> speaking of passion with a small letter
> and, crying widow, mourning not the Church

but a woman staring the sexless sea
for no ship's return,
and no fruit singing in the orchards.

Yet wailing with Cohen when the sun exploded
and darkness choked our nostrils,
and the smoke drifting over Treblinka
reeked of the smouldering ashes of children,
I thought what an angry poem
you would have made of it, given the pity.

But your eye is a telescope
scanning the circuit of stars
for Good-Good and Evil Absolute,
and, at luncheon, turns fastidiously from fleshy
noses to contemplation of the knife
twisting among the entrails of spaghetti.

So shall I say it is not eminence chills
but the snigger from behind the covers of history?
Let your words
tread lightly on this earth of Europe
lest my people's bones protest.

Most of the audience began to clap at the end of the poem but Stephen Spender
rose angrily and shouted that Litvinoff had grossly insulted Tom Eliot who was
the most gentle of men. He continued with great emotion and spoke with great
rapidity. Perhaps I did not hear Spender properly but he seemed to say something like: 'As a poet I'm as much a Jew as Litvinoff, and Tom isn't anti-semitic
in the least.' In the confusion of anger, Spender was not entirely coherent but
there was no mistaking his gutsy aggression towards Emanuel Litvinoff's attitude
as it was forcibly expressed in the poem addressed to Eliot. For his part, Eliot,
in the chair behind me, his head down, muttered generously, 'It's a good poem,
it's a very good poem.'

Mannie Litvinoff attempted to reply to Stephen Spender but Herbert Read,
with his chairman's hammer, violently struck the table and called for silence.
He firmly indicated that he wanted no further discussion on the matter and
would call on the next poet to read. There were a few lonely, scattered cries of
'Let Litvinoff reply, let him reply'. Most people, though, especially those sitting
in the vicinity of Eliot sat silent and awkward. Others plainly appeared to be
antagonistic to Litvinoff and had shouted 'Hear hear' when Spender had protested.

Litvinoff tried once more to reply to Stephen Spender's attack but Read,
anarchist and defender of free speech, now, presumably because of 'good taste'

and genuine feelings of loyalty to Eliot tyrannically censored all further discussion. There was something sad and ironic about the whole incident. In retrospect, something comical too.

As for Mannie Litvinoff, he felt hurt and rejected. He had been invited to read a poem and he had read a poem, a passionate poem, in his usual abrasive way and he had been treated as one who had come into a sacred place and had spat. Bitter as colonquitida, he quit the platform, his whole posture one of aggrievement and smouldering protest. He strode to the back of the hall and stood there, white and exhausted, while Herbert Read called on the next poet to read. During the polite applause that followed that next reading Mannie, with his wife Irene, moved through the door, and as unobtrusively as possible we joined them.[10]

Litvinoff had, *of course*, come into a sacred place prepared to spit, and he had spat. Which is what cultural anarchists were supposed to do. It is old anarchist Herbert Read's chairmanly opposition that needs to be explained and excused, as Abse tries to do. (Just a few years later Read would accept a knighthood.) The meeting's main reaction was perhaps explicable; a sort of cultural bomb had been thrown. (In conversation with me, Litvinoff claimed to have felt harshly personalized aggression and that he heard someone, in the Faber party allegedly, muttering, as he left with his extremely fetching and Gentile spouse, something along the lines of 'How did he manage to get a woman like *that*?') And, as anarcho-cultural events went, this one had the appropriate larger repercussions, set up the echoes it should, given its representative nature, its centrality within twentieth-century English anarchist being and action. Anthony Julius rounds off his sturdy diatribe against Eliot's anti-Semitism, *T. S. Eliot, Anti-Semitism and Literary Form* (1995), with reference to the episode, and a claim on the poem 'To T. S. Eliot' as model for his own critical work: it is 'a work of resistance as well as respect'.[11] More momentously, the affair is dwelt on by Iain Sinclair, poet and one-time marauding bookseller on the seedy margins of the London literary world, in his (now cult) book of cultural anarchic resistance, *Lights Out for the Territory* (1997): naturally dwelt on, for Sinclair is devoted to the idea of Litvinoff as a kind of anarcho-cultural warrior.[12]

Lights Out is a set of celebrations, memoirs, reviews and documentings of Sinclair's travels on foot, his flâneur life and times and encounters, as he traverses London, present and past. It is a set of 'psychogeographical' explorations, in the company of the black photographer Marc Atkins, a collection of essayistic recollections which is at the heart of Sinclair's so-called fiction, and placed, knowingly and self-consciously, by Sinclair at the centre of a whole group of such writings which engage with the people and places of

Lights Out. Round and round they go, Sinclair's obsessive written journeys about the same dark urban places, persons, obsessions: *White Chappell Scarlet Tracings* (1987), a re-creation of the Jack the Ripper murders, done in parallel with a wild picaresque of men from the book trade hotting round the country looking for rare books from Victorian times; *Downriver (or, the Vessels of Wrath): A Narrative in Twelve Tales* (1991), mythicizing the city of the river Thames, past and present, as a set of secretive places uncovered and unearthed, and of hermeticisms unsealed; *Radon's Daughters* (1994), another book-quest picaresque, plunging into the bibliographical under-world in a version of a secret-service/psychopathological thriller; *Slow Chocolate Autopsy* (1997), more stories, accompanied by Dave McKean's comic-book illustrated strips, about violent London, from the killing of the Elizabethan poet *maudit* Christopher Marlowe to the murder of Jack 'the Hat' McVitie by Mad Frankie Fraser, hit-man of the Kray brothers; *Lud Heat and Suicide Bridge* (1998), prose and poems in more celebrations of hermetic and murderous London, once more the imaginary map of Sinclair and his friend's low urban obsessions; *Liquid City* (1999), which revisits photographically the places and people of all of Sinclair's books (Atkins's photos, Sinclair's scripts). And as the journeys loop out from London in *Landor's Tower, or The Imaginary Conversations* (2001) they only confirm the continuing force of the same old clientele's presence – the people and places belted inescapably in by the M25 motorway that is the subject of *London Orbital: A Walk Around the M25* (2002).[13]

It is a dedicated, neurotic even, celebration of modern London anarchic tendencies and characters, a theatre of radical cultural anarchists and anarchizings. And it is Emanuel Litvinoff, and Litvinoff's kind, and Litvinoff's fundamental, genetic, Sidney Street concerns, rediscovered, reaffirmed, opened out. Sinclair's oeuvre is a constant tribute to Litvinoff's kind, to a loose group of the like-minded, writers who are, like Sinclair, obsessed with a dark, malignant, anarchic, *noir* London – Peter Ackroyd, Michael Moorcock, J. G. Ballard, Angela Carter, that sort of writer. Sinclair maps London as a very particular anthology of fellow celebrators of London Noir:

Writers, wishing to 'rescue' dead ground, will have to wrest it from the grip of developers, clerks, clerics, eco freaks, and ward bosses. We are all welcome to divide London according to our own anthologies: J. G. Ballard at Shepperton (the reservoirs, airport perimeter roads, empty film studios); Michael Moorcock at Notting Hill (visited by Jack Trevor Story); Angela Carter – south of the river, Battersea to Brixton, where she hands over to the poet Allen Fisher; Eric Mottram at Herne Hill, communing with the ghost of Ruskin; Robin Cook's youthful self in Chelsea, while his fetch minicabs between Soho and the suburbs (meeting Christopher Petit who is making the reverse journey); John Healy sparring down Caledonian Road towards the 'grass arena' of Euston; Peter Ackroyd dowsing Clerkenwell in quest of Dr John Dee; James Curtis in Shepherd's Bush; Alexander Baron in Golders Green (recalling his Hackney bolt-holes); Emanuel Litvinoff and Bernard Kops disputing Whitechapel and Stepney Green with the poets Bill Griffiths and Lee Harwood (author of *Cable Street*); Stewart Home commanding the desert around the northern entrance of the Blackwall Tunnel; Gerald Kersh drinking in Fleet Street; Arthur Machen composing *The London Adventure or the Art of Wandering*.[14]

Sinclair welcomes, indulges, pays generous tribute to a devotedly *noir* London and its aestheticizers. This is the London of the blackest of criminal generics, the darkest of fictional-detective makers – of Sinclair's associate Chris Petit, the film-maker, author of the *Psalmkiller*; and especially of Derek Raymond, anarchic Old Etonian con-man, crook, Soho soak and crime-story writer. J. G. Ballard's novel *Crash* (1973) and its direly sadomasochistic film version by David Cronenberg are granted ungrudging respect in these pages (Sinclair devotes a whole book to Cronenberg's *Crash*).[15] Sentimental Londons, not least sentimental East End Yiddisher ones of the kind produced by Wolf Mankowitz, are not approved.

> I overheard a drinking session head-to-head between Kray foot soldier, Tony Lambrianou, and old Etonian novelist, Robin Cook, on the subject of favourite films. Cook raved about his 18 viewings of the Brian De Palma remake of *Scarface*, while Lambrianou eulogised Carol Reed's *A Kid for Two Farthings*, a Mankowitz confection, concerning the quest for a unicorn in Fashion Street.[16]

Sinclair's London is hard. It is the London of leftist local historians and remembrancers, such as Raphael Samuel, the one-time communist and History tutor at Ruskin College, Oxford, founder and guru of the Ruskin History Workshops, long-time resident in a ramshackle Huguenot house in Spitalfields, a local memorializer obsessed by working-class ghosts, the radical past and presents of Spitalfields and Whitechapel, the memories and crookeries, the leftist politics and the violence of the East End.

Patrick Wright, connoisseur of lost and ruined England, another of Iain Sinclair's flâneur clique (*Lights Out* more or less ends with the night Wright got Emanuel Litvinoff talking 'in full flow' about 'Meetings with Canetti, alchemical investigations, John Lehmann and wartime poetry, trips to Russia, East End life and fictions' at the Bridewell Theatre off Fleet Street, the night Robin Cook gave his last public reading – 'Litvinoff, who insisted on

staying, was moved. "He's a real writer" ': shades of Eliot at the ICA),
Patrick Wright reports unfriendly Spitalfields gentrifiers labelling Raphael
Samuel 'That bloody anarchist'; and they had a certain point.[17] For this is
the Samuel who devotedly celebrated and romanticized East End bad boys,
political and otherwise, and typically put together *East End Underworld:
Chapters in the Life of Arthur Harding* (1981) – 'a wonder of transcription
and sensitive editing', says Sinclair, 'offering as incidental benefits, the freshest
portrait of the Jago, a criminal taxonomy of the Lane, and the strategies of
survival required to duck and dive from late Victorian times to the establishment of the Kray twins as voodoo deities'.[18] Harding was a petty villain
who hung out early in the twentieth century with local anarchists, Jews,
Russians, and was in and out of the Jubilee Street anarchist club-rooms and
the anarchists' pub in Hanbury Street, and who recounts the story of Gardstein
and his 'mob', 'the gang who murdered the city policeman at Houndsditch in
1910'. 'They were part of the landscape in Brick Lane', says Harding – a
criminal-political landscape on which feature prominently Harding's old
enemy Detective Sergeant ('Jew Boy') Stevens, the cop who claimed to
have actually set eyes on Peter the Painter, and Steinie Morrison, a fence and
a communist, who was falsely imprisoned on a charge of killing the man
who informed on the Houndsditch shootists.[19]

It is a weird London, this, of course, magical, hermetic, full of claimed
underground meanings and cryptic significances, a modern Kabbalism the
old rabbis of Whitechapel might have supposed endorsed by their visionary
secrecies, a large magical archaeological site striated by the leylines
allegedly joining together the churches of Nicholas Hawksmoor – the darkly
meaningful cityscape enthused over by Peter Ackroyd in his histories of and
fictions of darkest London, not least in *Hawksmoor* and his novels and
stories set in Victorian Ripper-land and in Clerkenwell Green, where the
Marx Memorial Library confronts the one-time home of Elizabethan mage
Dr John Dee.[20] It is a 'psychogeographical' landscape, according to Sinclair,
greatly focused in Bunhill Fields, where 'the spirit of William Blake, the
godfather of all psychogeographers' is thought to be palpable, where the
youthful Litvinoff mooched, and Atkins takes photographs, and Ackroyd
dreams his novels and biographies. But above all it is a traditionally violent
London, the London of East End terror and terrorists, the stamping-ground of
Jack the Ripper and the Kray brothers, those killers from the Carpenters Arms.

Sinclair is, of course, present for the funeral of Ronnie Kray, a kind of
East End carnival co-celebrated by the forces of law and order, the lawless
mobsters and their friends and neighbours. This is Litvinoff's spiritual and
political home:

Helicopters circling. Grey bullet heads in Brick Lane buffalo jackets bunch together on the west side of the street. Down at the far end, beyond the Carpenters Arms, you find the same knot of foot-stamping ghouls who used to wait outside Pentonville for the posting of the execution notice. This cul-de-sac and railway crossing, Hare Marsh, deserted on weekdays, pitched by Sunday traders, has been featured in works by two notable East End writers. It was the location for Alexander Baron's *King Dido*, his homage to Arthur Morrison, and it was photographed as a background to the author portrait on the dust-wrapper of Emanuel Litvinoff's *A Death Out of Season*. For Litvinoff the bridge and the railway arch had a peculiar significance – like a crossing point in Berlin, a rite of passage. Locations illuminated, as he points out in his autobiographical sketchbook, *Journey Through a Small Planet*, by memories of sexual initiation and battles fought.[21]

What Litvinoff recalls and brings into the light of modern memory is, again according to Sinclair, what the younger cultural anarchists in Stewart Home's Neoist movement, neo-Dadaist art guerillas (punkish descendants of Roland Penrose and the Thirties Surrealist terrorizers), are perpetuating. Home, author of a whole stream of vile, violent, occultic, sexually perverse stories and novellas – *Slow Death, Blow Job*, 'Frenzy of the Flesh', *Come Before Christ and Murder Love* – promotes cultural-punk aggressivity, aesthetic yobbery with violence, art criticism as violent action and resistance through the breaking-up of bourgeois exhibitions, and the like – and all done, or allegedly done, by a roster of radical-anarchic-aesthetic gangs Home variously initiates, invents, dreams up and fantasizes about: the Semiotic Liberation Front, avant-bardism, Glop Artists, DADAnarchism, Decadent Action (promoting 'exorbitant consumerism': anarchist guerila warfare along the High Street).[22] It would not be surprising to me if Home proved to be the author, and not just the editor, of *Mind Invaders: A Reader in Psychic Warfare, Cultural Sabotge and Semiotic Terrorism* (1997).[23] His art and art-activism are more extreme even than that of the taboo-breaking, graffiti-imitating artists Gilbert and George, 'The Plague Warriors', who live in Fournier Street, just off Cable Street – interviewed and photographed in *Liquid City* in yet another of the key locations on the Sinclair/Atkins map of oppositional cultural sites.[24] Home's terrorizings are certainly more violent than the bibliographical sabotage carried out by Sinclair's frequently featured friend Drif Field, the bicycled bookshop-raider and nuisance, author of the notorious *Drif Field Guide to the Secondhand and Antiquarian Bookshops of Britain*, or, for that matter, than Sinclair's own literary maraudings, as featured in *White Chappell Scarlet Tracings*.

Sinclair knows Home is an unreliable narrator of East End cultural politics. But he needs him for immoral support in his own campaigns and histories.

Home's shtick is alternate history, subverting myths to rewire received accounts of who was there and what they did ('Situated as it was on Stoke Newington High Street, the pub attracted the more presentable elements from among the Hackney anarchist community. While the punk-hippy-squatter axis would frequent less reputable establishments, members of the Class Justice Federation and all manner of syndicalists, bakuninists and the impossibilists were to be found in the Tanners').[25]

Sometimes one wonders whether Stewart Home is not Iain Sinclair, rather than just a youthful avatar. But whoever he really is, he is characteristic grist to Sinclair's texts in their kept-up performance of a rolling cultural anarchy roadshow; or group portrait with cultural anarchists.

Literally a group portrait, in Marc Atkins's photo of the Sinclair gang in *Liquid City*. There they are, lots of them, lined up outside the Krays' pub, the Carpenter's Arms, during the making of Chris Petit's/Iain Sinclair's film *The Cardinal and the Corpse* – Drif Field and Robin Cook, Chris Petit, Gerry 'the Scuffler', Brian Catling poet and sculptor, and 'The driver who drove the man who chauffered Jack the Hat [McVitie, the villain and Kray-gang murderee] under the river'. Emanuel Litvinoff had featured in the film, which was about East End writers and cultural operatives, and not least about his half-brother David Litvinoff, a good friend of Gerry the Scuffler. Emanuel Litvinoff was filmed walking his quarter, talking with Patrick Wright, being interviewed on the bridge that connects Hare Marsh and Pedley Street.[26] David Litvinoff had been a performance artist who once created a scandal at the ICA by appearing naked. He was the dialogue coach on the film *Performance*. And then he had simply vanished. And so he is absorbed into the Sinclair mythicizings of the Litvinoff region. Sinclair wants the absence of David Litvinoff to be read as a parallel to the legendary disappearance of the Jewish mystery-man David Rodinsky, a philosopher, or translator, certainly a reclusive bookish character, who was taken to be the 'caretaker' of the derelict synagogue in Princelet Street, where he had some sort of room upstairs.

This Rodinsky was brought to wider notice by Patrick Wright in a *London Review of Books* article of October 1987, reprinted in *A Journey Among Ruins*. *The Cardinal and the Corpse* had Patrick Wright leading Emanuel Litvinoff to Princelet Street and the synagogue, to put him visually into this childhood scene, this place now of absence, disappearance, in an attempt to stir his darkening memory. (Litvinoff, mind on other things, was not to be stirred on this occasion.) And it is the exemplary emptying out, the ruination, of these East End pasts which obsesses Sinclair. He eagerly joined in the drawing of attention to the empty room and its disappeared inhabitant in a *Downriver* story ('The Solemn Mystery of the Disappearing Room'), and then, more extendedly, with Rachel Lichtenstein's assistance, in the book *Rodinsky's Room*. The room, its haunted emptinesses, the old synagogue's mouldering outside, its neighbouring streets and façades, all feature strongly in Atkins's black-and-white photos in *Liquid City*. Here is a crime-story-type absence (Sinclair dwells, in *Rodinsky's Room*, on the common detective-story motif of the killing in the locked room). It is, of course, a very modernist absence. The title *Rodinsky's Room* is meant to remind you of Virginia Woolf's novel of unreachable, unknowable human absence, the negative epistemologies, of her *Jacob's Room*. But still the room remains a marker of a specifically Jewish absence For her part, Rachel Lichtenstein is intent on using the empty synagogue and the old Jew's room as a springboard for her larger quest for her ancestors and ancestral places in the Jew-emptied spaces of Eastern Europe. This ruined synagogue in London leads her back to the ruined synagogues and so on, out there. But for Sinclair the emphasis is emphatically a London one. And what moves him is the emptiness as an emblem of lost East End Jewish pasts, the disappearance of radical Jewish anarchistic life, the shaky hold on history that fading East End memories, the old stories, maintain.

What is clearly at stake is the life and memories of the Litvinoffs and their sort – a whole recall of an allegedly East End anarchistic past. It is all a murk now, a memorable murk, but undoubtedly a murk, and one sharply captured by the little essay, 'The Synagogue', attached in *Liquid City* to a blurry photo of Sinclair and Lichtenstein and somebody recording their impressions of Rodinsky's empty spaces:

Marc's framing rightly positions my collaboration with Rachel Lichtenstein, *Rodinsky's Room*, as cabbalistic theatre. Our task had been to mediate the disappearance of a hermit/scholar from the attic of this building. By this intrusion, we had become implicated, in very different ways, in the mystery. Our interrogator, earphone like a hammer against his head, finds that his left arm has turned into ectoplasm. What were we straining to hear? Nobody is there; not at the east end of the long room, the cupboard where the holy scrolls were kept. The click of the camera behind the technician's back imposes itself on the tape of voices. Rachel, heavily pregnant, becomes a Francis Bacon portrait. Paint combed with a razor. I am two-faced, explaining and performing. I remember the thrill of finding David Rodinsky's name written inside a spectacle-case in the cluttered attic. There's nothing here that resists explanation. The licorice pillar. The grille. Superfluous, half-cancelled human presences on their way into the dark.[27]

They all go into the dark. Where the Litvinoffs' childhood scenes, where their anarchic visions and memories, where Emanuel Litvinoff's narratives, and not least his anarcho-cultural narratives, were sited, there is now a hole, a gap, an emptiness – an absence to be supplied only by ghosts, memory, texts of memory and recall (including photographs), by imagination, story, fiction. This brand and branch of anarchism survives now only as an absence, and a fiction merely of presence. It exists, survives, now, only as fiction. And perhaps, the implication is, it only ever was.

Which brings us back to Conrad – whose *The Secret Agent* got so much about this anarchism right – its looseness, its mixed-ness as to personnel and political dreams; its exilic, diasporic nature, as an affair of foreigners, Jews, Russians; its city relations, its urbanism; its dependence on the packed-in crowd of the urban poor (the Professor, Conrad's 'Man of the Crowd' to rival Edgar Allan Poe's, with his self-authenticating pocket-bomb, needs the masses he despises); its secrecy; its cultic oddities (throw a bomb into the meridian, 'pure mathematics', astronomy? That's a lot like Stewart Home ranting about the fascistic British National Party getting on to the Isle of Dogs local council and thus corrupting the leylines of Greenwich and the Observatory); its relation to common-or-garden criminality, transgression, perversity (Verloc's porn-shop, Winnie Verloc turning killer); its natural presence in a detective novel, a crime story, a narrative of double agents. And of course *The Secret Agent* is a modernist detective story, an *anti-*detective story, in which the police and the criminals are morally inter-changeable. In characteristic modernist vein this novel arranges that the city, the characters, events, should appear in a constant haze, a blur (physically guaranteed by London's fog, or smog, and mist, its 'murky, gloomy damp-ness', its hazy gaslight) and that certainties should keep collapsing into the ironies of epistemological confusion and hermeneutic doubting. Anarchic London is *tenebrous*, a *maze, amazing, absurd* ('what is one to say to an act of destructive ferocity so absurd as to be incomprehensible, inexplicable, almost unthinkable; in fact, mad?'). The writing on this city's wall is only a flicker (the shadow of Mrs Verloc's raised knife-arm 'flickered up and down'). In such a rhetoric – maze, amazed, amazing, absurd, flicker, incom-prehensible, inexplicable, unthinkable – the epistemological confusion of Africa in *Heart of Darkness* comes home to London (it is as if the old Africa-hand Assistant Commissioner has brought it back with him). Stephie's swirling scribbles, lines of writing leading nowhere, are of course to be taken as allegorical of the writing and the world that contain him. Meaning remains obscured, *unreadable* – veiled as Mrs Verloc, wrapped up like Mr Verloc's brown-paper parcels (just what is it he trades in?). It does all indeed converge, as the novel's newspapers have it, on 'an impenetrable mystery'. And the anarchism that's central to this narrative partakes of this modernist absurdism; London anarchism is the very ground of the absurdism of this modernist hermeneutic. For the whole of the anarchist plot surrounding Greenwich is in fact a put-up job, and one descending into accident and farcicality. It is a 'sham', as the Assistant Commissioner twice says to Vladimir at the Russian embassy; it's 'real only by a fiction'. Which is, of course, just like the Sidney Street affair in Emanuel Litvinoff's novel – somewhere between an accident and a put-up job. Like the case of David Litvinoff, like David Rodinsky's room, like the East End world of Emanuel Litvinoff: it's all only an allegation of reality compounded by real absence.

The two most memorable 'anarchist' actions in England, the two biggest 'anarchist' events in British history, prove to be shams. Of course, the cultural wars and warriors which are the descendants and avatars of, and constant tributes to, the anarchist heritage of the East End can be real enough. The poems and bookshops and poetry readings, Drif Field's and Sinclair's book-shop raids, the novels and other texts which celebrate culturally anarchic dreams and actions, are real enough (even if Stewart Home's psychogeo-grapher levitating the Greenwich Observatory sounds rather far-fetched). But practising plagiarism and defying the commercialized world of author-ship by naughtily attributing every text to 'Luther Blisset',[28] and getting up the noses of T. S. Eliot and the men from Faber's, are not much by way of actual anarchic overturning. Cultural bombs are only metaphorically bombs. The anarchism of Sinclair and Home and their gang is a kind of political conjuring trick, a set of *jeux d'esprit*, merely semiotic games. They may have their force, but there *is* no John Dee in the cupboard in Ackroyd's Clerkenwell Green, and Blake and Bunyan lie mouldering on in Bunhill Fields for all Sinclair's or Ackroyd's or, for that matter, Emanuel Litvinoff's celebratory resurrectionist visits. All of which Emanuel Litvinoff more or less acknowledges in the second part of his trilogy, *Blood on the Snow* (1975). In this account, Peter the Painter and Countess Lydia escape from the ruin and shambles of Sidney Street and return to Russia, where a real revolution is taking place.[29] In Litvinoff's third part, *The Face of Terror* (1978), things go terribly wrong with and for both of them and for the real revolution they have actively furthered, as historical truth-telling requires.[30] But at least they have both entered the real world of politics, real revolutionary history and not just political sham and fiction. Though, of course, being main characters in Litvinoff's extended fictional memorializings, they have done that as well.

NOTES

1   See 'L. S. (Louisa Sarah) Bevington (Mrs Ignatz Guggenheimer) (also "Arbor
    Leigh") (1845–95)', in Valentine Cunningham (ed.), *The Victorians: An
    Anthology of Poetry and Poetics* (Oxford, 2000), pp. 881–3. Also, Hermia
    Oliver, *The International Anarchist Movement in Late Victorian London*
    (London, 1983).
2   T. S. Eliot, *After Strange Gods: A Primer of Modern Heresy* (London, 1934), p. 20.
3   Rachel Lichtenstein and Iain Sinclair, *Rodinsky's Room* (London, 1999),
    pp. 84–5.
4   Roland Penrose, *Scrap Book 1909–1981* (London, 1981), p. 75.
5   Ibid., p. 143.
6   Dannie Abse, *A Poet in the Family* (London, 1984 [1974]), p. 8.
7   All the details of Litvinoff's life are from Emanuel Litvinoff, *Journey Through
    a Small Planet* (London, 1993 [1972]).
8   Emanuel Litvinoff, *A Death Out of Season* (London, 1974 [1973]).
9   The title poem of the volume, 'The Untried Soldier', is a nicely autobiographical
    set of quatrains uniting Litvinoff's early life as casual labourer, union activist,
    street fighter, chaser of girls and conscript soldier: *The Untried Soldier*
    (London, 1942), pp. 38–9.
10 Abse, *A Poet in the Family*, pp. 130–3. Abse also recalls the occasion in his
    Intermittent Journals (Bridgend, 1994), p. 180.
11 Anthony Julius, *T. S. Eliot, Anti-Semitism and Literary Form* (Cambridge,
    1995), p. 218.
12 Iain Sinclair, *Lights Out for the Territory: 9 Excursions in the Secret History of
    London*, with illustrations by Marc Atkins (London, 1997).
13 *White Chappell Scarlet Tracings* (London, 1987); *Downriver (or, the Vessels of
    Wrath): A Narrative in Twelve Tales* (London, 1991); *Radon's Daughters: A
    Voyage, between Art and Terror, from the Mound of Whitechapel to the
    Limestone Pavements of the Burren* (London, 1994); *Lud Heat and Suicide
    Bridge* (London, 1998); *Landor's Tower, or The Imaginary Conversations*
    (London, 2001); *London Orbital: A Walk Around the M25* (London, 2002); Iain
    Sinclair and Dave McKean, *Slow Chocolate Autopsy: Incidents from the
    Notorious Career of Norton, Prisoner of London* (London, 1997); Marc Atkins
    and Iain Sinclair, *Liquid City* (London, 1999).
14 Sinclair, *Lights Out for the Territory*, pp. 145–6.
15 Iain Sinclair, *Crash: David Cronenberg's Post-mortem on J. G. Ballard's
    'Trajectory of Fate'* (London, 1999).
16 Sinclair, *Lights Out for the Territory*, p. 70.
17 Patrick Wright, *A Journey Through Ruins: The Last Days of London* (London,
    1991) – which includes a long tribute to the particular London-philia of the
    Sinclair mob.
18 Lichtenstein and Sinclair, *Rodinsky's Room*, p. 175.
19 Raphael Samuel, *East End Underworld: Chapters in the Life of Arthur Harding*
    (London, 1981), pp. 135–45, 172–3.

[20]   Peter Ackroyd, *Hawksmoor* (London, 1985); *The House of Dr Dee* (London, 1993); *Dan Leno and the Limehouse Golem* (London, 1994); *The Clerkenwell Tales* (London, 2003).

[21]   Sinclair, *Lights Out for the Territory*, p. 80.

[22]   See Stewart Home, *Neo-ist Manifestos* (Stirling, 1991); *Neoism, Plagiarism and Praxis* (Edinburgh, 1995); *The Assault on Culture: Utopian Currents from Lettrisme to Class War* (London, 1988); *Slow Death* (London, 1996); *Blow Job* (London, 1997); 'Frenzy of the Flesh', in Amy Scholder and Ira Silverberg (eds), *High Risk 2: Writings on Sex, Death and Perversion* (London, 1994), pp. 175–90; *Come Before Christ and Murder Love* (London, 1997).

[23]   London, 1997.

[24]   Atkins and Sinclair, 'Tea With the Plague Warriors, Fournier Street, 22 February 1999', *Liquid City*, pp. 206–7.

[25]   Sinclair, *Lights Out for the Territory*, p. 29.

[26]   Lichtenstein and Sinclair, *Rodinsky's Room*, p. 139.

[27]   Atkins and Sinclair, 'The Synagogue', *Liquid City*, p. 148.

[28]   See 'Luther Blisset' and Stewart Home, *Green Apocalypse* (London, 1995).

[29]   London, 1975.

[30]   London, 1978.

12

Anti-authoritarianism in the
Later Fiction of James Kelman

H. GUSTAV KLAUS

In Kelman's fiction anti-authoritarianism comes in many shapes and guises; neither is it the hallmark of the later novels alone. From the start of his literary career the author has displayed a radical distrust of the authority of the conventional narrative voice, with regard both to the cultural values behind the standard English usually adopted as the appropriate language for authoritative speech, and to the relation between that socially more acceptable 'superior' accent and the 'sub-standard' utterances of lower-class characters, sealed off by inverted commas in the dialogues. For Kelman even the best-intentioned working-class writing of the past is marred by this gulf within the narrative flow, for it tends to inferiorize the vernacular voices.

In his shorter fiction the author has circumvented the problem by overwhelmingly relying on first-person narrators. I have proposed the term 'speaker-narrator' for these 'I' voices to emphasize the oral demotic quality of their monologic digressions, and to draw attention to the blurring of the borderlines between natural speech and narrative discourse.[1] Several of Kelman's stories would lend themselves to a dramatization as radio or stage plays, dramatization not so much in the sense of acted drama – for there is little outward action – but of audible live performance. The author has, in fact, written a number of radio plays, and the longest story from his latest collection, *The Good Times* (1998), 'Comic Cuts', was first broadcast on BBC Radio 3.[2]

In the novels up to *Translated Accounts* there is no first-person narrator, but it is a measure of the success of Kelman's effort to obliterate, as it were, the narrative voice as an outside interfering agency that the reader still feels as if there is one. So frequently are we in the minds of the central figures, so compatible are the linguistic registers employed, that it becomes often difficult to decide who is speaking. In another defiant move Kelman has consistently, if not exclusively, chosen working-class characters as central figures for his narratives. What is more, from *The Busconductor Hines* (1984) onward he has represented some of them as highly literate and argumentative. That critics should have been baffled by such a portraiture tells against them. 'Working-class intellectuals are simply a fact . . . Why are we still having to argue that the literate class isn't logically distinct from the working class, that folk read and write literature from every social position?'[3] In 'Gardens go on forever', from *The Good Times*, a gardener has immersed himself in a work of German philosophy. On the way to work he reads out a sentence to his fellow passengers in the van, so as to 'get some higher thoughts into yer dreich existences'.[4] The workmates poke fun at the quotation but, importantly, not at the fact of his reading such a book.

However, this article is not primarily concerned with the formal exigencies of the embattled Kelman's literary politics. It is the thematic side of the novels *A Disaffection, How Late it Was, How Late* and *Translated Accounts*, their political edge and, especially, their interrogation of the working of state agencies and apparatuses, that I would like to discuss. The author seems to require the longer fictional form for this kind of sustained investigation, for *The Good Times*, published between these novels, does not contain comparable reflections on, or acts of defiance of, the ruling order. Although the ranters and railers against class iniquity or oppression are not totally absent from its pages, the prevalent mood is low-key and reflective, not because the 'good times' are dawning but because many stories focus on male–female relationships, with a delicate balance of frustration and promise.

Take the piece 'pulped sandwiches', which is set on a building site of the kind that we find in Ken Loach's film *Riff-Raff* (1991): small, with possibly subcontracted labour, poor tools and a 'spying' gaffer. The speaker-narrator of this story, an ageing builder, bitterly reflects on the changed working conditions:

> In the old days ye would have swung the sledge and nobody the wiser when ye stopped for a smoke, there wasnay nobody could tell except maybe they might have listened for the chip chip. But not this goddam hammer. Once ye stopped working they knew, they heard that silence. (p. 44)

Yet his distrust of the ganger is of no consequence. The story ends on a subdued, even docile, note when the narrator grudgingly accepts working overtime on a Friday evening, despite having a date with 'the missis'. By contrast, *Riff-Raff* works towards a dramatic finale. After the sacking of one builder, who complained about the unsafe working conditions on the site, and an industrial accident which kills or maims another, the film ends with a revolutionary beacon, reminiscent of the sabotage of the coal-mine by Souvarine the anarchist in Zola's *Germinal*. Two incensed construction workers set fire to the building, even though it will mean the loss of their jobs.

Nothing could be further removed from Kelman's method of story-telling. His narratives rarely culminate in such a dramatic climax. Just as their opening plunges the reader into an ongoing scene or dialogue, as in the case of 'pulped sandwiches', so they end inconclusively, with no particular point reached, or so it seems. They do not rely on plot, incident or conflict. Instead of elaborate lifelines they present glimpses or fragments of ordinary, mostly uneventful, certainly unspectacular lives. Of course, the difference is one not so much of political angles as of generic possibilities. Modern short fiction, from James Joyce and Sherwood Anderson onward, has largely dispensed with pivotal action and concentrates instead on episodes or discontinuous sequences of incidents. In the film medium the pressure to build scenes into a story, action, drama is immense. Even Ken Loach, known as he is for his sparse use of scripts, cannot escape the constrictions imposed by the genre.

It is, then, in Kelman's novels that we find characters in open conflict with authority. In *A Disaffection* (1989), this pronounced anti-authoritarianism rests on the shoulders of Patrick Doyle, a sickened teacher, a worrying intellectual, not on the 'fucking hopeless reactionariness' (p. 119) of his father, a factory worker, or his unemployed brother. Patrick's stance is established in four distinct, if closely related ways: his classroom behaviour; his view of the educational system; his attitude to his superiors; and his heroes from the past.

His classroom behaviour

The four classroom scenes in the novel are distributed over various age-groups, from first year to sixth year. But some common features of Patrick's conduct emerge. First he treats the children as equals, as would-be adults:

Right then, one more: Animi egestas! Immediate translation! Ian!
Is it to do with poverty of the mind sir?
Yes sir, precisely. Now class, the lot of ye, repeat after me: Our parents, who are the poor, are suffering from an acute poverty of the mind.
The smiling faces. (p. 24)

Underneath the obvious joke of returning the 'sir' to a first-year boy there is respect for the pupils, whom Patrick treats uncondescendingly, without in any way blinding himself to the different positions of teachers and kids. As might be expected, he is not only against the reintroduction of the belt, but also rejects the widespread notion that today's schoolchildren are being mollycoddled.

Secondly, Doyle sees in them individuals, not an amorphous group. He knows something about their family background and is not ashamed to connect it with his own:

> Hey Raymond, what does your da do for a living?
> He's on the broo just now Mister Doyle.
> Aw aye. What was it he worked at last?
> Eh he worked in a factory. [. . .]
> Patrick nodded; he looked at the rest then back to Raymond: My da's been working in a factory for the past twenty-two year – that's when he's no having fucking heart attacks. He's a real yin so he is, a right fucking numbskull. He's got a wee baldy heid and sometimes I feel like giving it a brush with a brillo pad.
> LOUD LAUGHING. (p. 194)

In such an atmosphere of frankness and mutual respect the students have no hesitation in questioning him about the motives for his decision to leave the school. Does he not let them down? And Patrick winces at the suggestion.

Thirdly, while Patrick is exacting in his use of philosophical sources he is clearly not bent on cramming knowledge into the children. As the narrator puts it: 'He was the kind of teacher who liked to spend an entire period on essential side issues' (p. 23). Argument comes before curriculum. His over-arching aim is to give them a 'proper grounding in reality' (p. 182): that is, make them aware of their own situation in terms of class and gender, and sensitize them to power relations in society and official versions of the 'truth'.

Finally, Patrick's classes are informal, relaxed. Several times the narrative, like a drama text, gestures to laughter and smiles as responses of the learners. It is the ironical twist of his phrases that prevents the incantatory sentences, in the manner of the Lord's Prayer, from becoming an indoctrinating chorus:

> Repeat after me: We are being fenced in by the teachers
> We are being fenced in by the teachers
> at the behest of a dictatorship government

at the behest of a dictatorship government
in explicit simulation of our fucking parents the silly bastards
in explicit simulation of our fucking parents the silly bastards
Laughter. (p. 25)

His view of the educational system

But what is it that drives a caring and committed teacher of the mark of
Patrick Doyle into resignation and depression? Why does he throw in the
towel? The answer is that with one-half of his being he is a disciple (or,
should one say, a prisoner) of Althusser (not named in the book) and, as
such, recognizes the limited reach of his efforts to instil rational argument
in the pupils. He leans towards the French philosopher's view of ideology
as a structural distortion of perception, fostered in us by the institutions
through which we are socialized from infancy onward. One of those institutions is the school; in fact, ideology requires an apparatus such as the
educational system and its practices in order to function, that is, to represent
'not the system of the real relations which govern the existence of individuals,
but the imaginary relation of those individuals to the real relations in which
they live'.[5] That is to say, we experience the real world and our place in it
not directly and clearly, but obscured through the workings of ideology,
which envelops social contradictions in a haze and interprets injustices in
the interests of the dominant class. Thus the teacher recruited by the state to
serve the educational apparatus becomes a cog in the wheel. All the critical
energy Patrick can muster, all the counter-interpretations aiming to retrieve
progressive impulses from reactionary canonical works of literature and
philosophy cannot detract from his complicity in keeping the lower classes
subordinate. When all is said and done, he argues, you still perform 'the
fencing-in job for a society you purport to detest right to the very depth of
your being' (p. 87). Following from this grim analysis, the position of a
radical schoolteacher becomes morally untenable. Here Patrick is in conversation with an uncomprehending colleague:

> [The] weans' heids get totally swollen with all that rightwing keech we've got
> to stuff into them so's we can sit back with the big wagepackets. It's us that
> keep the things from falling apart. It's us. Who else! We're responsible for it,
> the present polity. (p. 149)

It is this unresolvable conflict between commitment and betrayal, plus his
crippling loneliness, which drives Doyle to the verge of breakdown. Perhaps
in a country like Scotland, with its revered tradition of learning for all, the

proposition is particularly devastating that not just an individual dominie may be at fault, but the ethos of a whole profession.

His attitude towards his superiors

Patrick's tense relations with his superiors are the least of his problems, but they add another facet to his general hostility to the powers that be. His dubbing of the Deputy Head 'MI6' says it all. The feeling of being under constant observation, whether real or projected, is part of his paranoid state of mind, an obsession he shares with countless other characters in Kelman's universe (see the above-mentioned building worker):

> A head could be seen passing along the corridor: and slowly, going slowly, as though in an attempt to overhear the slightest piece of untowardity. Patrick indicated the head and the class turned to see it. Notice that head! he called. You're probably all thinking it's a spy from Mister Big's office. And fucking right ye are cause that's exactly the case, the way of things, how matters are standing, at the present, the extant moment. Arse. (p. 195)

Patrick's blood also boils when he thinks of Old Milne, the headmaster. He ignores an appointment with him, partly to show his disrespect, partly to avoid questions about his rumoured political views. In fact, when the interview eventually takes place all Patrick learns is that his transfer to another school has gone through. The ensuing altercations leave the reader wondering whether Patrick actually applied for the transfer, which he claims he cannot remember, or whether it is all a manoeuvre to get rid of him. Whatever the truth, the outcome strengthens Patrick's feeling that he is up against impalpable powers, and contributes to his decision to chuck the job altogether. He simply fails to turn up for the afternoon classes.

His heroes from the past

A Disaffection abounds with what critics, following Julia Kristeva, have called 'intertextual' references, a suspect term because it suggests movement from text to text without human agency. Some names crop up particularly frequently: Goya, Goethe, Hölderlin, Hegel (sometimes by implication when there is talk of dialectics) and the Pythagoreans. A mixed bag, no doubt, but the significance of the first four of Patrick's heroes should not be lost. Without exception they are contemporaries of the French Revolution. Mainlanders all of them, they were inevitably confronted with the turmoil of their times. Hölderlin and Hegel, born in 1770, belong to what one might call the generation of '89, that is to say they came of age in that 'dawn' in which it was 'bliss' to be alive (Wordsworth, also born in 1770, gets only one or two mentions, for reasons that will become clear in a moment). The upheaval they witnessed – Goya from very close quarters – appeared to herald the end of tyrannical rule and to hold the promise of universal liberation. Goethe had famously pronounced the beginning of a new era in the world's history after witnessing the cannonade of Valmy in 1792,[6] though he remained ambivalent about the French Revolution. Hegel believed the *Weltgeist* to have paraded on horseback in the person of Napoleon (born 1769). But with the excesses of the revolutionary terror, the endless wars and, finally, the triumph of reaction throughout Europe, 'the good times', far from being imminent, receded ever further into the distance. How to cling to the old ideals, whether and how to become reconciled with reality, was the question now agitating the disappointed liberal and revolutionary artists, writers and philosophers.

Kelman, born 1946 (though not Doyle, who is just under thirty in a novel presumably set in the mid-1980s), is a child of 1968. You did not have to attend university to be roused by the war in Vietnam, the invasion of Prague, the cultural upsurge of the Sixties and the student revolts in Europe culminating in May 1968. Once again, great promises, hopes, dreams, ideals, projects of liberation were in the air. But after the excitement, the high-flown rhetoric, the carnival, the sobering was not long in coming. In Britain it arrived in the figure of Margaret Thatcher, and the year in which she first assumed office (1979) also spelt the end, for the time being, of Scotland's dream of independence. Except for the revolution in sexual mores, all the great libertarian visions, all the projects of socialist transformation, came to be buried or disavowed. One can see the appeal of Althusser's disenchanted thesis to the politically disappointed generation of '68. Here, too, therefore, is the spectacle of confusion and resignation, of radicals making their peace with the world, some succumbing to cynicism, others, like Doyle, wavering between conviction and despair.

There are, then, also psychosocial reasons for Doyle's absorption in the generation of '89. He is haunted by Goya's 'black period' because its vision of horror corresponds with his own 'black' mood. Images of 'revolution and disease and starvation and torture and murder and rape' (p. 118) crowd his mind. No wonder that during his recurring bouts of depression he is, like Hölderlin, approaching the point of crack-up. Again, like Hölderlin or young Werther, who is infatuated with a betrothed woman, he is in love with a married woman; and like the great Romantic hero he contemplates suicide. Just as Werther's obsession, encapsulated in Goethe's phrase 'Krankheit zum Tode' (sickness unto death),[7] is more than an individual neurosis, but symbolizes a struggle against the oppressions of his contemporary life and the impossibility of obtaining freedom, so Patrick's psyche is the site of wider social and political conflicts.

Patrick considers himself a 'fucking no-user' (p. 199) because his teaching is not validated by his own political praxis. Contrary to some theoreticians he does not resort to the trick of selling his teaching as a political act. His decision to quit results from this frustration. So does the resolution: 'Facta non verba, from now on' (p. 186). And he challenges the pupils to do the same: 'Why dont yous go and blow up the DHSS office?' (p. 186). At the end of the novel Patrick, walking the streets in a state of drunken stupor, pictures himself smashing in the windows of every bank, building society and insurance company – 'anything at all connected with the financial institutions of the Greatbritish Rulers' (p. 335). Whether he will actually do it is another matter, just as it is uncertain whether the policemen on the other side of the road, who 'had appeared at the very thought of insurrection' (p. 336), want to arrest him. *A Disaffection* leaves, like so many of Kelman's works, nothing resolved.

But the appearance of the police is a reminder of that other, repressive, state apparatus, whose function it is not to secure consensus for the maintenance of power, but to exercise control, if need be by violence. The novel is interspersed with references to the 'polis'. Two are posted outside the school and the hint that Doyle 'went to uni and became a member of the polis' (p. 139) suggests that policing the masses and forging consent are two sides of the same coin.

If *A Disaffection* ends with *surveiller*, *How Late it Was, How Late* (1994) begins with *punir*.[8] After having kipped in the open the protagonist awakens, mysteriously with somebody else's shoes on, finds himself cornered by two plainclothes police ('sodjers') and, after a brawl, ends in a police cell, with a broken rib and his eyesight gone. As Ian A. Bell has noted in an early commentary, the opening of the novel is a substantial rewriting of Kafka's tale 'Die Verwandlung' ('Metamorphosis'), stripped of anything redolent of metaphysics.[9] Instead, the novel is grounded, in typically Kelmanesque fashion, in reality, the stark reality of the rough working class (as distinct from Kafka's equally ordinary, but middle-class existences). Sammy Samuels – the name recalls Kafka's Gregor Samsa and Milton's blind Samson Agonistes held prisoner by the Philistines – has not been transformed into an insect of sorts, but his life has undergone a no-less dramatic change. Sammy's hell is not a dream or nightmare, but a 'daymare' (the expression is from *A Disaffection*, p. 120). Eyeless in Glasgow, without a penny in his pocket, he gropes his way from the police station to his girlfriend's home, only to find it deserted. The body and its physiological functions, always important in Kelman, assume a tactile primacy, as he learns painfully – in more senses than one – to readjust to his new situation. Given his ordeal, Sammy surprisingly rarely succumbs to self-pity or sentimentality. But then he has never been spoilt by life. A semi-skilled construction worker, he has jobbed on building sites when jobs were going and been involved in crime when there were none. On two separate occasions he landed in prison, which he accepted in a stoic mood: 'Ye do yer crime ye take yer time' (p. 15). For years, surviving has been his only full-time occupation. So, in characteristically resilient manner, he sets about devising his 'wee survival plan' (p. 65):

> What can ye do but. Except start again so he started again. That was what he did he started again. It's a game but so it is man life, fucking life I'm talking about, that's all ye can do man start again, turn ower a new leaf, a fresh start, another yin, ye just plough on, ye plough on, ye just fucking plough on, that's what ye do, that was what Sammy did, what else was there I mean fuck all, know what I'm saying, fuck all. (p. 37)

If anything, this understates his astonishing feat of endurance. One source of strength is his irrepressible sense of ironic humour. Here he is propping himself against a wall for a rest during his groping journey home: 'He was gony stay there. So what if they tried to fucking lift him I mean what could they fucking charge him with? loitering with intent? A fucking good yin that, loitering with intent – intent to bump into a lamppost; bastards' (p. 44).

However, this parody of the discourse of legal authority cannot relieve the bitter insight that this is a society where mishaps are blamed on the victims rather than on the perpetrators:

> [H]is hand got a hold on the left side door; he stepped down, down onto the road; onto the road, he had to find the kerb fast, fast man come on, come on. One time there was this guy stepped off the pavement, Argyle Street on a Saturday afternoon for christ sake crowds everywhere and there was a bus coming fast on the inside lane and the fucking wing mirror fucking blootered him man right on the fucking skull, blood belching out; what a crack! the driver jumping out the cabin and wanting to help the guy but the poor bastard got off his mark immediately, probably thinking he had done something wrong man damaged company fucking property or something and the driver was trying to

get his name, so he got off his mark, staggering into this sprint – Sammy could see him yet, poor bastard, fucking blood everywhere. (pp. 85–6)

Just as Sammy is about to get his wits back he is arrested again and subjected to endless interrogation. But why single out a small crook for such special treatment? It takes Sammy and the reader some time to put two and two together. During the pub-crawl, which preceded his being beaten up and losing his eyesight in consequence, Sammy has been unfortunate enough to bump into a mate wanted by the police for some unspecified subversive activity. (As in Kafka, the absence of any definite charge only adds to the pervasive threatening atmosphere.) The mysterious Charlie Barr, a former shop steward, a political animal, perhaps a bomb-thrower, never turns up in the novel. But through this contact, Sammy has now himself become a suspect 'political' case, *puni et surveillé*, which explains the arrival of the Special Branch on the scene.

However, the police is only one of the implacable forces which Sammy, in his lone survival struggle, is up against. Once he starts seeking compensation or only re-registration, so as not to lose Community Gratuities, he gets caught in the bureaucratic machinery of other authorities. The questioning by the doctor is not accompanied by manhandling, the threats may be more veiled (benefit cuts), the insensitive formalistic procedures and protocols of a Kafkaesque bureaucracy are carried on in public rather than behind closed doors, but the intended effect of these methods is the same as that dished out by the police: the claimant is to be intimidated and discouraged, in short, disciplined. For Sammy, in this monstrously unequal battle with the tentacles of the (to him) invisible state kraken, it is all one. Does the doctor, he wonders, who lectures rather than examines him, collude with the police? On whose side is the exceedingly well-informed rep who offers to push his claim for compensation? The reader is made to share these uncertainties and anxieties through the narrative stance, which is completely restricted to the perceptions and rambling mindwork of a suddenly stone-blind man. His blackout regarding the details of his disastrous drinking tour makes for a patchy and fragmented picture.

One thing alone is certain: Sammy can trust nobody as he makes his stand against the police, medical and social security authorities. Even his drinking pals cut him, since word has been passed that politics is involved. It is not until the end that support comes movingly, if improbably, in the person of his fifteen-year-old son from his broken-up family. Familial relations, rare in Kelman's early fiction, *The Busconductor Hines* excepted, become a point of hope and succour in the later works, especially the short stories.

The end of *A Disaffection* saw the teacher running, in an imagined or real flight from the police. *How Late* also ends with the protagonist on the run, dodging his surveillance with the help of two teenagers. Cairns Craig entitled an essay on Kelman 'Resisting Arrest', even before the publication of *How Late*.[10] Hines and Tammas, the protagonists of the two earlier novels, were running up against the authorities, inspectors and 'polis'. But in the later fiction the resistance of isolated and terrorized individuals against the sinister and repressive forces of the state has become more desperate, more articulate (Doyle) and more ingenuous (Sammy).

Nowhere are state agencies more strongly identified as ruthlessly brutal instruments of terror than in *Translated Accounts* (2001), at once Kelman's most political and least tractable novel, if indeed 'novel' is an adequate term for a discontinuous narrative composed of anonymous eye/'I' witness accounts of life under military rule in an unspecified 'terrortory' (p. 149).[11] This country has a coastline and mountains, vendors of water and pumpkins. Some of its inhabitants drink wine, too. It might be Turkey, the Balkans in the 1990s, or Palestine in the 2000s; for geographical and political reasons – foreign observers *are* admitted – it cannot be Chechnya. The point is that it could be anywhere on the edge of the rich white world.

The first sentence sets the tone for much of what is to come. 'There were bodies strewn throughout the building' (p. 1). Chilling references to bodies, precariously alive, mutilated or dead, accompany the reader to the very end: 'The body now lying still. A carcass, corpse, yes' (p. 313). Destinies of anonymous people are reported in a faltering spoken English, providing stories or hints of intimidation, expulsion, separation of family members, internment, rape, torture, disappearance, atrocities ('babyonets', p. 40), executions. But we equally hear of little survival strategies, including desperate confessions of love and tenderness under impossible circumstances, and various acts of subterfuge and resistance against what are dubbed 'the authoritys' and 'the securitys'. The most memorable of these feats of resistance is embedded in one of the few accounts that is actually a story, 'a pumpkin story' (ch. 14), in which a pumpkin, or watermelon (the accounts differ), is thrown at a military official, splashing all over his 'insignia breast' (p. 124), for which the perpetrator immediately receives several bullets in his head. Occasional mentions of e-mails and the Internet, of Visa cards and 'corporate worldwide banking and finance operations' (p. 172), make it clear that we are in the present.

Pointers to state-inspired terrorist operations are not new in Kelman's work. Patrick Doyle reminded his fourth-formers that:

yous know there are people the same age as yourselves getting beaten up and tortured and killed in countries not all that far from here and I wont name them because if ye don't know what I'm talking about ye don't deserve to. People of twelve, thirteen, fourteen; they're getting tortured and murdered. (*A Disaffection*, p. 199)

And this hinted, among other places, at Ulster, where the British government was found guilty of torture and inhuman treatment by the European Convention on Human Rights. In an interview from the same year Kelman spoke of 'US terrorism in Central and South America, Asia, Africa, the Middle East' and of the refusal of 'liberal media people' 'to see things – to bear witness'.[12]

Displacing the action from a recognizable urban Scotland to an unknown distant region not only directs our attention to the naked repression existing in other corners of the globe; it also establishes a relation of guilt between the metropolitan centres and the peripheral zones, through either connivance with the local regimes or lack of solidarity with the victims. The link is provided by the frequent references to 'specialty individuals and professional expert people, lawyers, doctors, all professors and higher authoritys' (p. 80) visiting the country to investigate allegations of torture and summary executions. Kelman, steeped in the anti-expert Scottish common-sense philosophy, has only scorn for their mystifications and hair-splitting arguments, and for the advice these visitors have in store for people engaged in a struggle for life and death:

> At larger meetings in foreign countries our colleagues listened to conversations and leading statements . . . if this one or that one who is of fascist calling is also moral or has scruples derived from religious or ethical code, if a security is a 'kind security', or state official is just and fine a person in his own house, saying fine anecdotes to people, if torturers make jokes, these are witty people sensitive people, we must understand them.
>
> Colleagues entered into such discussion if one fascist was 'caring fascist', one racist was 'caring racist', what one torturer may be, one rapist, murderer of children, yes, murderer of children is 'caring murderer of children'. And if our colleagues said to them, But we know what securitys are, what are military operatives, what politicians of national government, lawyers, doctors, judiciary . . . They said to us, No you must listen. 'Official politics' is 'you must listen politics', constitutional activity operating by rules and regulating principles embedded into stone by all gods and infallible creatures. (p. 170)

In the novel 'colleagues' seems to have replaced the cautiously withheld, no longer valued or (by the translator) deliberately suppressed 'comrades'. An even more scathing criticism of the role of the foreign experts, and about the only instance of a bitter humour in these accounts, comes across in the 'lecture, re sensitive periods' (ch. 10). Here the usual scrambled transcription is compounded by legalese from an international lawyer, who has urged on the locals the case of a schoolgirl attacked in his own country by a vicious dog, with a view to instruct his hearers that stories of atrocities and murders must be taken with caution and scrupulously verified before a verdict can be given:

> And now of the child-victim, speak of her, this paragon child, puberty child in adolescence why she is walking home from school down this street and not another. What is her background. She is a child, she is female. She is reliable. Many girls do not distinguish easily as between fact, fiction. We know children, we were all children. Boys also, they invent fictions. Adults, yes, they too, it is a failing of all humans, tall tales. Mature responsible human adult citizens, who may have regard for stories, greater regard.
>
> And for some children it is true, authoritys advise us, that they have been naughty in the district and this dog-owning fellow, as one responsible and law-abiding citizen, will try to correct all anti-societal behaviour of these younger hooligan elements. He takes this societal burden upon his own shoulders, peacekeeper and moral strategist, what you may, asking no recompense. And what rewards. Calumny. It is not only children seeking revenge and of whom this girlish paragon is almost certainly one, or has friends she aids in such revenge, acting on their behalf.
>
> And at Hospital Casualty department, upon examination of this victim female paragon, did one so-called doctor or doctors verify existence of so-called bite, that teeth were responsible, that dogs were responsible, time of occurrence of bite, this teeth-wound, might it not have been older [. . .]
>
> Is his knowledge specialised knowledge. Perhaps he cannot distinguish dog bites one from another. Does teeth-wound indicate a dog in particular or could it be the teeth-wound of any dog found on planet Earth, dachshund to Rottweiler. Can first doctor distinguish between teeth of a dog and each other species of animal known to mankind. May not there be one unknown animal in lost jungles south of Borneo whose teeth markings are similar. Was one or more unusual animals discovered in vicinity of girl's village that day. (pp. 82–3)

This is the familiar Kelman, branding in a Swiftian rage the absurd casuistry of the legal profession. But *Translated Accounts* defamiliarizes even readers who have grown accustomed to Kelman's Glaswegian speaker-narrators, through a language literally tortured and strangled and disembodied, for there is no way that we can identify or empathize with the nameless individuals behind these collated abstracts of interviews and statements.[13] And yet, like one of his witnesses, Kelman is only too aware that 'the name of an individual is important' (p. 314). Making them anonymous is to heighten the pervasive atmosphere of fear, confusion, distrust and uncertainty that envelops these 'imperfect speakers'. Although the emotions and anxieties vented in their testimonies allow for some differentiation, the homogenized diction in which these are rendered effaces the fractured individual consciousnesses that struggle for articulation. As the fictitious Preface warns us, this may be the work of translators or transcribers who are not native English speakers, but it may also be due to modifications made 'by someone of a more senior office' (p. ix).

In an essay now collected in *"And the Judges Said . . ."* Kelman alludes to a gulf in understanding between the comfortably situated reader or spectator, whose senses may have been dulled by statistics, and the harassed victim of organized violence: 'Reports by refugees of atrocities are difficult to cope with. We are not used to such testimony, not unless, perhaps, the refugees are in flight from the same ideological enemy as ourselves.'[14] *Translated Accounts* illustrates this point through the foregrounding of language. The terrifying strangeness of the experiences reported here, hardly 'translatable' into the mother tongue, highlights the enormous difficulty of connecting with other people's pain. This is a matter not so much of the inadequacy of the translations as of the different positions of speakers and listeners. In the face of proliferating disasters and war zones, reported daily, in fact hourly on such channels as CNN, from across the globe, we may have reached a point of 'compassion fatigue', as the *Times Literary Supplement* reviewer put it.[15] By telling us their troubles in what has become a global language, interviewees address us directly, yet cannot count on understanding, far less help or solidarity. Kelman's novel must be one of the first to confront the political and linguistic implications of the rise of English as a lingua franca, itself founded on political and economic domination, and its uses in the non-print media. The questions that *Translated Accounts* raises can be formulated in general terms: under which circumstances are such utterances, statements, interviews, interrogations collected? Who transmits them to whom, with what intention and to which effect? In gesturing towards these questions, Kelman alerts us, once again, to the political uses made of language by those wielding power, and especially those in control of the communication channels.

NOTES

[1]   H. Gustav Klaus, 'Kelman for Beginners', *Journal of the Short Story in English*, 22 (1994), 127–35 (130).

[2]   For a discussion of Kelman's plays and their own anti-authoritarian thrust, see chapter 4 of my forthcoming monograph, *James Kelman* (Tavistock, 2005).

[3]   Kirsty McNeill, 'Interview with James Kelman', *Chapman*, 57 (1989), 1–9 (7).

[4]   James Kelman, *The Good Times* (London, 1998), p. 15. Kelman's works are quoted from the first editions: *A Disaffection* (1989), *How Late it Was, How Late* (1994) and *Translated Accounts* (2001); like *The Good Times* they were all published by Secker & Warburg, London. Page references are inserted in the text.

[5]   Louis Althusser, 'Ideology and Ideological State Apparatuses' (trans. by Ben Brewster), in his *Lenin and Philosophy and Other Essays* (London, 1971), pp. 121–73 (p. 155).

[6]   'Von hier und heute geht eine neue Epoche der Weltgeschichte aus, und ihr könnt sagen, ihr seid dabei gewesen' ('Here and now begins a new era in the world's history, and you can say that you were present at its birth' – my translation, HGK). Quoted in Wilhelm Bode, *Goethes Leben*, continued by Valerian Tornius, *1790–1794: Vereinsamung* (Berlin, 1926), p. 161.

[7]   Johann Wolfgang von Goethe, *Die Leiden des jungen Werthers*, Bk. 1, 12 August.

[8]   The reference to the French title of Michel Foucault's *Discipline and Punish* (English trans., 1977) does not, as in the case of Althusser's essay 'Ideology and Ideological State Apparatuses', necessarily imply that Kelman has read these works – neither Foucault nor Althusser is directly referred to in his volume of essays and polemics *"And the Judges Said . . ."* (2002) – but he was certainly familiar with the ideas expressed in them.

[9]   Ian A. Bell, 'Form and Ideology in Contemporary Scottish Fiction', in Susanne Hagemann (ed.), *Studies in Scottish Fiction: 1945 to the Present* (Frankfurt, 1996), pp. 217–33 (p. 231).

[10] Cairns Craig, 'Resisting Arrest: James Kelman', in Gavin Wallace and Randall Stevenson (eds), *The Scottish Novel Since the Seventies* (Edinburgh, 1993), pp. 99–114. Craig's title has, of course, more than one meaning: it also alludes to Kelman's restless characters (resisting 'a rest') and the initially unattractive idiom of much of the fiction.

[11] Drew Milne points to the ironic use of this and other terms in the novel: 'terrortory', perhaps a false pronunciation, invites a reading of 'terror Tory'. See his article 'Broken English: James Kelman's *Translated Accounts*', *Edinburgh Review*, 108 (2002), 106–15 (110–12).

[12] McNeill, 'Interview with James Kelman', 6.

[13] The idea of composing a novel on the basis of human voices comes up from time to time. Hans Magnus Enzensberger's novel *Der kurze Sommer der Anarchie* (1972) is a collage of interviews (oral history) and excerpts from contemporary (Spanish Civil War) sources. More recently, the exiled Byelorussian

writer Svetlana Alexievitch has said in an interview: 'One day, after finishing my studies of journalism, I had this idea of making a novel based on human voices' (*Libération*, 16 March 2003 – my translation, HGK). Contrary to Kelman, the author incorporates really spoken sentences from interviews.

[14] 'A Reading from the Work of Noam Chomsky and the Scottish Tradition in the Philosophy of Common Sense', "*And the Judges Said . . .*", p. 146.

[15] Keith Miller, *The Times Literary Supplement*, 8 June 2001.

13

Pimps, Punks and Pub Crooners: Anarchy and Anarchism in Contemporary Welsh Fiction

> Socialism and Communism, moving blindly on parallel lines are closely followed up by the werewolf of anarchy, . . . the dark creed of Destruction.[1]

The 'werewolf of anarchy' was a common bogeyman in British sensation fiction of the late nineteenth century. A hundred years later, one major trend in British fiction has let the wolf in the door and it now snarls on the hearth of contemporary society. The werewolf image is an apt one, suggesting as it does the double nature of anarchy, capable of metamorphosing from an optimistic political creed of fundamental human goodness and mutual aid to a marauding spectre of chaos and destruction: both faces of the creature are manifest in contemporary fiction from Wales.

The first wave of the Welsh industrial novel, ranging from works such as *Torn Sails* (1898), by 'Allen Raine', and *The Flower of the Dark* (1917), by Joseph Keating, to *Chwalfa* (1946), by T. Rowland Hughes, and *The Small Mine*, by Menna Gallie (1962), was often imbued with a strong socialist, class and nationalist consciousness. This type of Welsh novel is frequently seen as being epitomized by the 1930s texts of Valleys writers such as B. L. Coombes, Gwyn Jones, Lewis Jones, Jack Jones and Gwyn Thomas. Yet, despite the strength of anarcho-syndicalism in the south Wales valleys, none of these novels challenges the status quo from an anarchist perspective. Returning to our epigraph from the sensationalist novel of Richard Savage, one might see these writers as following the paths of socialism and communism, little realizing that the generation of writers to come would embrace the werewolf of anarchism.

But let us abandon metaphors and clarify what we mean by anarchist thinking. Sharif Gemie states: 'The key concept at the heart of anarchist thinking was the rejection of the state and of allied authority structures – capitalism, the church, the army – and the proposal that social life could be regulated according to the principles . . . put into practice by various "counter communities".'[2] Max Nettlau, furthermore, demonstrates how historical anarchism was a belief in the absolute freedom of the individual, liberated from all authoritarian and institutional shackles.[3] Anarchism entailed a thoroughgoing rejection of virtually all of the most hallowed traditions and institutions: the nation, democracy, the law, the monarchy, marriage and so on. At the same time, it was not simply a nihilistic repudiation of all givens but a positive adoption of alternatives: independence, freely given mutual aid, free federations and associations of people, cooperation and reciprocity. The kinds of anarchists demonized in novels such as Savage's were those who believed in direct action for the overthrow of the state, but such anarchists were always in the minority. Yet anarchism was always a 'philosophy of non-submission'; as the American anarchist writer Voltairine de Cleyre declared: 'I do not want to "love my enemies", nor "let bygones be bygones". I do not want to be philosophical, nor preach their inclusion in the brotherhood of man. I want to hate them – utterly.'[4] Such a philosophy of non-submission is notably present in a range of contemporary novels and short stories from Wales. Why this should be so at a time when devolution has brought limited self-determination to Wales for the first time in centuries is an interesting conundrum, one to which we will return.

John Williams, one of the most prominent exponents of the new wave of realist fiction from Wales, expresses mild surprise at this sudden efflorescence (flowering seems too decorous a term!): 'On a bright Welsh winter's day at the arse end of 2001 we unexpectedly found ourselves in the middle of a literary movement.'[5] It is certainly true that there is a marked similarity in the vision of Wales projected in a number of younger novelists' works, whether the setting is Cardiff, Swansea or Aberystwyth. Perhaps as an antidote to the increasing tendency of English middle-class holidaymakers to regard and use Wales as a pastoral retreat, Wales in these writers' works is a place of mean streets, dirt, violence, drugs and deprivation. As Niall Griffiths, another leading member of the new movement, asserts, 'there is a danger that Wales is treated as a giant theme park, the whole country a holiday home' and Griffiths goes further, claiming that Wales is still a 'colonised nation' despite the superficial manifestations of some of the trappings of government, in the form of the new Welsh Assembly.[6] For Griffiths's Aberystwyth characters, as for Williams's inhabitants of Cardiff's dockland, the Assembly seems to be at best an irrelevance, at worst an enormous swindle. Indeed, a number of the characters discuss the Assembly in proto-anarchist ways, dismissing it as yet another oppressive force in the lives of people who have already had their fill of exploitation and dispossession.

Williams's novel *Cardiff Dead* (2000) mocks the institution of the new Welsh Assembly; his characters laugh openly at it and repudiate the false pomp and tawdry regalia of its opening ceremony:

> In front of the bigger stage there must have been a good thirty thousand people. And there on the stage – you had to see it to believe it – was Shirley Bassey wearing a dress that appeared to be made out of the Welsh flag.
>
> Don't know which one of them started laughing first, Mazz or Lawrence, but after a moment they were both in hysterics, holding on to each other to keep from falling over. Then they started to notice the dirty looks they were getting from all the born-again Welsh patriots around them and that just made things worse . . .
>
> The next couple of hours Mazz just couldn't stop laughing, watching this absurdist panoply of Welsh cultural life unfolding in front of him. Tom Jones of course. Well, at least big Tom knows he's funny these days. But still, 'The Green, Green Grass of Home' – if the sight of Wales welcoming the brave new world to the sound of 'Green, Green Grass' didn't make you laugh, your kitsch bullshit detector had to be well out of order . . .
>
> 'Fuckin' hell, butt,' said Mazz once he'd recovered himself. 'Glad to be Welsh then?'
>
> '*Was ist das*?' said Lawrence in a dumb German accent and Mazz started laughing again.[7]

This is in fact a historically accurate account of the ceremony; Williams's narrative undermines its false nationalist rhetoric, pointing out the absurdity of a singer domiciled in Las Vegas and originally from Pontypridd extolling the 'green, green grass of home' (the false pastoral which the new movement repudiates). Shirley Bassey is a particularly interesting Welsh icon because, though for many years a tax exile, she actually originated in Tiger Bay, the old docklands which is nostalgically evoked in *Cardiff Dead*. The novel generally is anti-nationalist and profoundly anti-authoritarian. In this and his earlier short story collection, *Five Pubs, Two Bars and a Nightclub* (1999), the docklands characters live largely outside government systems, regularly breaking the law and traditional moral and religious codes. However, there is a palpable sense of community and a demonstration of mutual aid – the characters often help one another voluntarily. There is an anti-racist agenda at play here, too, and a suggestion that the relatively harmonious interaction of different races in the docklands society is something that ought to be celebrated at a national level, rather than the false glamour of the exiled superstars. Certainly, there is a political consciousness running through the novel, which cuts between 1999 and 1980; the main characters support rebels like Bobby Sands, who in 1980 was actively challenging and attempting to undermine the might of the British State and mocking its electoral system. Thus, the novel is simultaneously anti-British and anti-Welsh. However, the characters in general are not political activists – they are usually too stoned or drunk to take direct political action, and this dependence on drugs is another common facet of the milieu which this group of contemporary novelists is representing. As in Irvine Welsh's *Trainspotting*, these Welsh novels create worlds of counter-cultural groupings, often united by drug-taking, which virtually amounts to an alternative religion, such is the characters' devotion to it. The novels are also alike in their refusal to pass moral judgement on their characters' actions: in a quasi-naturalistic manner, they expose a world for us to contemplate, uncomfortable and squalid as it may often be.

Uncomfortable and squalid are adjectives which hardly do justice to the repulsiveness of *Sheepshagger* (2002) by Niall Griffiths, which is by far the most extreme of the contemporary Welsh novels discussed here. Ianto, the protagonist, is a slightly backward, dispossessed and desperate man, who commits three horrific murders in rural mid-Wales. Griffiths's creation is a kind of demented version of Iago Prytherch, R. S. Thomas's archetypal bleak-minded hill-farmer, and his destructive actions are partly motivated by his own sense of dispossession. There is a definite political dimension to this novel, which depicts an underclass of young Welsh people, addicted to drugs and violence. Certainly, they could be regarded as forming their own counter-community, if only because they could never be accepted into mainstream society. Ianto's horrible acts might also be seen as acts of anarchist protest and revenge against people he sees as having robbed him of his home and freedom. The style of Griffiths's work is remarkable, oscillating between an extreme dialectal demotic and a highly charged, poetic language, which is frequently archaic and arcane in vocabulary, occasionally toppling into the fustian. It is also clear that Griffiths is deliberately drawing not only on Welsh history but also on aspects of the Welsh literary tradition. The way in which he piles up increasingly ingenious and imaginative descriptions of things and people is reminiscent of the practice of *dyfalu* in medieval Welsh strict-metre poetry. Just as Dafydd ap Gwilym created a soaring flight of the imagination in his description of the seagull, so does Griffiths expend his formidable imaginative and linguistic powers in describing a sheep tick, which is painfully extracted from Ianto's back:

> Sunk in Ianto's skin and just visible beneath the blood-drained outer dermal layer as if frozen in cloudy ice is the capitulum with the prominent mouthparts, the pair of chelicerae curving in like tusks to the twinned skin-pricking digits and the central hyposteme, like the beak of some blood-sucking squid, serried with tiny recurved teeth and the pair of fat and stumpy palps hiding and protecting between them the terminal-pitted humidity-detecting organ with which the creature stalks its hosts, blueprint for foreign arteries hot with blood drawn and stored in this microscopic nodule athrob with antique thirst. Mud-born being, tiny vampire, its kind fevering the dreams of cave-sleepers and corn-walkers and dog-keepers. Little life-thief rooting itself in skin and from there psyche, waddling bloodsucker joining that host of horribles which seethe beyond the light of waking, in restless wait for the hands that hanker and the heads that yearn. Offspring of ooze, small slobbering issue of forest-floor rot brought to roost on Ianto's skinny back in this storm-shook shack gorging itself to bursting point as if it had sought and indeed found a hunger and a need as unslakeable as its own, as unassuageable as its own.[8]

Griffiths's writing is frequently reminiscent of Caradoc Evans's *My People* (1915), often regarded as one of the founding texts of Welsh writing in English, and equally shocking at the time of publication. Both texts are violent anti-pastorals which attack the most hallowed institutions of Welsh society and the hypocrisy and double standards which allow those institutions to continue to wield power. Like *My People, Sheepshagger* is undoubtedly imaginative and politically potent, but, also like Evans's masterpiece, it can hardly be regarded as a pleasure to read, despite the stylistic talent of both authors. The extremely graphic and extended descriptions of nauseating violence found in the pages of *Sheepshagger* mimic what people flock to see on the big screen in contemporary horror or so-called 'slasher' movies, and yet the description of these acts in words is somehow even more shocking than their visual representation. The primal scene of Anglo-Welsh literature, the rats eating away at Old Nanni's face in Evans's story 'Be This Her Memorial', from *My People*, is rivalled in horror by the interminable murder scene at the centre of *Sheepshagger*. Griffiths is clearly committed to an accurate depiction of what extreme violence actually looks like, describing the consequences of attack on the human body in lingering detail. A critic might be tempted to label this trait of his work as 'gratuitous' but it is very much a part of the horrible world Griffiths is creating for us – he will not let us look away, he rubs our noses in its gore and filth. As he himself has said: 'I get so sick of novels and films . . . where people are shot and they fall over. It shows nothing of the vileness of the two-edged sword of violence – where the person who commits an act of violence is diminished by it.'[9] The political impact of the violence is strong: Griffiths shows how a lifetime of dispossession, drug-addiction and social outcastness may create a monster like Ianto, the sheepshagger of the title, whose physical repulsiveness and sickening violence nevertheless do not prevent the reader from sympathizing with him right up until the end. What is perhaps even more shocking finally is that the small counter-community of survivors, who have been discussing their friend Ianto all the way through the novel, are revealed to be murderers as well – the murderers of Ianto himself. The underlying political message is clear: it is not just marginal half-wits like poor Ianto who are capable of acts of extreme vengeance and retribution, but more 'ordinary' people, like Danny and Marc and Griff. The vision is bleak; it is no accident that Gwenno, certainly the most sympathetic character in the novel, ends up in a psychiatric hospital.

Whereas Williams's novel rejects nationalism as an ideology, it is evident that there is a nationalist and class agenda underpinning the ideology of *Sheepshagger*, yet this radical rejection of English imperial domination of Wales, which in Griffiths's vision continues unabated, and the virulent attack (often physical) on the middle and upper classes, are frequently couched in anarchist terms. The counter-community itself practises mutual aid and consistently expresses complete lack of faith in any of the machinery of government: the legal system, the police, bailiffs, the new National Assembly and so on. Thus, the Welsh Nationalist undertones of Griffiths's rhetoric do not add up to a call for independence, such as is legitimized in the policies of Plaid Cymru, within a constitutional political framework. On the contrary, the kind of Welshness hankered for and lost in Griffiths's work is a kind of noble savagery, not a million miles away from the earthy life of Ianto the sheepshagger (who never does, incidentally, shag sheep: he has too much respect for animals – unlike humans). Such a Romantic view comes close to one aspect of traditional anarchist thought, as reflected in the title of the turn-of-the-century anarchist journal, *Mother Earth*. It was thought by many anarchists that true freedom meant not only throwing off the shackles of state and government but a return to the true freedom of Nature herself. Anarchism is fundamentally an optimistic belief that, left to themselves, human beings like other creatures will live in harmony. Clearly, Griffiths's portrayal of the forces of nature, which constitutes some of the most powerful writing in the whole novel, hardly shies away from showing nature as 'red in tooth and claw', but the cruelty of nature is ultimately seen as more acceptable than the false power-play and abuse of perverted middle-class imperialists.

Both novels discussed so far have been by male authors and contain a preponderance of male characters. It would be true to say that most of the contemporary Welsh novelists who write in this vein are men, though there are notable exceptions, such as Rachel Trezise, Trezza Azzopardi and Jennifer Rhead. This type of novel runs the risk of championing a macho aesthetic, which tends to marginalize women and gay men, as Christopher White has suggested recently is the case with Scottish writing of the 'gritty realist' school.[10] However, though many of these Welsh novels contain portrayals of brutal macho males, many of them also problematize the notion of masculinity, and of Welsh masculinity in particular. Chris Meredith observes that in Richard John Evans's *Entertainment* (2000) 'there isn't any portrayal of legitimised masculinity. No heroic worker . . . [the idea of] work as being definitive . . . is gone.'[11] In fact, most of Evans's characters are defined by their *lack* of work, but this is, for the younger generation, no longer a crisis of masculine identity, as it was for Meredith's own characters in the novel *Shifts* (1988) (which, along with Duncan Bush's *Glass Shot* (1991), may be regarded as one of the forerunners of the present literary movement) or for more popular representations of that sudden dilemma, such as the film *The Full Monty*.

Raymond Williams identifies the distinctive achievement of the Welsh industrial novel of the early twentieth century as portraying a 'working man's consciousness: his consciousness as a working man . . . industrial work, and its characteristic places and communities, are . . . not just a new "setting" . . . they are seen as formative'.[12] Most of the contemporary novels discussed here reject that formulation, with the possible exception of Lewis Davies's *Work, Sex and Rugby* (1993), which does foreground work and, in the character of Roy, has a picture of worker as hero or, rather, craftsman as hero. Lewis, the protagonist, is always content to be the labourer, mixing the cement, whereas he regards Roy's skill as a bricklayer with something like awe, an awe which the reader is invited to share. A similar admiration for the sheer efficiency of the mother's labour is also enshrined in the text. In this regard, Davies's novel, despite its surface post-modern cynicism, is actually much closer in tone to the earlier generation of Welsh industrial fiction, represented by authors such as B. L. Coombes, Lewis Jones, T. Rowland Hughes and Jack Jones. Conversely, Niall Griffiths redefines masculine heroism in the figure of Ianto; Griffiths describes the people he writes about as 'the chronically disadvantaged [who are] shat on and shat on and shat on again. They have a heroic quality.'[13]

Such an individual is at the centre of Richard John Evans's *Entertainment*, in the figure of Jason, an embittered and aggressive paraplegic who rages against his disability and likes nothing better than physically to attack a do-gooder. The novel mocks with savage black humour all efforts to 'improve the lot' of the underprivileged and disabled. Jason sees himself as a 'victim of the cosmic joke, the underdog, with a mission to show up the whole sham for what it was'.[14] Yet in the course of the novel there is an awakening to a kind of political consciousness; Jason gradually ceases to be a cynical nihilist ('I'm paraplegic. Possibly alcoholic. In terms of special needs, think in terms of a good hard shag' [p. 68]) and comes to acknowledge that his disability is inherently part of his identity, so that when someone dares to touch his wheelchair, he snaps 'Don't touch me.' Lewis Davies's novel *My Piece of Happiness* (2001) also deals in a challenging way with the lives of disabled people. Here, the main character, George, a social worker, eventually sets fire to the Social Services headquarters in an act of deliberate arson. His action could be seen as an anarchist rebellion against a state system which he has come to recognize as hypocritical and repressive towards the very people it pretends to look after. Specifically, George is protesting against the unwritten moral law that the young adults with learning difficulties whom he looks after must never have sexual relations. Thus, the novel challenges traditional society's moral values, traditions and institutions of state. Similarly, Evans's *Entertainment* undermines the authority of teachers and institutions of the welfare state, such as the Benefits Office. Arts workers who come to the Welsh Valleys from England to try to help disaffected and dispossessed youth to express their anger through community theatre are presented in grotesquely humorous terms, and yet it is only these characters who have a self-conscious idea of political action. Again, as in other texts, the native Welsh appear to be too busy getting drunk and stoned to notice that political action to change their lives might be a more effective and permanent escape.

This novel shows the poignant contrast between the previous generation of Welsh working men, such as Val, who was an active Labour supporter and trades union man, and his son, Philip, who is a cynical and rather pretentious layabout. Val's lifelong political belief does not help him when the bus company he has worked for all his life is privatized and he is made redundant. As his son Philip tartly observes: 'all that traditional Rhondda stuff . . . counts for precisely fuck all as he puts his signature at the bottom of his Job-Seeker's Agreement' (p. 157). His impotence is one of the saddest aspects of the book. As Richard John Evans has said: 'Philip sees his environment, the valley, as being post-everything . . . The industrial history that created the community is dead by the time he inherits it.'[15] Philip reflects gloomily on the way his country is being taken over by foreign high-technology commercial enterprises, simply because the Welsh are so ground down by poverty and deprivation that they will 'work for peanuts. For peanut shells. For the promise of peanut shells' (p. 8). But, unlike Val, Philip does not believe in traditional Labour politics; his attitude is more akin to anarchism in his complete rejection of authority and the institutions of state. He espouses a life of complete personal freedom. As Tony Bianchi observes, Philip is creating his own individual cartography of the valley: he 'could have drawn a map of all the quiet places in the valley where you could sit in a daze, feeling like a stray molecule in an amazingly complex circulatory system'.[16] Moreover, by the end of the novel, the principal characters form a little group outside the confines of the traditional family, which works on principles of mutual aid and protection. Philip can't belong to the real thugs (Minty's gang) nor can he bring himself to join the politically committed, affected English theatrical group led by Nussbaum, and 'he didn't want to be a 9 to 5er . . . So that only left the disaffected underclass intellectual' (p. 102). The novel has a naturalist timbre, since, in common with a number of the other novels discussed here, it passes no explicit moral judgement on the characters who live ostensibly immoral lives. As Richard John Evans says:

> The valleys . . . have got no unifying, cohesive social force, without the coal . . . On the one hand you've got the people who remember the days of coal and who remember a different, community-based Rhondda, and they're living right next-door to people who make their living out of drugs, but not as a moral choice. For them there is no morality to drugs . . . As their fathers would accept going underground and getting dust, these people take part in the economy they find themselves in.[17]

This is also true of Lewis Davies's *Work, Sex and Rugby*, a novel which displays a radical rejection of the institutions of state, capitalism, religion, marriage and nationalism. It is, nevertheless, more positive than later novels' excursions into Welsh urban grit, since the first-person protagonist, Lewis, is hard working and well brought-up – he even says thank you to his mam! His parents are 'decent' working-class people and his mother, particularly, is a paragon of efficient virtue, who even attends chapel on Sundays. Lewis is a labourer working with one of the most interesting characters in the book, the aforementioned Roy, who is an independent craftsman with proto-anarchist tendencies. Roy and Lewis work productively and cooperatively.

Roy is a dissident spokesman and would-be teacher to Lewis, his protégé – he ploughs his own independent furrow and has given up the alcohol which he sees as holding his fellow workers in bondage. He tries to open Lewis's eyes to this, too, and urges him not to play the empty games and rituals which capitalist society demands. Roy is also an important link with the past – a native Welsh speaker, whose education was curtailed because the British education system imposed on Wales could not teach him in his own language. He is bitter about that loss but has emancipated himself from the role of colonial subject. For him, cultural memory and communal networks are important (as they are in the community evoked in Raymond Williams's first novel, *Border Country* [1960]) but we can see that the younger generation are beginning to become deracinated and debauched, and to lose interest in any political solutions. Lewis is on the cusp: flirting with an alcohol-induced nihilism but still strongly drawn towards the 'decent' Welshness represented by Roy and his mother. At the same time, he also wants to escape from the narrowness of the valley – a trope which is so characteristic of post-colonial first novels (such as the early writings of V. S. Naipaul, George Lamming and Derek Walcott, which all express a similar longing to escape the confines of the island home). Unlike the work of Griffiths, this novel's main character is not dispossessed but has a strong sense of belonging to his community – he knows everyone, they know him and his parents and grandparents. Thus, the authentic portrait of Neath and Swansea that we are offered in this novel is much closer to the fictional world of an earlier generation of Welsh industrial novelists, such as Rhys Davies and Gwyn Thomas. Although Lewis is adrift and uncertain about his future direction in life, he is not as cynical or self-seeking as the characters in Griffiths or Evans. He is the offspring of the respectable *gwerin*, not of the drunk and abusive parents who inhabit the Rhondda of Rachel Trezise's novel, *In and Out of the Goldfish Bowl* (2000), for example.

Raymond Williams's classic account of the Welsh industrial novel draws attention to the way in which the novelists of the 1930s use the family as a form to structure their new kind of fiction. Contemporary Welsh realist novelists subvert this tradition by revealing how the family, which was often idealized and elegized after its destruction by outside forces in the classic Welsh realist novel, can actually be a repressive institution. This is particularly true of women writers' works, where the family is often bleakly painted as the site of abuse and neglect: Jennifer Rhead's *y.t. and his holiness* (1998), Trezza Azzopardi's *The Hiding Place* (2000) and Rachel Trezise's *In and Out of the Goldfish Bowl* (2000) are notable examples of this devastating revelation of the reality behind the cosy ideal. Trezise's account of the way in which Rebecca, the protagonist, is treated by the legal system when she is forced to give evidence against her sexually abusive stepfather is particularly harrowing:

> I was never asked whether I should like to take the child abuse matters to the court . . . Someone saw fit to answer the question for me: after all I was still only fourteen years old, and soon to be surrounded by policewomen, police doctors, police nurses, police social workers, barristers and judges.
>
> It began in a social centre on the outskirts of Pontypridd. That is where I would be interviewed, the interview would be recorded and played in the courtroom to shorten my presence at the actual trial . . . The floor was carpeted with soft toys . . . I wondered what the hell difference would social workers asking me if I knew what 'consent' meant, make? What is oral sex, where exactly did he touch? Where exactly did the liquid go? Did he know about me not starting my period? I tried to answer the questions with a minimal amount of speech . . . I didn't want to be there . . . I wondered why the hell I was there.
>
> Then a doctor and a nurse laid me flat, naked on a board, holding my feet together but my knees apart. They prodded me with various metal instruments and talked about my body as though it had no mind attached . . .
>
> Because I was a child, I would give evidence through a video link-up, so as not to be intimidated by the accused's face. This meant I would sit in a room at the back of the court where I could only see the judge and the two lawyers. However, the jury, the accused, and the public gallery could see me. My room was much the same as the one at the social centre, full of cuddly toys . . .
>
> The questioning began. 'Do you remember the video you made?'
> 'Yes.'
> 'You said during that interview that your step-father raped you, on an average of twice a week, do you remember saying that?'
> 'Yes.'
> 'An average of twice a week for a period of three years, is that right?'
> 'Yes.'
> 'So you are telling us that this man raped you three hundred times on average?'
> 'Yes, if that's what it works out as.'
>
> The judge interrupted the court to inform the lawyers that their wigs must be removed, because they can sometimes frighten child witnesses . . .
>
> Didn't they understand I didn't want to be here telling strangers how my step-father ripped that sweatshirt or how the bathroom lock came to be busted that time? Didn't they know that I was actually trying to forget the unforgettable? Didn't they know that all I wanted to do was shed my dirty skin and step out of myself?[18]

In the same way as John Williams reveals the sham behind popular notions of national identity in *Cardiff Dead*, so Rachel Trezise reveals the way in which a complacent legal system dupes the public into believing in its humaneness and justice through adopting superficial palliative measures, such as providing cuddly toys and not wearing wigs. Unsurprisingly, Trezise's novel is one of the most anarchic in the 'dark creed of Destruction' sense of the term. Her representation of the Rhondda is grim in the extreme, although again there is a hint (in the positive character of Rebecca's grandmother) that things were not always thus. There is a savage rejection of nationalism:

> The Rhondda was neither city nor country . . . The place where I grew up is physically as violent and as loud as any metropolitan dwelling, yet mentally the valley could be as compact as a West Virginian, out of time and date KKK town. I honestly could not understand or sometimes even want to know how we could actually stand up for the National Anthem and say we were proud to be residents. (pp. 70–1)

In the face of this despair, Rebecca, the first-person narrator of Trezise's novel, resorts to self-mutilation and silence. She comes to distrust language and to realize that whatever utterance she makes, she will not be believed. Language and the silencing of language is also a concern in a number of other novels, but for different reasons. The Welsh language often figures in many of these novels, if only as an absence or a loss of which characters are aware: Ianto, in *Sheepshagger*, for example, can speak only a few words of his native tongue, and this is figured as an element of his comprehensive dispossession. Most of the characters, though, have English as their native tongue and most of these novels try to give an accurate representation of actual speech. This entails both the rendition of dialect – strongly present in Griffiths's *Grits* (2001), where the ragtag group of characters speak in different dialects – and the representation of the casual obscenities which are like the punctuation of normal speech for many of these characters. The use of 'fuck' and its variants is particularly pronounced in the work of Griffiths who, like the Scottish writers James Kelman and Irvine Welsh, does not flinch from rendering the actual repetitive speech of his often inarticulate characters. It is noticeable that the decent *gwerin* of Lewis Davies and the older generation of characters of Richard Evans hardly swear at all. Because of its sheer volume, the swearing actually becomes purged of meaning and force, settling into being a mere marker of a common patois. Strangely, it might be seen as a badge of belonging – these people at least speak the same, self-chosen language, despite their diverse, painful origins. Often, these writers take pains to render Welsh dialects accurately, as in this snatch of conversation in the queue in the dole office at the opening of Evans's *Entertainment*:

> 'Tell you who I saw the other day – Ken.'
> 'Ken?'
> 'Ken Bins.'
> 'Oh aye.'
> 'He's gone to look old.'
> 'Lost a lot of weight.'
> 'Been ill, haven't he?'
> 'Oh hell, yeah. Death's door, like.'
> 'Pity. Got a lot of time for old Ken.'
> 'Bit of a wanker to his missus.'
> 'Ken? Yeah, bit of a wanker.'
> 'Smashing bloke, though.'
> 'Ken's all right.' (p. 8)

Not all the novels in this literary movement are as unremittingly grim as those of Evans, Trezise or Griffiths, however. *Aberystwyth Mon Amour* (2002) by Malcolm Pryce is a witty noir pastiche, set in probably the most unlikely location in the British Isles for a Raymond Chandleresque evocation of mean streets: Aberystwyth. It consistently and amusingly mocks Welsh traditions and notions of national identity and the fatherland. The local mafia consists of the Druids, who are a Freemason-like patriarchal organization made up of pillars of the Welsh community, and who are actually very nasty pieces of work. In fact, the authority figures – especially teachers – are singularly sadistic individuals, whereas the inhabitants of the demi-monde, including prostitutes and the private eye central character, form a community of mutual aid. The novel is consistently anti-religious, equating the chapel with the Druidic authorities. The private eye is more than willing to break the law and live a 'free' life outside its constraints – going to hide out in a caravan on Borth beach at one point. The novel is also very anti-war, undermining the way in which history is written by the victors in order to camouflage the sordid truth. In the novel a group of ex-soldiers live a tramp-like existence on the fringes of society (Borth beach, again) because they know the truth and they are unable to accept the lies of organized society any longer. The setting and plot are deliberately surreal, although Aberystwyth and its environs are accurately named and the topography is quite recognizable; underneath the outrageous burlesque, though, there does appear to be some serious political satire.

Another novel in this group which depends a great deal on humour is *White Powder, Green Light* (2002) by James Hawes, which is much more centred on middle-class life – in fact, the novel's version of the working class is pure caricature. Jane, the protagonist, is a university lecturer and a good middle-class girl, though she insists that she's 'not posh'. Much of the novel's comedy centres on the language – Jane's attitude to Welsh is initially quite arrogant and there is recurrent humour at the expense of the small number of people who actually speak Welsh; however, the plot as a whole traces a conversion experience for Jane, who eventually returns 'home' to Wales and begins to learn Welsh. Much of the satire is at the expense of London media types who live on cocaine and are completely artificial and affected. There is an act of anarchic subversion in the sub-plot, involving Skanky, who is homeless and pathetic but fancies himself as an eco-warrior – he blows up Soho from the cellars of McDonalds. But this seems to be unreal – no one appears to die – all the 'baddies' escape with blackened faces and carry on with their wheeling and dealing. It is like an explosion in a cartoon or a silent movie. The group of media types who hang around Groucho's and Soho House constitute the Crowd and are a parody of a counter-cultural group. Skanky is the only counter-cultural character, though Jane's final retreat to live in the wholly Welsh-speaking rural village of 'Tal-y-ban' (!) might be seen as a counter-cultural gesture. There is also satire at the expense of Welsh TV, which is run by a kind of mafia of Dai Hughes-Joneses and Aled Morris-Thomases, not unreminiscent of the Druids in Pryce's *Aberystwyth Mon Amour*. The annual Cymru-Wales Oscwr cere-mony is a source of humour, since there is usually only one nomination in each category and the viewing figures are miniscule. The Crowd in London are contemptuous but think a trip there might be mildly amusing: 'We can all come down and see them *being Welsh*.'[19] Jane's *Guardian*-reading friends in 'Muswell End' are horrified to learn that Jane's son, Bryn, goes to a Welsh-medium school: ' "He actually has to *speak Welsh*? My God, that's *ridiculous*," said her friend, who in earlier years had spent much time on Troops Out marches' (p. 194). Hawes has a deft hand at burlesquing the unconsciously imperialist assumptions of the English. But he also mocks the officialdom of the newly devolved Wales: '[they] hastily joined in the new Official Welsh National Toast, which the Welsh Assembly had recently declared was to be used on all formal and semi-formal occasions, by all official, quasi-official, or merely positively-inclined Bodies: – There we are then. – There we are then' (p. 116). There is a humorous episode during the Cymru-Wales Oscwr ceremony when the misanthropic Hugh Pritchard, Head of Public Relations at BBC Wales (English Language Section), tries to explain the identity of J. P. R. Williams (a prominent Welsh rugby player in the 1970s) to the Serbian delegate:

> – Jaypeeah? [she queries]
> – Oh, one of our old warlords, lovely, ha ha! Drink up then.
> – He defeated the enemies of your nation?
> – Aye, love, J.P.R. By Christ you should have seen him, tearing the English apart, year after wonderful year. He skinned their wingers every time.
> – Skinned their wingers? she asked, doubtfully. (Even to a strong girl from the Balkans, actually flaying enemy airmen seemed a little excessive.)
> – Aye. Tied them up in knots, turned them inside out and skinned the sods alive.
> – Alive?
> – Buggered them sideways. Great days, great days.
> – I see. He is dead now, this Jaypeeah?
> – No, he's a doctor.
> – Ah, she nodded. – Like our Dr Karadjic. (p. 54)

Despite the anarchic view of contemporary Wales evoked in these texts and notwithstanding the proto-anarchist sentiments and behaviour of many of their characters, these are, on the whole, not novels propounding a fully developed political ideology. Unlike Lewis Jones's *Cwmardy* (1937) or the brilliant and still underrated Welsh-language novel *Y Pla* (1987) by Wil Owen Roberts, which both persuasively propound fully fledged Marxist visions of Welsh society and history, albeit in completely different ways, the contemporary texts analysed here provide no solutions. Instead, in true 'post-everything' style, they anatomize the ravaged body of contemporary Wales and expose its sores for our contemplation . . . and instruction?

NOTES

[1]   Richard Savage, *The Anarchist* (1894), quoted in Haia Shpayer-Makov, 'A Traitor to his Class: The Anarchist in British Fiction', *Journal of European Studies*, 26 (1996), 299–325 (309).

[2]   Sharif Gemie, 'Anarchism and Feminism: A Historical Survey', *Women's History Review*, 5 (1996), 417–44 (421).

[3]   Max Nettlau, *A Short History of Anarchism*, ed. by H. M. Becker, trans. by Ida Pilat Isca (London, 1996).

[4]   Quoted in Karen Rosenberg, 'Hoisting the Black Flag: Review of *Anarchy! An Anthology of Emma Goldman's Mother Earth*', *Nation*, 274 (2002), 30–3 (32).

[5]   John Williams, 'Vulcanised, the new wave of Welsh fiction', *http://www.bloomsbury.com/Ezine/Articles*, p. 1.

[6]   Jon Gower, ' "Ianto's Story" – Interview with Niall Griffiths', *New Welsh Review*, 52 (2001), 12–13 (12).

[7]   John Williams, *Cardiff Dead* (London, 2001), pp. 56–7.

[8]   Niall Griffiths, *Sheepshagger* (London, 2002), pp. 116–17.

[9]   Gower, 'Ianto's Story', 13.

[10] Christopher White, ' "Don't Imagine Ethiopia": Fiction and Poetics in Contemporary Scotland', in *Nationals and Relations: Writing Across the British Isles* (Cardiff, 2000), pp. 56–70.

[11] Christopher Meredith, ' "The Dance of Misunderstanding" – Interview with Richard John Evans', *New Welsh Review*, 52 (2001), 7–10 (9).

[12] Raymond Williams, *The Welsh Industrial Novel* (Cardiff, 1979), p. 11.

[13] Gower, 'Ianto's Story', 13.

[14] Richard John Evans, *Entertainment* (Bridgend, 2000), p. 141. Further references will be inserted in the text.

[15] Meredith, ' "The Dance of Misunderstanding" ', 7.

[16] Quoted in Tony Bianchi, 'Maps and Travellers', *Planet*, 160 (2003), 66–74 (66).

[17] See Meredith, ' "The Dance of Misunderstanding" ', 8.

[18] Rachel Trezise, *In and Out of the Goldfish Bowl* (Cardiff, 2000), pp. 57–62. Further references will be inserted in the text.

[19] James Hawes, *White Powder, Green Light* (London, 2002), p. 210. Further references will be inserted in the text.

14

Lifestyle Anarchism and its Discontents: Mark Ravenhill, Enda Walsh and the Politics of Contemporary Drama

1.

British theatre in the 1990s was a highly contentious field, which provokes radically divergent public reactions and equally divergent critical responses. 'In the present decade', writes Ulrich Broich in 1998, 'hardly any new major play by a British author has been produced.' Broich underlines the widespread conviction that the theatre declined in the 1980s and that the decline, not accidentally, coincided with the Thatcher administration, but that its further decline in the 1990s can no longer be attributed to the Conservative government and to cuts in funding. Somehow, 'the creative energy, the innovative vitality of British theatre' have vanished.[1] Aleks Sierz, on the other hand, describes the same decade as 'the most exciting for new writing since the heady days sparked off by John Osborne's *Look Back in Anger* in 1956'.[2] With provocative writers such as Sarah Kane and Mark Ravenhill in the lead, 'shockingly radical in form and deeply unsettling in content', Cool Britannia's theatre 'had rediscovered the angry, oppositional and questioning spirit of 1956'.[3] While one critic laments the absence of innovative plays which might put an end to the ongoing crisis of post-1980s drama and theatre, the other celebrates the abundance of gifted authors and considers their polarizing plays to be on a par with those of the Angry Young Men. 'It was in-yer-face writers that saved British theatre.'[4]

Labelling one dominant strand of British theatre in the 1990s as 'in-yer-face', Sierz stresses provocation, aggression and confrontation as its dominant features. Although I go along with his positive outlook on the astonishing revival of British drama in the 1990s, a shift of perspective is necessary in order to get the plays' politics in view. If Sierz talks about politics at all, he is concerned either with a critique of identity politics, in the form of a postmodern questioning of some of society's most fundamental binary oppositions, or with the continuing value of modernism's shock of the new as a political agenda.[5] In opposition to that, I believe that the strength, vitality and attractive directness of some of the period's major successes of dramatic writing are due to their implicit critique not of identity politics but of some trendy versions of postmodernism, claiming the apparent dissolution of identity politics. This dissolution and the 'lifestyle anarchism'[6] which accompanies it are on the agenda of contemporary playwrights such as Mark Ravenhill, Sarah Kane, Patrick Marber, Irvine Welsh (or, rather, Harry Gibson adapting Welsh for the stage) and Cork-based Enda Walsh, to name but a few. On the following pages, I am first going to sketch out the criticism of postmodernism and lifestyle anarchism launched by Murray Bookchin and Fredric Jameson. Against this background, the political edge of contemporary drama – I have chosen Mark Ravenhill's *Shopping and Fucking* and *Some Explicit Polaroids* and Enda Walsh's *Disco Pigs* as examples – may be demonstrated.

In his 1995 pamphlet-like treatise, *Social Anarchism or Lifestyle Anarchism*, Murray Bookchin, trade-union activist, theorist and left libertarian, juxtaposes two contemporary expressions of anarchism: social anarchism and lifestyle anarchism. The main difference lies in social anarchism's prioritization of the social over the individual, which lifestyle anarchism rejects. With reference to anarchist thinkers such as Kropotkin and Bakunin, he draws the picture of an engaged anarchism as a political concept. Kropotkin's notion of anarchism as the 'left wing of all socialisms' and Bakunin's claim that 'the individual, his freedom and reason, are the products of society, and not vice versa' are the cornerstones of social anarchism.[7] At the heart of this version of anarchism lies the demand for a social revolution or, at least, a social revolutionary outlook, without which the freedom of the individual cannot possibly be achieved.

Competing with these collectivist views, there is an equally long tradition of individualistic anarchism, which shifts the emphasis from the utopia of a free society towards the utopia of the individual's autonomy. Bookchin claims that individualist anarchism strives for the autonomy of the presumably self-sovereign individual, while social anarchism's idea of freedom 'dialectically interweaves the individual with the collective'.[8] He sees an unbridgeable gap between the concept of autonomy of a Max Stirner, a Benjamin Tucker or a Margaret Anderson, on the one hand, and the collective freedom which revolutionary social anarchism fights for, on the other.

The fact that two anarchisms exist parallel to each other with completely different political outlooks (if one can speak of a political outlook at all regarding individualist anarchism) is a phenomenon intrinsic to anarchist thought. It is due to the fact that anarchism is an ideological blend or 'creative synthesis of two great currents of thought',[9] liberalism with a strong emphasis on individual autonomy and socialism with an equally strong emphasis on the collective. In this sense, David Goodway speaks of the protean nature of anarchism and views it 'as combining a socialist critique of capitalism with a liberal critique of socialism, a laissez faire liberal rejection of the state, both as status quo and as a vehicle for social change, with a socialist insistence upon human solidarity and communitarianism'.[10] Those anarchists who stress the liberty of choice and the liberty to do what one likes at the cost of social commitment have today, according to Bookchin, gained the upper hand to a point where 'the revolutionary and social goals of anarchism are suffering far-reaching erosion'. He fears that 'the word anarchy will become part of the chic bourgeois vocabulary of the coming century'.[11]

In addition to the much-quoted Friedrich Nietzsche of 'On Truth and Lie in an Extra-Moral Sense', Bookchin characterizes early individualist anarchists like William Godwin ('There is but one power to which I can yield a heartfelt obedience, the decision of my own understanding, the dictates of my own conscience'[12]) and Max Stirner as the forerunners of postmodern thinkers who promote the idea and the ideal of individualistic self-fashioning. Stirner's exclamation about truth and the individual – 'truth cannot step forward as you do, cannot move, change, develop; truth awaits and recruits everything from you, and itself is only through you; for it exists only in your head'[13] – is carried to its logical conclusion by Nietzsche, who describes the facticity and reality of truth to be a mere rhetorical trick: 'What, then, is truth? A mobile army of metaphors, metonyms, and anthropomorphisms – in short, a sum of human relations, which have been enhanced, transposed and embellished poetically and rhetorically.'[14] Bookchin considers these ideologemes to have laid the intellectual basis for the unholy alliance of individualistic anarchism and capitalist economy which makes up the episteme – to use the term of one of his dearest enemies – of contemporary culture and society. Thus he identifies integral elements of postmodernism, both in literature and in culture generally, with what he calls lifestyle anarchism, which today finds its principal expression in 'spray-can graffiti, postmodernist nihilism, antirationalism, neoprimitivism, antitechnologism, neo-Situationist *cultural terrorism*, mysticism, and a *practice* of staging Foucauldian *personal insurrections'*.[15] Bookchin labels as lifestyle anarchism everything he associates with the contemporary erosion of social anarchist thought and action; apart from the aforementioned, he particularly lays blame on the postmodern repudiation of grand narratives, Foucault's concept of power, anti-essentialism with its negative consequences for identity politics, the repudiation of Truth, the replacement of authenticity with various levels of representation and, as a result, the notion that freedom could be achieved on a personal rather than on a social level. All this adds up to the nihilistic asociality of postmodernism.

For self-styled postmodernists, or lifestyle anarchists, the achievement of individual freedom is no longer bound up with social change or even a revolution. Instead, it is relegated to an assumedly independent and private realm of culture and aesthetics. Bookchin recognizes that the co-opting of anarchism by culture, lifestyle anarchism, 'poses a real threat to the survival of anarchism as a social strategy'.[16] His argument is related to Fredric Jameson's famous dictum about postmodernism as the cultural logic of late capitalism.[17] Jameson describes aesthetic production today as integrated into commodity production generally. He highlights the tendency towards fragmentation in artistic styles and professional jargons, on the one hand, and in politics, on the other. The result of the one is an 'increasing linguistic fragmentation of social life itself', the result of the other the problem of micropolitics.[18] Cultural artefacts have turned into consumer goods and even subcultural movements and styles are being soaked up, their critical force rendered impotent by the mechanisms of the capitalist market economy as soon as they appear. While an earlier critical theory still insisted upon the semi-autonomy of the cultural realm, asserting the potential of cultural artefacts to mirror the world in such a way that not only flattering resemblances but also critical satires or utopian angst may be produced, the decisive change promoted by late capitalist postmodernism consists in the destruction of that semi-autonomy. The most devastating consequence of the commodification of culture is the loss of critical distance, without which no subversive, challenging or even negative stance can be taken.

Bookchin's lifestyle anarchists and Jameson's postmodernists fail to realize that individual and cultural autonomy are mystifying bourgeois deceptions, which are being subjected to the laws of the market-place. The well-known commodification of culture in late capitalist society thus results, for both Bookchin and Jameson, in an anti-political ideology of bourgeois anarchism 'that sets aesthetic satisfaction ahead of social reformation'.[19] However, Bookchin's angry condemnation of postmodernism in all its facets is far too general to be intellectually sound. He does not engage in a discussion about the merits of postmodern scepticism and the serious attempts at finding new ground for political action without adhering to the (often plausibly criticized) identity politics of a former era. Neither does he acknowledge the progressive impulses which the critical reception of Foucault or Derrida have triggered in the humanities. Nevertheless, the combination of Jameson and Bookchin – the first focusing primarily on the connections between late capitalism and postmodernism as a cultural condition, the second highlighting the fundamental opposition between a politically relevant social anarchism and a personalistic lifestyle anarchism – may lead one to approach contemporary culture and society with a fresh set of questions and ideas. Is there a way between the Scylla of lamenting the loss of traditional forms of social and political thought and action and the Charybdis of the arbitrariness of a fragmented micropolitics, which loses sight of the whole? What are the remaining possibilities of a critical cultural politics today? And where could its place be?

I suggest that the stage is a promising place to look for a critical cultural politics today. Here one can detect the attempt at a redefinition of a place or space from which a critique especially of the ideology of monadic self-realization, what Bookchin calls lifestyle anarchism, and its connection with capitalism may be launched. I suggest that contemporary playwrights, Mark Ravenhill from England and Enda Walsh from Ireland (together with several others not mentioned for lack of space), have started to map out a new terrain for a political theatrical practice that is at odds with neither postmodern individualism nor older forms of social commitment.

2.

Mark Ravenhill's debut as a playwright, *Shopping and Fucking* (1996), provoked a scandal, mainly for its title, but it turned out to be one of the Royal Court Theatre's most successful plays of the 1990s.[20] Right from the start, his reputation as a shock writer has stood in the way of appreciating the profound morality and social vision displayed in his representations of contemporary society. If an earlier generation had developed the 'state-of-the-nation' play – often epic in scope, spanning decades – to criticize the politics of their time, it is consumerism and its effects on the individual which are on the agenda in Ravenhill's plays. 'He is concerned to trace what happened when we turned from a nation of shopkeepers to a nation of shoppers.'[21] Ravenhill is less concerned with the superficialities of the will to consume than with the deep impact on the individual of a world in which even love relationships are just one more consumer good. Mark in *Shopping and Fucking* considers relationships with other people as dangerous and enjoys sex only when he has paid for it. The very idea of the social is no longer available to the monads who people Ravenhill's plays, isolated characters who do not realize that their credo – 'we're not letting the world get to us' (Tim in *Some Explicit Polaroids*, p. 273) – is turned into self-mockery every time they shop.

When Robbie in *Shopping and Fucking* is questioned about what he thinks lies behind all that is good in the world, he comes up, rather surprisingly, with 'a father' but is corrected by Brian, the drug dealer, until he gives the proper answer: 'Money' (p. 48). The desperate and unspecified longing for origins, for connections and a place in the world suddenly shines through, but is immediately countered by the apparent facticity of the real, which bows to one God only: money. (In the final scene, Brian teaches Robbie that money is civilization and vice versa: 'The getting is cruel, is hard, but the having is civilization' (p. 87).) A dialogue summarizing well-known commonplaces about the postmodern condition again evokes the world we have lost and again ends with the disillusionment of the omnipresence of market relations:

> ROBBIE: A long time ago there were big stories. Stories so big you could live your whole life in them. The Powerful Hands of the Gods and Fate. The Journey to Enlightenment. The March of Socialism. But they all died, or the world grew up or grew senile or forgot them, so now we're all making up our own stories. Little stories. It comes out in different ways. But we've each got one . . . It's lonely. I understand. But you're not alone. I could help. I'm offering to help . . .
> GARY: A helping hand. What do you wanna do that for?
> ROBBIE: For a fee . . . Pay me and you'll get what you want . . . It's got to be cash. (p. 66)

Ravenhill stages postmodern issues without either praising or condemning them. For the characters in his plays, postmodernism is not an option which they may take or leave at will but the status quo of a post-Thatcherite world, in which individuals are turned into Stirnerite unique beings, whether they want to or not. Ravenhill manages to represent the fragmentations of contemporary society without losing sight of the whole. The postmodern privatization of public knowledge'[22] and its turn towards 'little stories' are not praised as the golden path to avoiding the totalizing effects of grand narratives, but exposed as the ideology of an unfettered global capitalism which makes resistance impossible.

With *Some Explicit Polaroids*, first performed in September 1999, Ravenhill's set of plays about globalization, consumerism and the lifestyle anarchism of the 1990s, almost a tetralogy including *Shopping and Fucking, Faust is Dead* and *Handbag*, comes full circle. The play is set in contemporary London and focuses on the differences between people's attitudes and values twenty years ago and today, especially with respect to political radicalism and the long-term changes initiated by Thatcherism. It is vaguely based on Ernst Toller's *Hoppla, wir leben* (1927), which tells the story of Karl Thomas, who returns home after eight years in a mental hospital following his participation in the 1919 revolutionary uprising. Just like Thomas, who does not come to grips with the conformist attitudes of his former fellow revolutionaries, Nick, in *Some Explicit Polaroids*, is at a loss to understand the world around him, after fifteen years in prison for attempted murder of a capitalist entrepreneur. When he calls on Helen, a former friend who has turned into a New Labour councillor, she does not want to be confronted with their radical pasts, with the fact that she once suggested to Nick that a 'class traitor', a concept which no longer exists, should be killed. At the point when Helen has to leave for a meeting they start to quarrel about politics, and this soon develops into a discussion about their respective world-views. When asked what the meeting is about, Helen explains that she is involved in the planning of timetables for the buses. Nick immediately mocks the pettiness of it and asks what has become of the 'big targets: Why are there shitty estates? Why are they there in the first place? / HELEN: Oh yes. Come the revolution, down they come. But while we're waiting . . . / NICK: Let's fiddle with the fucking bus timetables. So fucking petty' (p. 238).

Ironically it is the enforced fifteen-year absence from society which has made it possible for Nick to stick to the ideals in the name of which he committed the crime. Imprisonment, assumedly imposed on people to make them think differently about what they did, achieved exactly the opposite. Helen, on the other hand, experienced Thatcherism at its worst. She exclaims that 'prison must have been fucking heaven compared to what it's been like out here'. In order to explain to Nick and herself how she changed from holding radical political convictions to rearranging bus-timetables and competing for a seat in the House of Commons she points out:

> Stuff we've seen. Communities disappear. Greed and fear everywhere. Start of with a society and end up with individuals fighting it out . . . Everything gone. Not all at once. Not some great explosion. Not one day you can see what's happening and fight back. Long dull pain. Every now and then thinking: 'How did we get from there to here? How did we let this happen? It can't get any worse.' But it does. On and on . . . And you do start to make concessions . . . You can't be fighting all the time. You get so fucking weary of always being angry . . .

And now finally there's the chance to do something. Too late for something big. Too much lost for any grand gestures. But trying to pick up the pieces. (pp. 280–1)

Helen explains her own development as a continual self-mutilation. She claims not to have anything in common with Nick any more, as she has 'cut bits out of myself. Bit by bit, another belief, another dream. I've cut them all out. I'm changed. I've grown up. I'm scarred' (pp. 281–2). This is the first clash in the play of two different world-views, one that radically calls into question the conditions of capitalist society as such, but from the social seclusion of the prison cell, and another one that has arranged itself with the once-despised system, at least to an extent which makes life within society bearable. In the course of the play, both characters realize that they will not be satisfied with their positions in the long run.

Even though Helen has altered her convictions, she is still able to acknow-ledge Nick's thoughts and feelings. Scene 3 stages a meeting of Nick and Nadia. They lack any common ground in their approaches to life. She celebrates the individualist philosophy that 'we all have our own journeys that we're travelling' (p. 238). She is caught in a disastrous relationship with Simon, who beats her up frequently, but when Nick encourages her to fight back – 'Men. You can't let them . . . you've got to make a stand' – she responds by 'thinking positive' and by asking Nick not to generalize (p. 253). Her refusal to judge a particular situation in the light of a larger context makes it impos-sible for her to make a stand. Generalizations don't mean anything for her. Making a stand is a form of self-assertion, and generalizations are a necessary part of it.

Nick soon realizes that he is a dinosaur in 'happy world' (p. 268). Locked away since 1984, the year of the disastrous miners' strike, he is unable to find his way along any more. Some crucial change in the self-understanding of the individual in society seems to have happened during his absence, some deep-cutting paradigm shift which prevents Nick from understanding both his old mates and the younger generation. Confronted with people who refuse to draw any connections between their own situations and larger social issues, Nick is at a loss, even though he tries to adapt. He is an inhabitant of a world, the truths, values and commonplaces of which have evaporated. His world is 'very nineteen eighty-four' (p. 269), as Tim condescendingly teaches him.

What Tim, on the other hand, fails to understand, in the eyes of Nick, is the very situation he (Tim) finds himself in, the material conditions of his own existence. This is partly a result of his being wrapped up in the ideology of lifestyle anarchism, partly due to a redefinition of the term *responsibility*. This term which used to stand for the obligations the individual owes towards her/his surroundings is redefined in strictly personal terms. It is now placed in a coordinate system of what one may call a late capitalist existentialism. Nick, on the other hand, is taught by the rest (apart from Helen) that the issues he considered worth fighting for before 1984, and still does today, have lost their urgency, not in reality, of course, but for the individual, as if these were different realms.

Even in personal relationships, post-1984 people try to avoid getting affected. The isolation of the individual and the sense of external untouchability is bought at a high price, namely the impossibility of authentic ideals, feelings or even love. For Victor and Tim, happiness is defined by the avoidance of seriousness and responsibility on all levels, particularly in human relationships. Their own relation is based on cash – Victor is Tim's Russian sex-slave – and the fact that Victor acts out a fixed role. 'You take this seriously, you're out' (p. 283) is Tim's threat when he senses that Victor is no longer merely interested in money but develops feelings for him as a human being. In the course of the play, Nadia and Victor both realize that the freedom, independence and liberty they thought they enjoyed was in fact monadic isolation, that the happiness at which they aimed was nothing but meaninglessness:

> NADIA: Everything is terrible. Nothing means anything. There's nobody out there. I'm alone in the universe. (p. 282)
>
> . . .
>
> VICTOR: I wish we knew what to do. I think maybe inside us, if we were allowed to have feelings we would know what to do. (p. 294)

The play ends with Tim dead, Victor planning to go to Japan to make a lot of money and Helen and Nick reunited, after Nick has had a conversation with his victim, Jonathan, of more than fifteen years ago. Jonathan is the perfect example of a successful new economist, believing in the dynamics and the ultimately redemptive functioning of the free market's invisible hand. Nick, on the other hand, feels empty and tired, with all his ideals questioned and ultimately meaningless in this brave new world. His confrontations with three different lifestyles and world-views – the radical turned bourgeois (Helen), the lifestyle anarchist (Nadia, Victor, Tim) and the anarchic capitalist (Jonathan) – have left him confused and disoriented. He has lost the belief in the big targets, and now Helen feels like having to rekindle political ideals and radicalism in Nick.

Ravenhill's plays do not present any clear answers, nor do they have a message, in the usual sense of the word. Nevertheless, they seriously attempt to represent the current state of moral and political confusion, which is the result of the evaporation of one set of values without the advent of new ones. Lifestyle anarchism is practised by several of the play's characters, but in the end Nadia experiences her 'own path' simply as threatening isolation, while Victor longs for feelings. Both have the sense that something is missing, only they are not at all able to name what it could be. *Shopping and Fucking* and *Some Explicit Polaroids* not only represent and ironize the pitfalls of a globalized postmodern world, but offer the vision of an alternative or, rather, the surviving will to believe in alternatives. Even though reality has lost the status of objectivity and is now not more than the sum total of some explicit Polaroids, which do not add up to a larger picture, the absence of that larger picture is experienced as loss. It is music which, for Brian in *Shopping and Fucking*, represents the unrepresentable: 'You feel it – like something you knew. Something so beautiful that you've lost but you'd forgotten that you've lost it. Then you hear this . . . Hear this and know what you've . . . l-l-l-ooost' (p. 45).

3.

In several of his plays, Enda Walsh adopts a different perspective to describe a similar problematics. It is one major issue in his work to call into question the possibility of dialogue on stage and in contemporary society. Thus the two protagonists of *Disco Pigs* (1996) create their own language to 'make a whirl dat no one can live sept us two', while the hero of *misterman* (2001) talks to himself most of the time, inventing and recalling dialogues which no longer take (or never took) place.[23] Articulation, etymologically the action or process of jointing, of bridging gaps, of bringing into contact, is here shown to serve opposite ends.

Walsh depicts a society where social exchange is present only as remembrance or utopian hope, a society where language produces monadic individuals in confrontation with (non-existing) communities, against which they define themselves.

Pig and Runt, the disco pigs, are two seventeen-year-old inhabitants of Pork Sitty (Cork City) who have almost completely isolated themselves from the rest of society by highly asocial behaviour and by speaking an artificial language, which only the two of them fully understand. Always together, and always on the look-out for alcohol and the next victim, their relationship has grown more and more hermetic as the number of mutually committed crimes increases. This set-up does not allow for social criticism on the part of the characters, criticism of a society which turns human beings into monads. Quite the opposite: Pig and Runt are radicals not due to oppositional attitudes but by pushing to an extreme the mechanisms of isolation at work in the modern world. Enda Walsh demonstrates how the communicative character of language may turn into its opposite and serve only to increase the sense of isolation.

The play starts with the birth of Darren and Sinead, who simultaneously 'bounce inta a whirl of grey happiness'. One day, playing animals on a farm, they turn themselves into Pig and Runt, and from that moment they act out their self-chosen roles as outcasts. Most of the action takes place on their seventeenth birthday. They do what they always do, drift from one night-club to the next, get drunk and play their favourite game: Runt chats up somebody only to pretend to be molested by him, Pig interferes and beats up the apparent intruder. Later on, as a birthday present, Pig takes Runt to the sea, 'da big blue, da colour of love'. Runt experiences the beauty of nature for the first time and is so overwhelmed that, probably for the first time as well, she has doubts about her existence. 'I wanna walk inta da sea an neva come back. I wan ta tide to take me outa me an give me someone differen' (p. 17).

Later the same night, they come across the Palace Disco, a posh and expensive night-club. Once inside, they are overwhelmed by the shiny chrome and the number of well-dressed people. Runt dreams of a peaceful encounter with another man, but when it actually happens, Pig is convinced that Runt is staging another violent game for him. She desperately tries to keep him back, but in the end the other guy is dead. This initiates Runt's flight.

> An Runt race good dis time! Mus ged away! No mo all dis play an pain! . . . An it well ovur, drama fans! Jus me! Jus da liddle girl all aloneys! An I wan Pig an I wan for all da buzz an all da disco we do dance but hey ho an wadda ya know I wan fur sumthin else! Sumthin differen! Sumthin differen! Fuckin freedom!! Jus me!! Jus da Runt!! . . . Jus me an da big big colour blue. Dat colour blue! . . . An I look a da sun crep up on my pal Pork . . . Cork . . . An Runt she alone now. But is okay now, is all righ. An I watch . . . da liddle quack quacks . . . I look . . . at the ducks . . . as they swim in the morning sun . . . in the great big . . . watery-shite . . . that is the river Lee. – Where to? (p. 29)

Runt struggles free of the cocoon-like relationship with Pig, turns into Sinead again. Her attempts at socializing have led, at first glance, to an even more complete isolation, but the recovery of an understandable English marks a step towards reintegration, or at least the realization that the 'sumthin differen' she longs for is to be found only if the basic prerequisite for social inter-course, a common language, is re-established.

While in Ravenhill's second play the differences between competing world-views and politics are explicitly put on the agenda, the two disco pigs have no contrasting 1984 counterpart at their sides. They are born into con-ditions in which, literally right from the start, that is right from their birth, defining themselves as social beings is no option. Society does not seem to exist at all except as a negative foil, as a fateful conglomeration of equally unconnected others. Thus, even traditional political activism can be interpreted only in these parameters, which happens when Pig, confronted with Sinn Fein activists in a pub, asks the 'fookin weirdos' whether they 'shouldn't be out plantin bombs an beaten up ol ladies' (p. 22). For Pig and Runt, the com-bination of the ideologies of happiness and wilful anarchic isolation indeed ends in nihilistic asociality. The autonomy they seemingly enjoyed was based on the rejection of the very idea of the social, while the 'fuckin free-dom' Runt longs for in the end can be realized only in society. 'Where to?', Sinead's final question in the play, is a signifier not only of desperate lack of orientation but also of the urge to start the search for 'sumethin differen'.

4.

Both Fredric Jameson and Murray Bookchin, in their analyses of postmod-ernism, stress the loss of the possibility of critical distance, without which no subversive, critical or even negative stance can be taken. Jameson speaks of the discursive heterogeneity without a norm in advanced capitalist societies; of the faceless masters who continue to inflect the economic strategies which constrain our existences; and of the absence of any great collective project and the unavailability of the older national language itself. The plays which I have presented pick up the issues which theorists and activists like Jameson and Bookchin raise. The brutal realism with which Ravenhill and Walsh set to work can be interpreted as an expression of unease and anger, a search for a critical stance which, at the moment, is very unsure about its direction. What these plays show is that contemporary drama does not cele-brate lifestyle anarchism, even though it often stages it. Quite the opposite: never mind the absence of didacticism, it stresses the disastrous con-sequences both for the individual and for society if the ideology of lifestyle anarchism is put into practice.

Bookchin is surely right in claiming that certain forms of postmodern relativism are pitted against the principle of hope (to use Ernst Bloch's phrase) that marked the radical theory of the recent past. I am far from arguing that we are on the verge of a new radicalism, launched by the staging of a few plays; not only the relative marginality of the medium of theatre, as compared to other media, speaks against it. Emma Goldman was exaggerating, in the early days of the twentieth century, when she claimed that 'drama is the vehicle which is really making history, disseminating radical thoughts in ranks not otherwise to be reached'.[24] Now, in the early days of the twenty-first, when great social truths are no longer readily available, it would be absurd to argue thus. Nevertheless, a utopian, even a romantic, element in contemporary drama aims at a re-politicization of the stage. Although the recovery of utopian concepts is performed negatively, it is performed. That means that we are confronted with an absence, a feeling of loss, rather than anything positive to strive for. It is no longer the romanticism of Shelley's 'unacknowledged legislators of the world' or of Saint-Simon's men of the imagination who will open the march. But even if contemporary poets and playwrights are not in the position to create positive utopias and provide visions of Eden, 'where to?' is at least an urgent question that calls for an answer. 'Trying to pick up the pieces', as Helen says in Ravenhill's play, might be more than nothing. The new drama succeeds not only in attracting large numbers of young people, people of an age group which would not have set foot in a theatre fifteen years ago. More importantly, it succeeds in reminding the public that once there was a principle of hope, that once there was a utopian vision, where today there is only the unnameable big, big blue. In this sense, it is worth considering the stage as one site which contributes to the recovery of a critical cultural politics today.

NOTES

[1] Ulrich Broich, 'British Drama in the 1990s and David Hare's *Skylight*', in Jürgen Kamm (ed.), *Twentieth-Century Theatre and Drama in English* (Trier, 1999), pp. 213–23 (p. 216). D. Keith Peacock shares Broich's pessimism but, on the other hand, argues that the development of British theatre in the 1990s, especially its 'increasing isolation from the social and political life of Britain', is still a consequence of the successful 'cultural shift initiated by Thatcherism'; *Thatcher's Theatre: British Theatre and Drama in the Eighties* (Westport and London, 1999), p. 217.

[2] Aleks Sierz, *In-Yer-Face Theatre: British Drama Today* (London, 2000), p. xi.

[3] Ibid., p. xii. Broich also notes the will to provoke, but even with regard to form, an apparently objective category, the gap between him and Sierz could not be wider. Broich describes the same authors' works as 'more or less conservative

in form, written for quick and easy consumption' (p. 315) – the exact opposite of Sierz's acclamatory judgement.

4   Sierz, *In-Yer-Face Theatre*, p. xii.

5   Ibid., p. 9.

6   Murray Bookchin, *Social Anarchism or Lifestyle Anarchism: An Unbridgeable Chasm* (Edinburgh and San Francisco, 1995).

7   Quotes in Bookchin, *Social Anarchism*, p. 6.

8   Ibid., p. 12.

9   Peter Marshall, *Demanding the Impossible: A History of Anarchism* (New York, 1992), p. 639.

10   David Goodway (ed.), *For Anarchism: History, Theory, and Practice* (London and New York, 1989), p. 1.

11   Bookchin, *Social Anarchism*, p. 3.

12   William Godwin, in Bookchin, *Social Anarchism*, p. 5.

13   Max Stirner, *The Ego and His Own*, vol. 2, ed. by James J. Martin (New York, 1963), p. 352.

14   Friedrich Nietzsche, 'On Truth and Lie in an Extra-Moral Sense' (1873), in *The Portable Nietzsche*, ed. by Walter Kaufmann (New York, 1959), pp. 46–7.

15   Bookchin, *Social Anarchism*, p. 19.

16   David Weir, *Anarchy and Culture: The Aesthetic Politics of Modernism* (Amherst, 1997), p. 262.

17   Fredric Jameson, 'Postmodernism, or The Cultural Logic of Late Capitalism', in *New Left Review*, 146 (1984), 53–92.

18   Ibid., 65.

19   Weir, *Anarchy and Culture*, p. 262.

20   Mark Ravenhill, *Plays 1* (London, 2001). The volume includes *Shopping and Fucking, Faust is Dead, Handbag* and *Some Explicit Polaroids*. Page references will be inserted in the text.

21   Dan Rebellato, 'Introduction', in Ravenhill, *Plays*, p. x.

22   Ibid., p. xvi.

23   Enda Walsh, *Disco Pigs and Sucking Dublin* (London, 1997); Enda Walsh, *bedbound and misterman* (London, 2001). Page references will be inserted in the text.

24   Emma Goldman, 'The Modern Drama: A Powerful Disseminator of Radical Thought', in *Anarchism and Other Essays* (New York and London, 1911), pp. 248–63 (p. 249).

Index